Dear Reader:

The book you  rom the St. Martin's True Crime Library, the imprint the *New York Times* calls "the leader in true crime!" Each month, we offer you a fascinating account of the latest, most sensational crime that has captured the national attention. St. Martin's is the publisher of perennial best-selling true crime author Jack Olsen, whose SALT OF THE EARTH is the true story of how one woman fought and triumphed over life-shattering violence; Joseph Wambaugh called it "powerful and absorbing." Fannie Weinstein and Melinda Wilson tell the story of a beautiful honors student who was lured into the dark world of sex for hire in THE COED CALL GIRL MURDER. St. Martin's is also proud to publish two-time Edgar Award-winning author Carlton Stowers, whose TO THE LAST BREATH recounts a two-year-old girl's mysterious death, and the dogged investigation that led loved ones to the most unlikely murderer: her own father. The book you now hold, SCREAM AT THE SKY, is also by Carlton Stowers, and follows the forensic trail of a cold-case serial killer, and the twist that apprehended him.

St. Martin's True Crime Library gives you the stories *behind* the headlines. Our authors take you right to the scene of the crime and into the minds of the most notorious murderers to show you what really makes them tick. St. Martin's True Crime Library paperbacks are better than the most terrifying thriller, because it's all true! The next time you want a crackling good read, make sure it's got the St. Martin's True Crime Library logo on the spine—you'll be up all night!

Charles E. Spi

Executive Edit

OUTSTANDING PRAISE FOR CARLTON STOWERS AND HIS TRUE CRIME ACCOUNTS

SCREAM AT THE SKY

"It cannot be recommended for the faint of heart . . . the author is as methodical and skillful as Little in the forensic reconstruction of an investigation and trial that provided closure for five families and judgment and a sentence for a killer who eluded justice for 15 years."

— Washington Post Book World

"Carlton Stowers gets it exactly right . . . SCREAM AT THE SKY offers compassion for the victims as well as a balanced, warts-and-all view of each . . . thanks to John Little, their murders were avenged. Thanks to Carlton Stowers, they will not be forgotten."

— Austin American-Statesman on *Scream at the Sky*

Stowers "deftly portrays investigators' increasing tenacity and Wardrip's trail of deceit and violence, elements contributing to the tension as readers wait for the law to catch up with a bizarre and maddeningly fortunate murderer."

— Kirkus Reviews

"The book becomes increasingly suspenseful as Little quietly builds his case against the sanctimonious Wardrip, whose composure crumbles when he's finally confronted on his old misdeeds. Stowers demonstrates sensitivity toward the many survivors of Wardrip's crimes, yet at heart this is a gory, effective meditation on the evil sometimes committed by 'ordinary' men and the great efforts necessary for justice."

— Publishers Weekly

"Stowers presents the murderer as a multidimensional character. Forget 'investigative' TV series. SCREAM AT THE SKY is better than *CSI* or *Law & Order*, because it's about the real thing." *— Arizona Republic*

MORE PRAISE FOLLOWS...

Also by Carlton Stowers

Open Secrets

Careless Whispers

Sins of the Son

To the Last Breath

SCREAM
AT THE SKY

FIVE TEXAS MURDERS AND ONE
MAN'S CRUSADE FOR JUSTICE

CARLTON STOWERS

St. Martin's Paperbacks

SCREAM AT THE SKY

Copyright © 2003 by Carlton Stowers.

Cover photographs: Landscape by John Halpern; Faryion Wardrip courtesy Wichita County District Attorney's Office; Terry Sims courtesy Catie Reid; Toni Gibbs courtesy Jeff Gibbs; Ellen Blau courtesy Murray Blau; Tina Kimbrew courtesy Robert Kimbrew.

ISBN: 0-312-99819-8
EAN: 80312-99819-6

Library of Congress Catalog Card Number: 2002033282

Printed in the United States of America

St. Martin's Press hardcover edition / January 2003
St. Martin's Paperbacks edition / August 2004

St. Martin's Paperbacks are published by St. Martin's Press, 175 Fifth Avenue, New York, NY 10010.

10   9   8   7   6   5

For Pat

. . . who continues to make things worthwhile

The triumph of justice is the only peace.

—Robert G. Ingersoll

It is easy to utter what has been kept silent,
But impossible to recall what has been uttered.

—Moralia

PROLOGUE

In history's grand scheme it cannot be measured as a great passage of time. Yet in the fifteen-year span about which you are to read, a lifetime of events, major and minor, changes large and small, occurred.

For most caught up in today's high-speed, old-millennium-to-new advances, it is difficult to think back to that winter when 1984 turned into 1985 with any degree of accurate recall. The bitter north Texas storms that rolled in on dark and ominous clouds, spilling snow and sleet, have now mingled with similar stretches of frigid weather that visited in subsequent years. Memory, though one of the remarkable miracles of life, is seldom foolproof, rarely exact.

Inasmuch as our past is a series of good, bad, and indifferent happenings, we recollect selectively and generally, leaving great spaces blank. New memories constantly crowd out old; modern sights and sounds mask those of bygone days. We remember, but seldom with the benefit of perfect recall.

The passage of time will do that. In the memory bank it all blurs.

Such is not the case of the people you will read about

in these pages. There is a period in the lives of those who populate this story that is as real and vivid today as it was almost two decades ago. For them, time stopped and a series of dark and ugly snapshots were indelibly etched in their minds. No passage of years, not the most supreme of efforts, has erased the endless nightmares with which they have been forced to live out their lives.

These are people who can still remember the smell of the flowers that filled the churches and funeral home chapels, the newly turned dirt at gravesites, and the ever-lingering taste of the bilious anger directed toward whomever, whatever caused their lifelong anguish. The pain of great loss and unfounded accusations remains. So do the long years of frustration and unanswered questions.

Memories, often the sweet fountain of our treasured nostalgia, can also be the cauldron of our greatest fears and anxieties. They do not pretend to be fair. Too often, in fact, they are the reason that in the throes of our darkest sorrows, we sometimes find ourselves wanting to . . .

scream at the sky.

THE SETTING

Wichita Falls, Texas, sits on a barren plain to the north-west of the Dallas–Fort Worth metroplex, home to just over 100,000 residents whose civic consciousness is routinely assaulted by the good-natured jibes of friends throughout the state. Biting, windswept winters give rise to the old joke that the only thing separating it from the North Pole is a barbed wire fence. Then, in the summer, its consecutive days of 100-plus–degree heat are relentless, so much so that a 100-mile bicycle race it annually hosts is appropriately called the Hotter 'N Hell Hundred. The NFL Dallas Cowboys did their preseason training on the campus of its Midwestern State University for several summers before it finally occurred to management and the coaching staff alike that the brain-baking July and August temperatures were no doubt contributing factors to the recent string of miserable seasons of the once-proud America's Team.

Despite its name, there are not even any falls in Wichita Falls—unless one counts the man-made one on the edge of downtown. Among its premier tourist attractions is a structure known as "the world's smallest skyscraper," a historical landmark that begs explanation unless you read about it in a long-ago *Ripley's Believe It or Not*. Back in 1919, at the height of the oil boom that visited the region, an out-of-town promoter reportedly sold $200,000 in stock to investors who believed they were buying shares in an enormous building project that would provide badly needed office space. What they weren't told was that the blueprints they were shown were drawn to a scale of inches rather than feet. What resulted was a slender, four-story building one-twelfth the size expected—just 40 feet tall with rooms measuring only 10 by 17 feet. There was not even a stairwell leading to the top three floors. The con man, legend has it, quietly stole away with the investors' money, and today the eighty-three-year-old structure serves as monument to greed and folly and as a comfortable roost for pigeons.

Scamming aside, it was apparently well built. The "skyscraper" was among the downtown buildings that managed to survive the monstrous tornado that leveled 20 percent of the city back in 1979.

It was, historians point out, another kind of natural disaster that destroyed the city's namesake. Before a devastating flood in 1886, the nearby Wichita River featured a picturesque series of five-foot falls near where pioneers had battled Caddo, Comanche, Kiowa, and Wichita Indians for settlement rights. The falls, alas, were washed away by the flood, and it was not until a century later that city fathers decided a man-made waterfall was better than none at all.

The delay most likely resulted from the fact that people were too busy getting rich to be concerned with such matters. With oil strikes in nearby Electra and Burkburnett, Wichita Falls became the prototype of a Texas boomtown. Even today it is a city populated by numerous millionaires who had to do nothing more than endorse royalty checks from the nation's leading oil companies to fund the building of their mansions.

And while local residents might pass the time with jokes about their hometown, maligning by outsiders prompts quick and angry response. When *Texas Monthly* magazine published a tongue-in-cheek article on the "worst occupations in Texas" and listed "full-time resident of Wichita Falls" among its choices, the editorial offices were bombarded with complaints. Members of the media who chuckled when *Advertising Age* magazine recently selected Wichita Falls as "America's Most Average City" were quickly reminded that not every community in the state aspires to the social-climbing, anything-for-a-buck, self-important attitude of places like, say, Dallas and Houston.

In truth, Wichita Falls is a modern, progressive city with thriving businesses, an air force base that contributes greatly to the economy, a respected university, an award-winning newspaper, a fine library, damn good high school football teams, and residents who can trace their local lineage back for generations. It is not a place to make fun of.

It is, residents will tell you, a quiet and low-key city, a great place to raise a family, free of worry over many of the nightmares that stalk the streets of the nation's major cities.

A safe place. Until that winter when 1984 spilled into 1985 and the good-natured joking ceased and the easy smiles disappeared. The city had come under assault from a nameless, faceless evil—and its young women were dying.

THEN . . .

CHAPTER ONE

The December morning air, crisp and cleared by recent rains, was still and silent, not yet disturbed by early risers who would soon turn the new day into frenzied preparations for work, school, as well as last-minute holiday preparations. For a welcome change, there was not so much as a hint of the taunting north Texas wind that generally sent the region's winter chill factor plummeting. As nurse Leza Boone drove through the modest Wichita Falls neighborhood, Christmas lights winked from many of the windows and morning papers still waited to be retrieved from front yards along Bell Street.

Returning home from work at the Bethania Regional Health Care Center, she was tired yet surprisingly energized. Normally after a double shift her thoughts would have focused on nothing but a quick shower and sleep. Instead, her mind was racing with other plans. With Christmas just four days away, there was still shopping to do and friends to drop in on. She loved the season and on that Friday wished she could set aside weekend plans to study for an end-of-semester exam she was scheduled to take at nearby Midwestern University. That coworker and fellow student Terry Sims had volunteered to stay over at the small frame house she was renting and her help would make the academic drudgery more bearable. In exchange, Leza had promised to accompany her friend and house-guest on a shopping trip for a bicycle that was to be Terry's Christmas present for her twelve-year-old sister, Catie.

The young women had become acquainted shortly after meeting on the Midwestern campus. Then, when they began working at the hospital, Leza as a respiratory therapist, Terry as an EKG technician, the friendship had quickly grown. They shared common interests and, on those occasions when Terry worked late at the hospital and had early classes the next day, she had welcomed the invitation to spend the night at Leza's instead of driving all the way across town where she lived with her great-grandmother.

Leza, in fact, had mentioned their becoming roommates, but Terry had gently dismissed the idea. Maybe someday, she had said.

Someday, Leza knew, when her friend's responsibility to her family was not so keenly felt.

At age twenty, Terry Sims had already been functioning in an adult role for years. Throughout her teenage years she had cared for her siblings, sisters, Vickie and Catie, and brother, Tony. Terry had been only thirteen months old and Vickie newly born when their father, a minor celebrity on the local stock car racing circuit, died in an automobile accident. Following an argument with his wife, he had stormed from the house on a July evening in 1965 and was speeding along a Wichita Falls street when the police attempted to pull him over. Rather than stop, he led the patrol car on a high-speed chase that had ended when he hit a bridge embankment while driving in excess of 100 miles per hour.

For his wife, Marsha, suddenly widowed at just seventeen, the experience was overwhelming. Leaving Terry to be cared for by her great-grandmother and baby Vickie with her grandmother, Marsha had left Wichita Falls. Almost two years passed before she returned, married to a hairdresser and with their infant son, Tony. Insisting that she was ready to settle down and resume a constructive family life, she reclaimed the daughters she'd left behind. The new marriage didn't last long, however.

Marsha next married a medical equipment salesman who persuaded her to move her children to Fort Worth. Soon she had given birth to Catherine, her third daughter, whom everyone would call Catie. And less than a year later she was again divorced. Marsha married for the fourth time in 1977, moving to Dallas. It worked out no better than her previous attempts. By 1980 she was divorced again and making plans to marry a man who wanted her and the children to accompany him to Springfield, Colorado.

While her troubled relationships continued, she had built a growing reputation as a first-rate hairdresser. Once she had even been called on to do actress Farrah Fawcett's hair. While Marsha pursued her career, the children returned to Wichita Falls to live with their grandparents.

In her absence, it was Terry who assumed many of the responsibilities of child rearing. Though the great-grandparents offered steady support and comfort, Terry was the one who routinely helped with homework and science projects, cooked preschool breakfasts, washed and ironed clothes, and, when they caused childish mischief, was quick to take the blame for them. When sister Catie had tearfully pointed out that she was the only girl trying out for the junior high tennis team with a hand-me-down racquet, it was Terry who quietly used some of her own savings to purchase a new one. While the other youngsters had moms and dads cheering them on at their Saturday morning soccer games, Catie had only her big sister.

That Terry enjoyed little of the social life that accompanies the teen years seemed never to bother her. Already determined that she would one day become a doctor, she had pledged her life to the role of caregiver. An acolyte at the neighborhood St. Stephen's Episcopal Church and a straight-A student in high school, she planned to work her way through college.

Well into her sophomore year on that December in 1984, it had not been easy. Not only were there the younger kids to watch out for, but occasionally her mother would suddenly resurface, returning to Wichita Falls with a new hard-luck story even sadder than the last Terry had heard. And while others in the family considered Marsha a lost cause and dismissed concern for her, it was Terry whom she could still depend on for a "loan" when her rent payment came due, to take her shopping for badly needed groceries, or to go on visits to the doctor.

Leza Boone knew little of her friend's background. Terry had never spoken about the constant moves as a child. What Leza did know was that Terry was the most selfless and energetic person she'd ever met, constantly giving to and doing for others.

The previous day, in fact, she had brought Catie with her to the hospital chapel where a list of needy children in the community was posted. After letting her little sister pick a couple of names, they had then driven to a nearby Target store where they purchased toys along with a large box of chocolate candies to be distributed among fellow workers at the hospital.

Finally, before dropping Catie at her great-grandmother's home, Terry had stopped at the post office to mail her Christmas cards.

Only in recent months had she seemed to focus more time on her own needs, belatedly sampling the delights of independence and experiencing some of the fun her friends took for granted. She'd bought her first car and begun taking karate lessons, even returning from a kick boxing tournament in Lawton, Oklahoma, with her first trophy. And while she had vowed no interest in developing a serious relationship, she had begun dating more.

She and Leza had worked the 3 P.M.-to-11 P.M. shift on that Thursday and then made a late-night stop at the home of girlfriend Sue Whitaker and her mother, June, to exchange Christmas gifts. It was shortly after midnight when they finally arrived at Leza's house and she handed the door key to Terry. Having volunteered to work the late-night shift, Leza had to return to Bethania.

Only as they pulled into the narrow driveway at the side of the house had Leza realized that her car was in need of gas. Terry suggested that her friend drive her car back to the hospital.

As she backed into the darkened street, Leza watched Terry hurry through the drizzling rain toward the welcome glow of the front porch light. Reaching the steps, she brushed the dampness from her hair and turned to wave.

It would be the last happy moment Leza Boone would experience for years to come.

On her return home that Friday morning, Leza knocked at the locked door and called Terry's name but got no response. She waited a minute and tried again. Finally assuming her guest was simply sleeping soundly, Leza walked around the corner to the residence of her landlord and asked his wife if she might borrow his key.

The moment the young nurse opened the front door, a chill that had nothing to do with the early-morning temperature raced through her body. Her normally neat living room was in disarray. Books had been swept off the coffee table and lay open on the floor. Sofa cushions and magazines were scattered about. A stereo speaker was overturned. The key chain that held the house key she'd given to Terry just hours earlier lay on the floor.

As she stood in the doorway, her eyes scanning the small room, Leza was suddenly aware that she was not breathing and forced herself to inhale deeply. "Terry?" she finally called out. "Terry, you okay?"

When her eyes fell on the crumpled pink smock and pants that lay beneath the coffee table, Terry's tennis shoes and eyeglasses on the carpet nearby, then a blood-stained wad of Kleenex tissues, she knew the answer to her question and quickly fled the house.

Hysterical, she ran back to the landlord's house, where his wife met her at the front door. "Something bad has happened," Leza screamed. "I'm scared. Something really bad's happened." The woman woke her still-sleeping husband, and in a matter of minutes he was hurrying toward the house he'd been renting to the young nurse for the past year.

What William Walbrick saw as he entered made him sick to his stomach. While Leza and Mrs. Walbrick waited on the front porch, he had walked through the living room and down the hallway, past the front bedroom, finally reaching the open door to the bathroom. There, lying in a pitch-black pool of blood, he saw the nude body of a young woman he'd occasionally seen in the neighborhood. He didn't know her name, only that she was a friend of Leza's who had always acknowledged him with a smile and a wave. And now she was dead.

"Call the police," he said to his wife as he returned to the front porch. Leza Boone threw her arms into the air and screamed so loudly that people in the neighborhood began pouring from their homes to see what had happened.

A growing crowd of onlookers had already gathered by the time the Wichita Falls police began arriving at 1509

Bell Street. Officer David Bynum, first on the scene, found no evidence of forced entry. The front door locks, he wrote in his field notebook, were the type that automatically fasten whenever the door is closed. The door could be opened only with a key or by someone already inside the house. There was a good chance, he had already determined, that the victim had known her killer and willingly let him in. During his initial walk-through of the house, the officer had not found a weapon.

Soon the small house was filled with investigators. Detectives Joe Shepard, Jerry Riley, and Dennis Huff were in charge of the evidentiary search. Sergeant W. J. Mienzer photographed the crime scene and Bill Horton from the Wichita County District Attorney's Office moved from room to room, videotaping everything from the bloody tissues found in the living room to blood spots found on the bed linens and, finally, Terry Sims's bound and blood-soaked body, which lay in the bathroom.

As Detective Shepard slowly made his way through the house, taking note of every bloodstain, every item out of place, a mental picture of what had transpired in the early-morning hours began to form. Standing in the doorway of the bathroom, looking down on the lifeless body, he took only cursory note of the stab wounds visible on the woman's chest and back. What commanded his attention were the bruises on the forehead and cheek and along the bridge of the nose. There was a distinct laceration evident on the lower lip. Then there were the victim's small hands, which were still tied behind her back. Deep gashes crisscrossed her fingers—defensive wounds indicating she'd tried to fight off her attacker. With that he turned and walked to the front of the house, trying to imagine the horror Terry Sims had been subjected to in the final moments of her life.

The violent struggle, he knew, had begun in the living

room, very near the entrance. The first blood droplets, in fact, were only four feet from the front door. Silently viewing the overturned furniture, the scattered clothing, the bloodstained carpet, he could imagine the attack beginning with angry and powerful blows from a fist, maybe some blunt object. Then his mind's eye turned to scenes of a knife being wielded, the victim frantically grabbing at it even as it was being aimed at her chest.

The battle had continued into the bedroom, where specks of blood on the sheets and pillow hinted that a sexual assault probably had taken place. The detective examined the yellow extension cord that connected the heater on the water bed to an electrical outlet. A piece of it had been cut away and used to bind the victim. At the foot of the bed lay the victim's purse and wallet.

He slowly followed the blood trail down the short hallway that returned him to the bathroom. There, he knew, the final cruelties had been played out. Blood was smeared on the side of the bathtub and on the wall by the light switch. Splatters were evident on the nearby sink and on the wall above where the body lay on its left side, nude except for socks, eyes closed, hands tightly bound behind her back.

The detective shook his head, then turned away. So much blood, he thought, so much rage.

He wanted to speak with Leza Boone to see if she had any idea who might have committed such an atrocity. Outside, he breathed fresh air into his lungs and surveyed the circus that had gathered. Beyond the yellow crime scene tape, neighbors, young and old, stood, watching and whispering. Television cameramen were pointing toward the house, reporters wandered among the crowd getting reaction to the nightmare that had visited their neighborhood.

Leza, however, was nowhere to be seen. She was, he

was finally told by a patrolman, en route to the hospital. She was returning to Bethania Regional Health Care Center, not as a nurse but a patient suffering from severe shock.

Across town, a solemn-faced police officer stood on the front porch of the picturesque old home that occupied a sprawling corner lot on Lake Park Drive and Easy Street. He had been assigned the task of reporting Terry Sims's death to her seventy-five-year-old great-grandmother. Beda Wingrove was traditionally a late sleeper and often chose to ignore the arrival of visitors she was not expecting. The officer had knocked and rung the doorbell steadily for almost fifteen minutes before she finally responded.

When told of the tragedy that had occurred, she looked as if she might faint, and the officer helped her to a chair in the living room. He asked if there was someone he could call to come be with her. "Thank you, no," she whispered. "I need to make the calls myself."

As matriarch of the family, she had always been a woman of great strength and stern will, dating back to the days when she had spoken out for women's rights long before it was fashionable to do so. After the death of her husband in 1968, her resolve to see that her family remained tightly knit and well cared for only grew. She was the one all others came to for help, be it financial or advice on personal matters. Now, however, as she sat alone, pondering the impossible, she could barely muster the strength to dial the office number of her son-in-law, Gill Bridgens. "Terry is dead" were the first words she managed.

The drumbeat of bad news had begun sounding throughout the family.

Marna Bridgens was at the family lakehouse in nearby Bridgeport, busy with holiday preparations, when her husband appeared unexpectedly in the living room. He'd left the office of his welding company in Wichita Falls and picked granddaughter Vickie up at the home of friends, then sped toward the lake. The look Marna saw on his face immediately signaled that something was terribly wrong.

Tears began rolling down her cheeks as he held her, telling of the call he'd received from her mother and a subsequent conversation with the police. "We need to get to Wichita Falls," he said. "Your mother's asked that you take care of the funeral arrangements."

It was the first time Marna could recall that her mother had not automatically assumed control of a family tragedy—even the death of her own husband—and provided strength for everyone else to draw from.

"Catie's down at a friend's house," she said. "I've got to tell her."

At first the young girl refused to believe what she was hearing. She had been with her sister only two days earlier and everything was fine. Terry had been so happy. She couldn't be dead. No one would want to hurt her. Everyone loved her. Through confused tears Catie begged not to have to accompany them to Wichita Falls, as if by keeping her distance she could avoid the reality of the tragedy.

Marna phoned the parents of the friend Catie had been visiting, briefly explained the situation, and asked if they would keep her until they returned.

It was as they were preparing to leave that the distraught youngster moved away from her grandmother's hug, the look on her face more serious than Marna had ever seen. "Who did this?" the young girl asked.

"Honey, we don't know."

Catie was silent for a moment. "Whoever it is," she finally said, "I hate them."

En route to Wichita Falls, Gill Bridgens was stopped twice for speeding.

Terry's aunt, DeeDee Peters, was at her desk in a downtown Denver office when her husband, Bob, called. "There's something we need to talk about," he said, "but not over the phone."

What Bob did not mention was his concern for her driving alone once she heard the news about Terry. Or that he'd already spoken with his wife's boss, explaining the need for her to cut short her workday. "I'll be there in a few minutes," he said, ending the conversation before she could begin asking questions.

Later, as they drove toward their suburban home, he had to repeat himself three times before DeeDee acknowledged that she understood what he was saying. Finally he had shouted it at the top of his voice. "Terry has been killed," he said. "Someone murdered her."

Numb, she fought for some kind of response. She had talked on the phone with Terry, the godmother of her 16-month-old son, less than a week earlier, listening as she cheerfully spoke of work and school and plans for the holidays. Her voice had been so full of life. And now she was gone? Murdered?

"What," she finally asked, "will we do about Christmas?" At home she had two sons, twelve and two, who had been talking of nothing but the visit from Santa Claus for days.

"We've got to go to Wichita Falls," her husband replied, mustering a firmness to his voice that he hoped masked the helplessness he was feeling. The days ahead, he knew, were going to be traumatic and would darken holiday seasons for years to come.

In Texas, a futile effort to locate Terry's mother was under way. The last anyone had heard, she had left California, had moved for a while to North Carolina, and had recently been living in Amarillo. The Wichita County Sheriff's Department, alerted to the need to contact her, had faxed information to departments throughout the state, asking help in finding a mother who needed to be informed of her child's death.

Once more, it seemed, Marsha had vanished.

The basement of the Southwestern Institute of Forensic Sciences in Dallas was, as usual, teeming with activity, signaling that death pays no mind to the holiday season. Bodies, rigid and discolored, lay on gurneys that had been wheeled from the nearby cold storage room, awaiting attention from the half dozen medical examiners on duty.

Dr. Allan Stilwell had been assigned to perform the autopsy on the body that had just been delivered from Wichita Falls. A man who had done over 3,000 such procedures during the course of his career, he had never ceased to be puzzled by man's endless inhumanity to man. He'd seen the nightmarish results of jealous rages, drunken disputes, murders bought and paid for, and had long ago ceased trying to assign any logic to the indignities he labored over. His job, which he did well, was simply to determine the cause of death. The rest was up to the homicide investigators.

Such detachment, however, did not mask the rush of emotion he felt as he looked down on the nude and violated body of the young woman. She was so small, weighing only ninety-four pounds, and once so pretty. Now, however, her auburn hair was matted in blood, the sparkle of her brown eyes dulled. He took note of the slender gold rings on three of the damaged fingers, a small chain around her neck with its flower pendant, a watch that continued to keep time, and the tiny pierced earrings that were still in place.

Even in death, the M.E. was aware of the faint scent of the young woman's perfume.

Soon he was making note of the bruises to her face, the deep cuts on the fingers of each hand, and, finally, the series of stab wounds to the chest and back, the story of the final moments of her life unfolding before him. The cuts on her hands, he observed, were classic defense wounds. At some point she had likely even grabbed the blade of the weapon with her left hand. There were eight stab wounds to the chest, one that had penetrated the left pulmonary artery, causing severe internal bleeding. Others had lacerated both lungs, causing their collapse. The three deep stab wounds on the back, he believed, had occurred after the victim had been tied and was already immobile.

The blade of the weapon, he concluded, had one sharp edge and was approximately an inch in width and approximately four-and-one-half inches long. If he had to guess, the victim's killer had arrived armed with some kind of hunting knife.

While his examination revealed no obvious signs of forced sexual activity, he could not rule out the possibility that the victim had been raped. As part of his normal routine in such cases, he took oral, vaginal, and anal smears to be sent along to trace evidence analysts and serologists.

There was nothing in the science he practiced to indicate just how long the struggle had lasted, but he was reasonably sure that Sims had lived less than five minutes after the artery leading to her heart had been punctured.

And experience suggested one other thing: The severity of the defense wounds told him that the young woman had been convinced from the outset of the struggle that her attacker had planned to kill her.

•   •   •

Back in Wichita Falls, investigators had already begun brainstorming, trying to determine a motive for the crime and compiling a list of possible suspects. Not only was their list frustratingly short, but the motives were limited. At first blush, the murder appeared to have been triggered by some jealous rage, the cruel work of a spurned boyfriend. Or, perhaps, the young woman's death was the end product of a drug deal that had gone bad.

The suggestion that Terry had been in any way involved in drugs immediately angered her friends and family. Leza Boone, interviewed in her hospital bed, insisted that neither she nor her friend were drug users. Terry's sisters quickly told detectives the same thing. So, for that matter, did the toxicology report from the medical examiner's office: There had been no drugs or alcohol in Sims's system at the time of her death.

Still, with little else to go on, the police doggedly pursued the drug angle, interviewing Catie and asking if she'd ever accompanied her sister to any place where she might have purchased drugs, calling Vickie to the police station to ask if she knew whom Terry had bought drugs from. It was when they placed crime scene pictures on the table in front of her, suggesting such bloody savagery was common to drug transactions that had gone awry, that Vickie's anger erupted, her words echoing against the walls of the interview room. "My sister did not do drugs," she yelled. "She didn't know any drug dealers."

What, then, about jealous boyfriends?

In recent months, Terry had been seeing a Midwestern student named Mark Thomas, occasionally going out with him for dinner or a movie. Once she had accompanied him and his father on a weekend deep-sea fishing trip off the coast of Mexico and had returned home to tell friends that the experience had been a nightmare. She had been seasick the whole time. Mark, the police quickly learned, had been out of town on the night Terry was attacked.

Investigators also asked Beda Wingrove if Terry had mentioned any problems she might have been having with a man she had recently met. The police had learned that another female student, Toni Gibbs, had filed a report just weeks earlier in which she stated that the same person had been making unwanted advances toward her and was threatening a sexual harassment suit.

And then there was a young respiratory therapist named Donnie Ray Goodson, who also worked at Bethania. From Leza, they learned that Goodson had briefly dated her, then Terry. Both young women had broken off their relationships with him several months earlier, but he had continued to call and occasionally drop by Leza's house, particularly when he knew Terry would be staying over. So persistent had he become that Terry had complained to a superior who ultimately forbade Goodson from even going onto the floor of the hospital where she worked.

During an interview with the police, he had freely admitted his attraction to Terry but insisted he had nothing to do with her death. Though she had made it clear she did not share his romantic interest, they had remained friends. He had, in fact, been asked to serve as a pallbearer at her funeral.

Yet even before Terry was buried, Donnie Ray Goodson had emerged as the police's prime suspect.

Because Terry's body was being held in Dallas until the results of all testing were complete, Christmas was fast approaching, and the search for her mother was still ongoing, funeral services were delayed for almost a week.

DeeDee and her husband, after a series of calls to Wichita Falls, had finally agreed to celebrate Christmas at home with their children before making the trip to Texas. Still stunned by the news of her niece's death, DeeDee had been idly thumbing through mail that arrived just a day after her husband had come to her workplace with the terrible news. Among the envelopes was one addressed with familiar handwriting. It was Terry's Christmas card.

Mixed with the numbing sense of loss was a dark cloud of guilt that settled over several members of the family. Vickie, perhaps the most headstrong of the children, had finally wearied of her mother's vagabond lifestyle and left home during her junior year in high school. Seventeen at the time, she lived with various friends, found work as a waitress in a downtown snack bar, and managed to graduate from high school. Busy with her own survival, she had not seen her older sister since Terry attended her nineteenth birthday party the previous June.

Like Vickie, seventeen-year-old Tony had opted to pursue life on his own. After an endless string of arguments with his mother, she had finally ordered him from her house. He'd lived for a time with his father, then drifted from the home of one friend to another. Dropping out of high school, he began playing drums and singing for a local rock band.

On the night his sister was killed, he'd stopped by the garage apartment in back of the Wingrove home to say hello. Seeing that she was not at home, he had waited for an hour or so before it occurred to him that she was probably at Leza's. He briefly considered going over there but eventually had dismissed the idea. In the days after her death, he would be tormented by his decision, obsessed by the idea that if he'd made the drive over to Leza's he might somehow have prevented the tragedy that occurred there. Despite the insistence from others in the family that he would not have been able to save his sister and might, in fact, have been killed himself, Tony withdrew.

It was on Christmas morning that Beda Wingrove answered her kitchen phone and heard the operator ask if she would accept a collect long-distance call. Marsha, assuming her family would follow tradition and gather at the Wingrove house, was calling from Amarillo to wish everyone a merry Christmas. Beda cut her granddaughter short, telling her to come to Wichita Falls as quickly as possible. In a chilled, monotone voice, she explained that Terry had been murdered. "You should be here for the funeral," she said.

Stunned by the news, Marsha was silent for several seconds. She was crying by the time she managed to speak. "I don't have any money," she said. "How am I going to get there?"

For more years than she cared to remember, Mrs. Wingrove had lent her troubled granddaughter financial assistance, helping with bills, clothing, and food for the children. Twice she had purchased automobiles for her. She'd not done it for Marsha's sake but for the children's.

"What am I going to do?" Marsha pled.

"You're going to do the best you can," Mrs. Wingrove replied, "just like the rest of us are doing." And with that she hung up the phone.

At the Owens & Brumley Funeral Home, Marna had begun the grim task of making arrangements. Helping her through the necessary decisions was a pleasant young funeral director named Bob Mason. What she did not know—and what he chose not to mention—was that years earlier he had been part of the ambulance crew summoned to the scene of the automobile accident that had claimed the life of an old school-days friend: Terry's father.

•   •   •

With only two days remaining in 1984, the funeral was conducted at the St. Stephen's Episcopal Church. Staff members from the hospital, students from high school and college days, teachers and instructors joined the family inside the small church. Speakers were set up near the entryway for those who were unable to find a seat inside.

In attendance, wearing a black dress, her slender face drawn and pale, was Terry's mother. A former brother-in-law, living in nearby Iowa Park, had wired Marsha bus fare and had picked her up at the station.

In the weeks to come, members of the grieving family felt little relief from the oppressive gloom that had settled over them. Beda Wingrove soon wearied of visits from investigators, their meaningless questions and apologetic admissions that the case was at a standstill, and finally refused to see them. Marsha remained in Wichita Falls after her daughter's funeral but seldom saw the family. Neither Vickie nor Tony made an effort to contact her.

Gill and Marna Bridgens had retreated back to their Bridgeport lake house, there to focus their attention on the needs of the fragile Catie. They traveled to Wichita Falls only to make occasional checks on Mrs. Wingrove. The routine had become heartbreaking. Once a woman busy with family activities, volunteer work, and gin rummy games, Beda rarely moved from her chair in the living room, even when her daughter or grandchildren came to visit. Her appetite had disappeared. So, Marna began to fear, had her mother's desire for living.

Marna found each trip more distressing, leaving her with a feeling much like that she'd had following Terry's funeral. An aching weariness would invade her body, rapidly growing into a feeling of overwhelming exhaustion. Every movement—a step, even a gesture—was accomplished only after what seemed monumental effort.

It was on a mid-January evening, following yet another visit punctuated by long and discomforting stretches of silence, that Marna walked onto the front porch where her husband waited. "Let's go home," she said. They were the last words she would speak until later that evening when, nearing Bridgeport, Gill pulled into an all-night service station for gas.

Marna forced herself to step from the car and stretch her legs. Breathing in the cold night air, she turned toward the lighted interior, watching as a bored cashier leaned on the counter, thumbing through a magazine while waiting for her husband to come inside and pay his bill. Looking at the window, her attention was drawn to a small poster that had been attached with Scotch tape. On it was the picture of a smiling young woman, dressed in a starched nurse's uniform. Above the picture, printed in bold block letters, was a single word: MISSING.

Slowly Marna approached and stared at the poster. How, she asked herself, was it possible that there could be so much grief, so much tragedy in the world? She stood, shaking her head, too weary for more tears, until her husband approached, placed his arm over her shoulders, and walked her back to the car.

As they rode into the night, Marna sat in silence, trying to remember the name of the missing woman: some other family's nightmare, someone else's lost child. Finally she closed her eyes tightly, trying to summon the picture on the poster back to her mind's eye.

"The girl's name was Toni Gibbs," she finally whispered.

It had been another bad idea, like so many he'd come up with during the course of his going-nowhere life. Bad ideas, bad choices, and bad relationships had haunted him for as long as he could remember. The late-night walk was supposed to calm him, allow him a brief escape into the crisp darkness, away from his misery and anger. Walking had helped before. But now the cold rain assaulted him like torturous pinpricks, adding to his discomfort, burying his already blackened spirit beneath a new and dense layer of despair that even the booze and pills could no longer scare away.

As he walked, hands buried deeply in his pockets, his painful outcries echoed into the darkness, unsuccessful in summoning compassion from those in the neighborhood who were enjoying the peaceful sleep he had not known for years.

At age twenty-eight, everything positive about his life had been a lie, a fantasy invented to convince others that he was something more than he was. He bragged of scholarly achievements during his school days, hiding away the truth that he had not only been a terrible student but had dropped out before ever receiving a diploma. He spoke of heroics in the military when, in fact, he'd been nothing more than a cook's aide before being discharged under less than honorable conditions. Back in the civilian world, he found nothing but menial jobs and mounting financial problems.

When his boasting failed to impress, he reached out for sympathy. The fifth of nine children, he told heartbreaking tales of growing up in a tiny house on the wrong side of the tracks, physically abused and unloved. It was just another in his lengthy list of lies. The home his machinist father and telephone operator mother had provided was middle class and loving.

Whatever demons haunted him had not been born at home. Yet they were real, blinding all hope as he had wandered aimlessly through the quiet residential neighborhood.

It was when he had seen the young woman standing on the porch of the small house on Bell Street that the anger boiled to an uncontrollable level.

CHAPTER TWO

The murder of Terry Sims had occurred just ten days before new Wichita County District Attorney Barry Macha, a native son still basking in the glow of a landslide election victory, was sworn in. Awaiting the first day of 1985, when he would officially take office, the lanky and ambitious young attorney was forced to satisfy his curiosity about the case like the man on the street. Macha had resigned his position as an assistant district attorney to campaign, so he had been out of the loop. He read the newspaper reports of the investigation, watched the television coverage, and listened to the law enforcement community gossip that suggested the case was dramatically lacking in clues and viable leads.

Like a tethered racehorse, Macha was feeling frustrated. The case, he knew, would be waiting on his desk the day he reported for work. But, he wondered, what would have transpired? He'd campaigned on the promise of being a hands-on prosecutor, yet he knew that by the time he could claim authority over the case much of the important work would have been done.

His greatest regret was that he had not been able to attend the crime scene along with the local police. In his years as a prosecutor, he'd reached the conclusion that a firsthand look at the spot where evil had been played out was invaluable. One could read police reports, review photographs, and listen to witnesses, but nothing offered the degree of awareness that came from being on the scene during the infancy of an investigation. It was an unpleasant task but one he embraced. To those who questioned him about his philosophy, his answer was simple: If you go to the crime scene and see the absolute horror that was done, he would say, you won't forget it; you won't ever forget what your job is.

Still in the early stages of his career, Macha had already arrived at the disturbing awareness that man's cruelty knew no boundaries. The first homicide he'd ever been called out on was a double murder of two teenage girls. He'd encountered the smell of death the minute he walked into the house that night, long before entering the bedroom where the young victims lay side by side on a bed, gunshot wounds in the backs of their heads. It had gotten only more difficult when he arrived at the scene of the murder of a seven-year-old boy whose throat had been cut, his small hands still locked into fists filled with twigs and weeds that his stepfather had dragged him through prior to his death. He'd viewed the body of a child scalded to death in a bathtub, the end results of barroom brawls, and tragic aftermaths of domestic confrontations.

In time, Macha came to subscribe to the theory that at every murder scene a residue of violence remained long after the crime had been committed.

The death of Terry Sims offered a personal ingredient and, though not needed, an additional incentive to solve the case. While Macha had not known the victim, her cousin, Billy Gahagan, had been one of his best friends since boyhood. As a youngster, Gahagan had even lived with Macha and his adoptive parents for a time. As adults

they had played on summer league softball teams together, and Macha had served as best man at his friend's
wedding. At the time, Macha had told Gahagan that when
he married, he could anticipate being asked to return the
favor and be his best man.

Sims's death, Macha knew, had been a severe blow to
his friend.

Some in the law enforcement community viewed Macha's
election to the position of D.A. with great enthusiasm,
impressed by his almost tunnel-vision dedication to the
prosecution of cases while an assistant. A tireless worker,
the lights in his courthouse office were often the last
turned off in the evenings. He regularly rode along with
patrol officers and was fascinated by any new advance-
ments in investigative techniques. A few of his detractors,
however, quietly wondered if the overachiever attitude
might only be a signal that he was using the D.A.'s office
as a political stepping-stone. Regardless, they all agreed
that the former Eagle Scout, All-State baseball player at
Notre Dame High, and two-sport standout at Midwestern
was clearly driven.

It was a state of mind for which Macha offered no
apologies. Even before being accepted into the University
of Houston's law school, he'd known that he wanted to be
a felony prosecutor. And from the moment he passed the
bar exam, his career had been on a fast track. On his first
day as an ADA back in his hometown he found himself
seated in a courtroom, serving as the second-chair prosecutor in a murder case.

Young, single, still living in the home of his Catholic
parents, Barry Macha quickly fell into the routine of a
workaholic. He didn't play golf, had no hobbies, and so-
cialized little. What he did was prosecute murder cases,
one after another. And he rarely lost.

When he'd finally had the opportunity to review the police reports on the Sims case, he found that they included no mention of any physical evidence that might be assigned to the perpetrator. Not a single witness had come forward to suggest any abnormal activity in the neighborhood on the night of the crime. The authorities, he learned, had no suspect other than Donnie Ray Goodson, the young hospital worker who had known both Sims and Leza Boone. Yet there was nothing that placed him at the scene of the crime.

Though he kept it to himself, Barry Macha had a gut feeling that the first high-profile case of his new career was going to be difficult to solve.

What he was not aware of at the time was that yet another horror story was already in the making.

CHAPTER THREE

For Danny Wayne Laughlin, working at the Stardust Club was more than a job. It was a source of heart-pumping energy and excitement, fueled by the jangle of country music, the free-flowing laughter, and the dim neon that made the pretty girls who came to dance and drink even prettier.

All personal troubles that haunted the twenty-four-year-old ex–army enlistee vanished in the evenings when he reported for his job as a bar-back, assigned to run stockroom errands for the bartenders, see to it that an ample number of clean glasses was always on hand and make sure the beer kegs didn't run dry. It wasn't the glamour position he would have preferred and the money wasn't that good, but it was a definite step up from the janitorial work and brief stint as a male stripper that he'd had since his discharge.

Working at the club provided him a respite from real life's disappointments and two-dollar woes and put him on more equal footing with the young and the beautiful. In the cavernous Stardust, with the music playing and everyone having a good time, he comfortably mingled with the rich college kids and the young working men and women with careers that far eclipsed his own. The Stardust, one of two popular country-and-western dance clubs in Wichita Falls, was upscale and friendly. Innocent flirtation was not only tolerated; it was expected. And Danny took full advantage.

On the nights between Christmas of 1984 and New Year's, the crowds were larger than usual; each of the eight bars located in the club were doing landslide business while the dance floor was packed with holiday season customers. One evening as he returned from a trip to the stockroom, Laughlin lost his balance in the elbow-to-elbow congestion, breaking a fall by bracing himself against one of the small tables near the stage where minutes earlier a local country singer had been doing his best to imitate Garth Brooks.

Laughlin's eyes met with those of a smiling young woman with frosted blond hair. "Hello, Georgy Girl," he said as he righted himself.

It was several minutes later when the woman, a bemused look on her face, approached the bar where he was busy replacing an empty beer keg. "Why did you call me that?" she asked.

"What's that?"

" 'Georgy Girl.' "

Laughlin laughed, placing his elbows on the bar and leaning toward the attractive stranger. "Remember the TV show *My Three Sons*?" he explained. "There was this actress on it—I don't remember what part she played. But in this one episode she sang the song 'Georgy Girl.' You just reminded me of her. And of that song."

The woman gave him a puzzled look, then shrugged. "Just wondered," she said as she turned to walk away.

And though he found himself immediately hoping that the opportunity to talk more with her would eventually present itself, Laughlin never saw her again. He didn't even learn her name. That would only come weeks later, after a flyer with her photograph on it was posted near the entryway to the club.

She was Toni Jean Gibbs, and she had been missing since January 19.

In the weeks preceding the new year, the twenty-four-year-old registered nurse at Wichita Falls General had confided to family members that she had been receiving unsettling late-night calls at her Raintree Apartments home. Sometimes they were obscene, filled with lurid descriptions of sexual fantasies described by a male voice; on other occasions the caller simply would breathe heavily into the phone, saying nothing. Finally he had begun accurately describing how she had been dressed on the day prior to his call. Concerned that she might be the target of a stalker, she bought a can of Mace to carry in her purse and even talked with her brother about the best kind of handgun to carry for protection. She had, she said, considered going to the police to see if they could place a tap on her phone.

With the murder of Terry Sims still fresh in their minds, female workers at both Wichita Falls hospitals had become particularly wary of the night. Since reports of Sims's death, in fact, nurses at both Bethania Regional and Wichita Falls General had reported harassing phone calls much like those Gibbs had described. At Bethania alone, twenty-five female employees, most of them nurses, reported such calls. Wary hospital officials had gone so far as to institute a policy that required security guards to escort nurses to their cars in the parking lot after work.

It was when Toni Gibbs, always a prompt and reliable employee, failed to report for her Saturday night shift—11 P.M. to 7 A.M.—on January 19 that Peggy Horn, supervisor of nurses, phoned her apartment several times in an effort to reach her with no success. Finally, at three in the morning, the concerned supervisor contacted a friend with the police department, asking if it would be possible for someone to check Gibbs's apartment. In short order a deep night patrol officer was at the Barnett Road address, knocking several times on the door of Apartment 2047. He got no answer. After calling in a request for a description and license plate number of Gibbs's car, he then walked through the apartment parking lot but was unable to locate it.

Also receiving calls from the supervisor of nurses were Toni's brothers, Walden and Jeff, who immediately drove to her apartment. Having no more luck than did the investigating officer, they promptly filed a missing persons report on their sister and telephoned their parents in Clayton, New Mexico. W. L. Gibbs and his wife, Donnie, left for Wichita Falls immediately to join in the search for their daughter. Upon their arrival, the distraught couple announced that they were offering a $1,000 reward for any information leading to their daughter's whereabouts. They also hired a private investigator to aid police in the investigation.

It seemed impossible that only weeks earlier they had visited the city under much happier circumstances, delivering a Christmas gift of a new stereo system to Toni's apartment. As they walked through their daughter's vacant residence, both noticed that the stereo was still in place, where her father had helped install it. In fact, that there was nothing missing or out of place in their daughter's apartment only heightened the mystery of her disappearance—and fueled their fast-growing apprehension.

The only thing they could not find was their daughter's R.N. pin, which she always attached to her uniform, and the heart-shaped locket she regularly wore. Something, they instinctively knew, was terribly wrong.

．　．　．

In a quiet suburb on the southern edge of town, a young
bricklayer named John Little peered through the window
of his home into the overcast January morning, sipped
from his coffee cup, and resigned himself to an idle
weekend. No construction crews, he knew, would brave
the bitter temperatures and frozen roads to work. The previous night's blizzard, which had left a twelve-inch blanket of snow in its wake, had been the first of the winter
season, signaling to those who call north Texas home that
their world would be at a virtual standstill until things
thawed. He turned his thoughts to spending time indoors
with his wife and newborn son. And while they still slept
he poured himself more coffee and turned on the television to catch the early news.

Minutes later he was in the bedroom, gently shaking
his wife. "You aren't going to believe what's happened,"
he told her.

A solemn-faced newscaster had reported that a young
nurse had been reported missing. Even before her name
was mentioned, Little recognized the woman in the photograph that had appeared on the TV screen. Little's wife
and Toni Gibbs had once been members of the same
sorority at Midwestern University. Little's older brother
and Toni's ex-husband had been friends. He remembered
once being invited to a party at Gibbs's house. And though
he'd not known his hostess well, he'd liked her. She had
been outgoing and personable, bright and attractive.

And now there was clear concern that something horrible might have happened to her. Little had heard it in the
tone of the newscaster. "This doesn't sound good," Little
told his wife.

It marked the first time in his life that someone he personally knew was the focus of such ominous attention. He was uncomfortable, overwhelmed by a sudden need to do something. But what?

By midmorning, as the sun broke through and began to thaw the roadways, it was announced that the local police were organizing search parties in the parking lot at the university. Anyone willing to help was urged to report.

Little immediately telephoned his brother.

For the remainder of the day they walked side by side with somber strangers, across frozen fields near Toni's apartment, along the muddy shoreline of the lake, up and down alleys and through deserted parking lots. And by the time the early-winter darkness approached, they had found nothing.

Early the following week—on a Tuesday morning— Wichita Falls police patrolman Sam Dobson radioed in to report that he had located Toni Gibbs's '84 Chevrolet Camaro parked in the 2000 block of Van Buren, miles from her apartment. Inside the locked automobile were the young woman's purse and driver's license. The only thing missing were the keys to the car. If there was any thought that she might simply have traveled from Wichita Falls on the spur of the moment, neglecting to tell anyone, it vanished immediately with the officer's discovery in the quiet residential area.

Publicly the police were continuing to investigate a missing persons case; privately they were becoming increasingly convinced that they might well be looking for evidence of Wichita Falls' first homicide of 1985. While a search of Gibbs's abandoned car had showed no signs of a struggle, there was a faint smudge beneath the door latch on the driver's side and a tiny stain on an interior armrest.

Forensic testing soon revealed them to be blood.

Police detectives, pulled from cases they were working to focus on the search for Gibbs, quickly found themselves chasing a ghost. From interviews at Wichita Falls General they established that the last time Gibbs had been seen was early Saturday morning, as she left the hospital following her shift. A door-to-door canvass of her neighborhood provided nothing. No one had seen or heard anything suspicious or out of the ordinary.

Continued ground and helicopter searches of the areas near her apartment and where her car had been found only resulted in more dead ends. There was a brief flurry of excitement when police telephoned from nearby Burkburnett to report that pieces of a nurse's uniform had been found in a barrow ditch along the highway just west of the city, but it was quickly determined that it was not the type Wichita Falls General nurses are issued, and the strange discovery led nowhere.

A Wichita Falls radio station appealed to the public to donate to a reward fund that the station executives hoped might encourage someone with knowledge of Gibbs's disappearance to come forward. And, in short order, psychics from as far away as Dallas began calling to volunteer their services.

"We're grasping at straws," Charles Trainham, a major in the police department's Criminal Investigations Division, admitted during a late-January press conference. Despite the presence of bloodstains on and in Gibbs's abandoned car, he said, the police were continuing to view the matter of the woman's disappearance as a missing persons case.

Though he did not say so, his experience told him that would soon change. Only the absence of a body stood in the way of officially designating it a homicide investigation. The only real conviction in his voice came when he assured members of the media that there seemed to be absolutely no link between the December murder of Terry Sims and Gibbs's disappearance.

The Arctic freeze that had visited north Texas on the night of Toni Gibbs's disappearance, causing the chill factor to dip below zero, lingered for weeks, an unwelcome winter guest that caused much of the city to move in slow motion. Businesses opened but received few post-holiday visitors. School attendance was drastically down as mothers opted to keep their children home. Many residents ventured beyond their indoor comfort only if the need was essential.

For days, Charlie Harris, a repairman for the Texas Electric Service Company, had put off replacing a faulty transformer on the southern edge of town. Finally, on the afternoon of February 15, he felt the chore could be delayed no longer and, braving still-freezing temperatures, drove to a location just a mile beyond the Wichita Falls city limits.

Turning off Highway 281 and parking on a rutted, still muddy West Jentsch Road, he left the warmth of his truck and began walking across a scrub-brush pasture in the direction of the troublesome transformer. He never reached it. The sight he soon walked up on was one that would haunt him for weeks to come, filling restless nights with flashbacks of the horror that blocked his path.

Lying in the knee-high grass, partially hidden by the jagged limbs of several small bushes, was the nude body of a young woman. Harris, fighting a sudden rise of nausea, ran back to his truck and called the police on his mobile phone.

Toni Gibbs, missing for almost a month, had been found.

By midafternoon Jentsch Road had become a law enforcement parking lot, lined with vehicles hurriedly driven to the scene by Wichita Falls police, sheriff's deputies, and

Department of Public Safety troopers. Since Gibbs's body had been discovered in Archer County, jurisdiction, by law, switched to the sheriff's department of the neighboring county. Immediately, Archer County deputy sheriff Carl Enos, the senior officer at the scene, placed a call to Texas Ranger Bill Gerth, whom he considered one of the premier crime scene investigators in the country.

A law enforcement official with thirty years experience, eighteen of them as a member of the state's elite law enforcement agency, it was Gerth, headquartered in Wichita Falls, who took charge of what was now a homicide investigation.

For the no-nonsense, baritone-voiced Ranger, who had long ago lost track of the number of murders he'd investigated, visits to crime scenes had gotten no easier with passing years. There was always that almost palpable residue of violence that seemed to linger over the area like an invisible cloud. And there was the question, not spoken but always the same: What kind of evil hatred could have boiled to such a degree?

Officers silently parted as Gerth, his familiar white Stetson pulled low on his forehead, approached. Standing over the body, he said nothing for several minutes as his weary eyes carefully explored the horror before him.

The victim lay on her back, arms stretched above her head, her legs slightly spread. Her feet and hands showed signs of frostbite. Her head was turned slightly to the left, as if trying to avoid eye contact with those looking down on her. That, however, was only illusion. Toni Gibbs, left to the elements, insects, and predators that roamed the remote pasture, no longer had any eyes. Parts of her left arm and left leg had been gnawed away. Gerth would not need to wait for a coroner's report to know that varmints had cruelly feasted on the body. Or that the wounds visible on the victim's chest were a result of her having been repeatedly stabbed. Moving forward for a closer look, he saw a gaping gash on the inside of one hand. A defense wound. He noticed that a fingernail on the other hand had been broken. She had fought for her life, the Ranger immediately knew.

The watch on her wrist was stopped at 10:15. One gold ball earring was still in place. And matted in her hair was the heart-shaped locket her mother had searched for weeks earlier in Toni's apartment.

Looking at the scratches crisscrossing her legs, Gerth made his first comment. "It looks like she might have been dragged here," he said. With that he scanned the field, his attention coming to rest on a rusted-out, abandoned trolley car less than a hundred yards away. "Either that," he added, "or she somehow managed to crawl this far before she died."

Almost by rote, Gerth began calling out assignments to the nearly thirty officers on hand. One group was assigned to walk the pasture, side by side, with metal detectors, searching for a weapon or any other evidence that might be connected to the crime. Another was assigned to place crime scene tape around the area where the body was discovered and await the arrival of the justice of the peace and medical examiner. Others were assigned the task of videotaping the scene.

Gerth and Deputy Enos led a group who walked up a slight incline toward the old trolley car. In short order it was apparent that the attack which ended Toni Gibbs's life had taken place there.

Despite the fact that a welcome sun had returned, the dank and trash-littered interior of the old trolley was hidden in shadows, forcing the men to briefly wait at the doorless entrance as their eyes adjusted. Once they did, answers to their questions came quickly. Blood spatters were obvious along the rotted floor and on the wall near where they stood.

A rumpled nurse's uniform lay just a few feet away. A bra and Gibbs's jacket had fallen through a crack in the floor and lay on the ground beneath the trolley. Her shoes, still laced, were visible through one of the gaping holes in the floor.

Gerth reached through the crack, pulled out the leather coat, and began searching for identification. In one pocket he found a single penny. It was the bloodstained uniform that told him what he already knew. Stitched in blue letters on the left breast was Toni Gibbs's name.

Exhaling a heavy sigh, Gerth turned to District Attorney Barry Macha, who had just arrived, and said, "A lot of violence took place here." With that he began assigning the tasks of a thorough collection of the evidence.

The D.A. bit at his bottom lip as he looked into the blood-spattered trolley, the image of Gibbs's ravaged body still fresh on his mind. Long before returning to his car, leaving the task of evidence collecting to the officers on hand, Macha knew he would get little sleep that night.

By day's end there would be discoveries beyond the interior of the trolley. At the entrance to the pasture, two Bic pens and a crumpled dollar bill were found beneath a small mesquite bush near the barbed wire fence that bordered the property. Attempting to reconstruct the harrowing events that had transpired in this pastoral setting, Gerth imagined Gibbs tossing the items from the car as it turned off the road into the pasture, hoping they might serve as clues to those who would ultimately search for her.

What troubled the officer most, however, was the location of the body and the questions it raised. In light of all the evidence left behind, it seemed unlikely that Gibbs's killer would have bothered to move her before fleeing the scene. And that fact created an image that chilled the veteran Ranger. A heartbreaking picture of the victim, nude and fatally wounded, crawling through the frozen pasture toward a place to die played in his mind's eye.

It was almost dark when John Little, returning home from a day of bricking the exterior of a new house that was under construction, walked across the yard, stopping to respond to the barked greeting of his dog in the backyard. His wife, he then noticed, was standing at the front door, her face ashen as she clutched their child to her breast. She had obviously been crying.

The local television news, she explained, had just ended. "They found her," she said as her husband reached out to embrace her.

He had reached out to women all his life, hoping they would hear his whispered cries for help, that they might understand the dark depression that was as much a part of him as the lifelong shyness he'd battled against. His mother had agonized over the constant sadness she'd seen in his eyes, wondered at the cause of the endless flow of tears that seemed to come without the slightest provocation. The father, also perplexed, wondered why this was his only offspring who could not seem to find his place in the world.

As a child, many of his playmates had been female. The girls who did pay attention to him did so out of pity, drawn to his troubled and sensitive nature, his wounded spirit. To some, he was a latter-day James Dean without the haunting good looks. Unkempt, tall, and lanky, he was not someone any hoped would ask them to the prom.

They did, however, like the fact that he seemed always to have pot and beer that he was willing to share.

Yet in time he came to dislike them all. They were all users, takers, their role in life to eventually disappoint and discard him. It was a mind-set that followed him into adult relationships. Even into a marriage that he had re-

gretted from the moment he said the vows. By then, however, the disappointment had evolved into something more tangible, more volatile: anger. Thus it did not surprise him when the pretty young woman at work had remained distant and aloof when he'd tried to make conversation.

No longer seeking understanding, no longer fantasizing of finding comfort and conciliation, he simply wanted revenge.

CHAPTER FOUR

The autopsy told of the nightmare Toni Gibbs had been subjected to before her death. At the Southwestern Institute of Forensic Sciences in Dallas where the body had been taken, Medical Examiner Roger Fossum softly dictated his findings into the microphone that dangled above the stainless steel table on which the body had been placed, making note of the general appearance of the corpse, the clear evidence of damage done by animals and insect infestation. Remarkably, because of the freezing temperatures to which the small body had so long been exposed, there were no signs of lividity or rigidity.

It was, however, the multiple stab wounds that commanded Fossum's greatest attention. A deep wound on the upper left side of the young woman's chest had penetrated the lung, causing a great amount of interior bleeding; others had passed through the diaphragm, spleen, kidney, and stomach. One of the three stab wounds to her back had penetrated the lumbar spine. The gashes on Gibbs's left palm and thumb that Bill Gerth had earlier noticed were obviously defense wounds. A lengthy list of other superficial cuts, scratches, and bruises was evident.

And spermatozoa were detected in the victim's vagina and anus.

The young woman's attacker had clearly brought a great deal of rage to his task.

In the weeks following Gibbs's disappearance, Danny Laughlin grew increasingly obsessed with the young woman he had spoken to only briefly. To friends and coworkers at the Stardust, he talked of her constantly. He spoke of how friendly she'd seemed and how pretty he thought she was and kept up with the progress of the investigation in the newspaper and on television. And while none of his fellow workers could remember ever seeing Laughlin and Gibbs together, he seemed determined to convince anyone who would listen that they had, in fact, become friends in the weeks prior to her disappearance. He'd been trying to convince her to go out with him, he insisted, but she had turned him down. Even her fantasized rebuke, it seemed, had done nothing to cool his fascination. He told of first assuming she was another of those young women who, probably from a prominent family, looked down on others. Most of the really pretty ones, those who wore nice clothes and jewelry and looked as if they'd come to the club straight from the beauty shop, were that way. He'd seen hundreds like that in the Stardust. But Toni, he decided, wasn't like that at all. Watching her with those she came with or met at the bar, he'd decided she was one of those rare women who wasn't completely self-absorbed. On occasion, he said, he'd been sure she was stoned when she'd arrived.

Then, as the weeks passed following the announcement that Gibbs was missing, Laughlin's conversations took on a darker tone. "They'll never find her," he grimly confided to a friend. "She's dead and cut into pieces that are probably scattered all over the place."

When the woman's body was finally located, it seemed to heighten Laughlin's interest in the case. No sooner were details released of how and where Gibbs was found, than the attention-hungry bar-back had a new story to tell, one that again put him in close proximity to the dead nurse.

While in the army he had acquired an Alaskan gray wolf–tundra wolf mix as a pet. He'd named it Diablo and had brought it with him when he moved to Wichita Falls. Laughlin boarded the wolf and a small lion cub he said he'd also bought at a wildlife park on the southern edge of town, visiting them almost daily, often taking them into rural areas for exercise on weekends.

On February 10, the Sunday before Gibbs's body was found, he confided to several friends, he had been in the very pasture where the newspapers reported the murder had occurred, allowing Diablo and Ruthie, the lion cub, to romp in the open spaces. He'd even stood near the abandoned old trolley car, once climbing atop it for a good vantage point from which to keep an eye on his frolicking animals.

"If Gibbs's body had been out there at the time," he suggested, "I'm sure I would have seen it. Diablo and Ruthie were all over the field that morning."

One who was not impressed by the coincidence Laughlin had described was a friend named Anna Guerieri. "Danny," she said, "this is getting pretty scary. I'm afraid that you're going to get yourself involved in this if you keep talking about it. You need to leave it alone."

The warning went unheeded. Soon the fact of his visit to the pasture where Gibbs's body had been found was known to several workers at the Stardust. The attention it earned him became a drug. Soon he had yet another story to tell.

While results of the victim's autopsy had been kept

from the media, another female friend of Laughlin's who worked at Wichita Falls General was passing along rumors she'd heard at the hospital. In short order he was talking of the gruesome fact that animals had eaten away parts of Gibbs's arm and leg. He also had it on good authority that she had been raped. Not all of Laughlin's "inside" information was accurate, however. It was his understanding, he confided to several people, that Toni Gibbs had not only been stabbed but shot twice with a .22.

"That's the part that kinda worries me," he observed. "I had a couple of .22 rifles until not long ago. Somebody broke the windows out of my pickup and stole them." The theft, which he said he'd reported to the police, had come shortly after Gibbs disappeared.

Those to whom he confided such information didn't know what to make of Laughlin's blind determination to inject himself into the life and death of someone he had barely known. He was, they knew, eccentric—who would own a wolf and a lion cub as pets?—and attempted to disguise his low self-esteem with often-outlandish stories of sexual conquests or big deals he had in the works. The one thing that was common knowledge about Danny Laughlin was that he seemed to have an insatiable appetite for attention. He was loud, boisterous, and on more than one occasion had displayed a hair-trigger temper. Divorced, he had girlfriends, but it was highly unlikely that someone like Toni Gibbs would have given an always-broke bar-back the time of day. So why had he fixated on her and the investigation of her murder? Why was he risking the danger of involving himself in an unsolved crime? Unless, perhaps, he'd had something to do with it.

Dana Gearardo, with whom he'd been living off and on in recent months, had begun to wonder. Though Laughlin had never even hinted that he had in any way been involved in Gibbs's disappearance or death, she found herself contemplating the possibility that her boyfriend might be a killer. Weary of his constant talk about the crime, her anxiety grew daily, until she finally told him she wanted him to move out of her apartment. "We can still be friends," she said in an effort to soften the pain of her decision. "I just don't think we should be together all the time." She was relieved that he'd taken it so well. In fact, his response immediately sparked a tinge of regret. Danny had never treated her badly, had never raised a hand to her. He had, in fact, done everything he could to take care of her since she'd moved to Wichita Falls, doing mechanical work on her old car to keep it running, often having breakfast prepared when she woke, and sharing responsibility for keeping the apartment clean. Sex with him had always been gentle. And, god, how he loved that wolf. Diablo was more like Danny's child than a pet. For every shortcoming he had there was a balancing positive to his nature.

Surely there was no way he could have murdered someone.

The young man with the shoulder-length hair and mustache was not unknown to those investigating the case. In the days after Gibbs's family had filed a missing persons report, Wichita Falls police had conducted interviews at the hospital, in her neighborhood, and at places she'd been known to frequent. Learning that she visited the Stardust on a regular basis, the police had made it a point to speak with employees of the club. While a few thought they recognized Gibbs from the picture they were shown, only Laughlin could actually remember her. But since he'd spoken to her only once and had not even known her name, his input was judged to be of little or no real value.

That would change shortly after the body was found

when a Stardust employee, jailed overnight in nearby Henrietta on a driving-while-intoxicated charge, mentioned that a coworker at the club had been talking a great deal about the case. In short order the information reached Bill Gerth. A computer background check soon indicated that before moving to Wichita Falls, Danny Wayne Laughlin had, shortly after being discharged from the army, been arrested by police in Kansas City as a suspect in an attempted rape.

"We need to talk to this guy," the Ranger said.

It was on a mid-February Saturday that Laughlin returned to the Fillmore Street apartment he'd recently moved into and found the card of a Wichita Falls police officer attached to his door. Written on the back of it was a request that he phone at his earliest convenience.

"I bet I know what they want to talk to me about," Laughlin told a friend who had stopped by.

"You gonna call them?"

"Hell, I guess I'd better." Danny shrugged.

The following afternoon he telephoned the police station and quickly learned that his prediction had been accurate. Though surprised word had reached investigators that he'd been in the pasture where Toni Gibbs's body had been found, he readily admitted taking the wolf and lion cub for a run. "I kinda figured you guys would be calling me," he added.

"Why's that?" the officer replied.

"Well, from what I've been hearing, that girl they found out in the country was killed with some kind of .22, and I had two rifles stolen out of my pickup just before she disappeared. I've been worried that maybe it was one of my guns that was used."

Though puzzled by his caller's willingness to insert himself into the investigation, the officer, aware that there was no evidence a gun had been used in the crime, laughed. "Well, I really don't think you've got much to worry about," he acknowledged. "Unless, of course, they come after you with chains and shackles."

The following day, however, yet another police officer contacted Laughlin. Stopping at the young man's apartment, Detective Joe Shepard, assigned to the case since Gibbs's disappearance, asked him to come to the police station to further discuss the matter. "How's the twenty-sixth sound to you?" he asked.

"Works for me."

It was only after the detective left that Laughlin, who had begun a search for a new, better-paying job, realized that he had scheduled an appointment with the Texas Employment Commission for that day. He phoned a surprised Shepard to ask if it would be okay for him to come in a day early.

"This guy," the detective said to Gerth, "is anxious to tell us something."

By the time he arrived at the police station, the confident demeanor Laughlin displayed over the phone had turned belligerent. Why, he wanted to know, had the police been following him in unmarked cars for the last several days? And, even before being asked, he made it clear he would not consent to a polygraph test. "I've taken them before," he said, "when I was interviewing for jobs, and I've never passed one." Looking across a small table at the unsmiling Bill Gerth, he nervously moved about in his chair, repeatedly clasping and unclasping his hands.

"Son, nobody's asking you to take a lie detector test," Gerth said, "and as far as I know there hasn't been anybody following you. Why would they?"

"Because I was out in that field . . . out there where they found the body." And with that Laughlin again recounted his weekend trip to the pasture with Diablo and Ruthie. He'd gone out early in the morning, he said, and had stayed only a couple of hours since the day had suddenly begun to turn cold.

"You ever go around that old trolley car?"

"Yeah, I climbed up on one side of it a couple of times to see where my animals were." He had not, however, looked or gone inside. And, no, he'd not seen Toni Gibbs's body as he followed Diablo and Ruthie through the pasture.

Gerth leaned back, folding his arms, silently staring across at the young man for several seconds before speaking again. "Then how is it you told people that part of the woman's arm and leg had been eaten away by varmints?"

"That policeman who called me, I think maybe he told me that," Laughlin replied.

Gerth, already advised of the content of the phone conversation, had been assured no mention of Gibbs's body or evidence collected had been made.

"Tell me about Toni Gibbs," the Ranger said.

During the two months he'd worked at the Stardust, Laughlin said, she had come in a couple of times a week, usually on weekends. On a couple of occasions he thought he'd seen her snorting cocaine or speed with some of the friends she'd been with. One night, he remembered, she got into some kind of argument with a couple of guys at one of the pool tables. The last time he'd seen her was on a Sunday night.

"You saw her in the club the night after she was reported missing?"

Laughlin nodded. "Yeah, I'm pretty sure."

"See her leave that night?"

"No."

"You and her ever go out?"

"We'd made a date to," Laughlin said, "but then she disappeared."

The cocky tone had returned to his voice. "I tell you who you guys ought to be looking at," he said. And with that he gave the name of a Stardust bartender with whom he'd been having problems. "This guy," Laughlin continued, "hates women. He's always making crude and obscene remarks about them. He's always talking about how his favorite thing to do to women is, you know, fuck them in the ass, really humiliate them.

"I once saw him kick one of his girlfriends in the head . . . and she was eight months pregnant at the time. He's the guy you should be talking to."

Gerth nodded as the young man spoke, yet kept the question that was suddenly playing on his mind to himself: Did this arrogant kid sitting across from him know that Toni Gibbs had been assaulted anally?

Long after the interview had ended and Laughlin had left, Gerth sat with Police Captain Roy Wynn and Major Charles Trainham, who had listened in on the questioning. They collectively agreed on three things: Danny Laughlin had a greatly inflated ego. He had not been telling the truth. And they damn sure would be talking to him again.

Two days later, following a second interview with Gerth, Laughlin began talking with friends about seeing to it that his pet wolf was returned to Alaska. He had, he said, voluntarily given hair and blood samples to the police and had finally agreed to take a series of polygraph tests. He'd even allowed a search of his apartment. "They're going to arrest me pretty soon," he told Dana Gearardo. "I'm pretty sure of it."

For the first time since he'd begun talking of Gibbs's disappearance and murder, Dana detected a note of genuine concern in Danny's voice. Whatever game he was playing, she knew, had gotten far out of hand.

Laughlin's worry was justified. What he'd not been

told was that on each of the three polygraph tests he'd taken, he had shown deception.

Checking his military records, officials found that his army career had not been nearly as distinguished or exciting as he'd led friends and coworkers to believe. Most interesting, in fact, was his disciplinary record during his three years of service. He had regularly disobeyed orders from commanding officers, gotten into fights with other enlisted men, and on at least one occasion resisted arrest by Military Police officers. He had been assigned to counseling for his verbal outbursts, and there was a dismissed claim that he had, in a fit of anger, once threatened his wife after she had informed him she was filing for divorce.

During his year-long stay at Fort Richardson, Anchorage police had considered Laughlin and a friend of his the prime suspects in a lengthy series of residential burglaries. Laughlin was never convicted despite the fact that his wife had told police during one of the numerous disturbance calls made to their home that there were items from over twenty burglaries hidden inside. A female investigator also said that Laughlin had been a suspect in a robbery-rape that had occurred near the base where he was stationed. "We just never could make anything stick," the investigator told the Texas authorities. "And, frankly, I was glad to see him discharged and out of here." It was her guess, she said, that Danny Laughlin left Alaska with seven or eight thousand dollars' worth of jewelry taken in the burglaries her department had investigated.

Even his story about owning the lion cub was apparently a lie. When Wichita Falls officers went out to the wildlife zoo to take hair samples from Laughlin's wolf for comparison to animal hairs that had been found in Gibbs's abandoned car, they met a woman named Elaine Bennett who told them she had boarded her young African lion at the same zoo. "Danny occasionally played with the cub when he'd come to exercise his wolf," the woman said, "but as far as I know he never owned a lion himself. And he never took mine out to run with his animal."

It was soon rare that a day would pass without Laughlin being aware that he was being watched. It was unusual for him to emerge from his apartment and not see an unmarked police car parked on the street. On several occasions the driver would lift a camera to the car window and snap a quick series of photographs. Seldom was he not followed when he made the early-evening drive to the Stardust. When he went to speak to the manager of a Gibson's warehouse about a job the Employment Commission had steered him to, he was surprised to be asked if there was anything in the immediate future that might make it necessary for him to miss a considerable amount of work. The manager obviously knew something Danny didn't.

Archer County District Attorney Jack McGaughey and his Wichita County counterpoint, Barry Macha, had, after numerous discussions, decided to convene a grand jury to further investigate Laughlin's possible involvement in Toni Gibbs's murder. Neither anticipated that an indictment would result, but both felt that it might add to the pressure Danny Laughlin was no doubt feeling. His answers under oath, they hoped, could provide some forward momentum to another homicide investigation that seemed headed toward a dead end.

A half hour's drive south of Wichita Falls, one is quickly removed from the urban world and set in a cattle country that has changed little since the days when all cowboys rode horseback. Archer County is a rolling mural of scrub oaks and mesquites, barbed wire fences and grazing whiteface Herefords. Were it not for the fact that a small residential portion of Wichita Falls lies within its boundaries, the 8,000 population figure it claims would be much less.

Archer City, the county seat, is home to 1,807 people. Mingling among its farmers and ranchers is Pulitzer Prize–winning author Larry McMurtry, who has provided the world of literature such novels as *Lonesome Dove* and *The Last Picture Show*. The movie version of the latter, a coming-of-age story set in the 1950s, was actually filmed in Archer City. Its liberal peppering of profanity, infidelity, and the bare breasts of a young actress named Cybill Shepherd had caused more than a few local eyebrows to be raised. Only in recent years, in fact, has McMurtry been forgiven his ribald transgressions and restored to status as the community's favorite son. That came after he began a downtown facelifting effort by purchasing a half-dozen vacant buildings on the square and filling each with books, new and used. His thriving enterprise now lures a steady stream of buyers and the curious to town. At the local Dairy Queen, framed dust jackets of his lengthy list of best-sellers grace the walls.

Late on the morning of March 8, 1985, a nervous Danny Laughlin sat in one of its booths, drinking coffee while waiting until it was time to report to the city's old native-stone courthouse where the grand jury would hear evidence gathered on the Gibbs murder. He had not slept at all the previous night.

What the grand jury members would hear later that afternoon was a series of rambling and confusing explanations of why Laughlin was not a potential murder suspect but, rather, an attention-hungry young man who had been lying about his involvement with Toni Gibbs and her case from the start.

Dana Gearardo, who had ordered Laughlin out of her

apartment when she feared that he might somehow be involved, explained how, just days later, he had come to her and admitted that he had not been truthful. He'd said that he was out in the field where Gibbs's body had been found only in some twisted attempt to renew her interest in him. "He told me that he lied," the nervous young woman told the eleven grand jury members, "that he'd never been out at that field and didn't really know anything about what happened to that girl. He said all the information he'd gotten and had told to me had come from talking with other people."

Danny, she knew, had lied to the police about being out there. "I told him, 'If you're going to lie to me, that's fine. But you shouldn't have done it with the police.'"

Long before Laughlin took the stand to finally admit that he had not been truthful about being in the field, the district attorneys were resigned to the fact their earlier assumption had been correct: No indictment would be forthcoming on that day. But despite a lack of any tangible evidence, they remained convinced that the young bar-back was involved in Gibbs's death. The how and why, however, were still masked in a tangle of lies and half-truths.

When the long afternoon in the grand jury room ended, the only crime they could prove Laughlin had committed was that of giving a false statement to a police officer.

Wichita Falls D.A. Barry Macha was particularly frustrated. The murders of Terry Sims and Toni Gibbs remained dark mysteries, nowhere near resolution.

In truth, however, his impatience and concern were little different from that felt by law enforcement officers throughout the country. In nearby Fort Worth, for example, authorities were facing much the same dilemma, investigating a year-long series of disappearances and deaths of young women. And despite far greater manpower and resources than Wichita Falls, they had not yet made a single arrest.

Just days after Laughlin's grand jury appearance, in fact, the nude and decomposing body of a young mother of two had been found by a construction worker in a wooded area on the eastern edge of town.

The woman, named Debra Taylor, had been missing for almost a week.

CHAPTER FIVE

Nikkie Standifer rarely had either time or the inclination to read a newspaper and seldom arrived home from her job in time to watch the local newscast on television. What little she knew about the murder of Toni Gibbs had come from overheard bits of conversation from her coworkers. Only when she learned that the young woman's body had been found in a pasture less than a mile from her rural home did her interest in the crime increase. And even then she remained quiet about something she'd seen just days before the grim discovery.

It wasn't until an evening in early April, while she and her husband were having a drink in a Wichita Falls bar, that she mentioned it. A friend of her husband had joined them at their table and eventually the conversation turned to the murder investigation.

"You know," she finally said, "one afternoon I saw some guy messing around out there by that old trolley."

When she noted that it had been only a short time before Gibbs's body was found, the men immediately began pressing her for more details.

It was midafternoon on a February weekend, she said, and she was en route to visit a girlfriend. As she had turned off the highway onto Jentsch Road, she noticed a car parked near the gate that led into the pasture. In the distance, near the old abandoned trolley, she saw a young man, wearing jeans and a heavy coat. "He had a really big dog on some kind of rope or chain," she said, "and when I slowed down he looked in my direction for a second, then turned away."

Thinking nothing of the brief encounter, she had slowly continued along the still-frozen road. After a half-hour visit with her friend, she began her return home and saw that the automobile was still parked at the entrance to the pasture. She had looked for the man and his dog but they were nowhere in sight.

"I think," her husband's friend said, "that you need to tell the police about this."

By the time she decided to do so, Standifer had racked her memory for the exact date she had seen the man in the pasture. The best she could come up with was that it had been on the first weekend in February, either Saturday, the ninth, or Sunday, the tenth.

Few cases he'd worked in his lengthy career had so frustrated Bill Gerth, causing his generally low-key demeanor to turn sour and testy. A much-anticipated offender profile he'd requested from a trusted forensic expert in the New Mexico State Police Academy only added to his darkening mood. It suggested that the person who had raped and murdered Toni Gibbs was, in all likelihood, not a serial rapist. Thus it was unlikely that the same person had killed Gibbs and Terry Sims. The man they were looking for in connection to the Gibbs murder, the report indicated, had probably committed the crime in a sudden rage resulting from a deteriorating relationship with a wife or girlfriend. If he hadn't already, the killer would likely leave town shortly.

Gerth had read the report a half-dozen times before resigning himself to the fact it offered no new insight, nothing that would point him in the direction of the killer.

And then he was told that a woman named Nikkie Standifer had telephoned.

Unnerved by the fact that a half dozen stern-faced officers were crowded into the small police department interview room, Standifer replied to Ranger Gerth's questions in soft, measured tones. Again she told of her trip out Jentsch Road that afternoon, describing the car she'd seen parked there. It was a gray two-door, she recalled. Not knowing much about automobiles, she had no idea of the make or model. "There was some kind of square sticker on the rear window," she said.

Asked to describe the man she had seen in the field, she remembered him as tall and slender, with short brown hair. She didn't recall him having a beard, but he might have had a mustache. As she passed, he and the dog were approximately twenty-five yards away, walking in the direction of the old trolley car.

"Ma'am," Gerth finally said, "would you mind taking a little ride with us?"

They had driven into a residential area in the northern part of town before the Ranger explained the purpose of the trip. "If you see anything that looks familiar," he said, "let us know." Slowly driving through a neighborhood populated by modest frame houses and small apartment complexes, they passed a number of cars parked in driveways and alongside the curb as they approached 1612 Grandview. In its driveway was a gray Chevrolet Monte Carlo. In the rear window was a rectangular sticker.

"That," Standifer said as she pointed, "might be it." As Bill Gerth parked on the opposite side of the street to allow her a better look, a dog appeared at a side gate leading into the backyard, barking loudly at the passersby. The woman's eyes widened. "That's the dog I saw out in the field," she said.

What she did not know as the Ranger drove away, back in the direction of the police station, was that the residence where the car was parked belonged to Dana Gearardo, Laughlin's one-time girlfriend. The car was Gearardo's. And the dog Standifer had identified was Diablo, whom Dana had been boarding since Danny had moved into his own apartment.

Minutes after returning the woman to her car, Gerth was on the phone to the Archer County district attorney. "He lied to us," he said. "Laughlin *was* in the field. We've got a witness."

The drumbeat of new information that had the potential to finally get the investigation off high center soon reached Barry Macha's office. Giving false statements to a grand jury, he knew, was a felony offense. Still, proving that Danny Laughlin was a murderer loomed as a difficult task. Convincing a jury that he had committed perjury, on the other hand, was now a real possibility. "The short stick we've been fighting with," the D.A. said, "has just gotten a little longer."

Police in Wichita Falls and neighboring Archer City, meanwhile, had also been busy. While investigating burglaries of two small businesses and several homes, they had received a tip from a confidential informant who insisted that Laughlin had committed the crimes. Additionally, it was learned, Laughlin was in possession of property—including a .25-caliber pistol—taken during the burglary of a residence in nearby Lawton, Oklahoma.

Not only, it appeared, was he a liar, he was clearly the thief that authorities in Anchorage had said that he was.

Thus, on the first week in May, Danny Laughlin was back in front of the Archer City grand jury. And while he

again swore that he had not visited the field where
Gibbs's body was ultimately found, the eyewitness statement of Nikkie Standifer undermined his denial. This
time he was indicted, not only for committing perjury but
on burglary charges as well.

Still, it was not what Gerth or the district attorneys in
Archer and Wichita counties were after. Even as he was
being transported to jail, Laughlin steadfastly insisted
that he knew nothing of Gibbs's murder. "Hey, I can tell
you where I was that day," he said. "I can prove it."

No one expressed any interest in what they were certain would be still another lie.

Resigned, Laughlin changed the subject. Would they,
he asked, give him time to see that arrangements were
made for the care of his wolf before he was taken to jail?

The small, antiquated Archer County jail offered few
amenities to its prisoners. No television, not even a radio.
Rarely did the menu go beyond bologna sandwiches,
weak Kool-Aid, and tepid coffee. Visiting hours were
sporadic and the accommodations for the few who came
were discouragingly spare and uncomfortable. For those
locked inside, life became a slow-passing blur of night
and day.

There Danny Laughlin would stay to await his trial.
The murder investigation, meanwhile, had all but ground
to a halt. Officials in both counties had interviewed and
reinterviewed those to whom Laughlin had spoken.
Crime scene evidence had been reviewed so often it was
set to memory. Searches for something, anything, that
might have been overlooked did nothing more than add to
the frustration.

In Wichita Falls, meanwhile, memories of the brutal
murders of Gibbs and Sims had begun to dim. With the
arrival of spring, a new energy appeared on the city

streets. Newspaper headlines no longer blared the names of those killed, nor did editorials angrily demand justice. Aside from occasional calls to investigators from the families of the two victims, hopeful that some progress had been made, days would pass without so much as a mention of the unsolved crimes.

And then, on a late June morning in 1985 as he prepared to attend the daily routine of his office, it all came rushing back for Barry Macha. He had agonized over the cases, a day rarely going by when thoughts of them—and a credo he'd adopted back in his days as an assistant D.A.—didn't enter his mind. What he had vowed years earlier was to always keep in mind the pain felt by family members who had lost a loved one to a violent crime. In his mind, it was them for whom he was working.

A call had come from Ed Java, an employee at Central Bail Bonds. "I've got a fella in my office," he told Macha, "who has some pretty interesting information on the murder of that nurse." The man, he said, had briefly occupied a jail cell with Danny Laughlin.

The skeptical Macha was told that the man's name was Harry Harrison. "We just posted bond on several cases against him in Tarrant County," Java said.

"What's he got to say?"

"That this guy Danny Laughlin told him about killing Toni Gibbs," the bondsman replied. "Want to talk to him?"

"Can you have him in my office tomorrow morning?"

Macha immediately phoned the Archer County D.A.'s Office to alert Jack McGaughey, then spent much of the remainder of the day trying to determine just who Harry Harrison was. Over the course of his career, Macha had developed a healthy wariness of jailhouse testimony, viewing it as generally self-serving and therefore unreliable. If Harrison was in search of some kind of "deal," everyone would be wasting their time.

By day's end, Macha's concern about the man who would visit him the following day was dramatically reinforced by the fifty-four-year-old Harrison's criminal history. Dating back to his days as a teenager, his rap sheet told the story of a career criminal, from robbery, to assault with intent to murder, to aiding and abetting a rape. Should he wind up in prison on the charges he was facing in Fort Worth, the environment would be nothing new. He'd already served six- and ten-year sentences. Add the fact that he'd received an undesirable discharge certificate from the army, and it was clear Harry Eugene Harrison fell far shy of model citizen status.

Still, Macha had difficulty masking his excitement over the possibility, however remote, that a break in the case might soon result.

Seated on a couch in the district attorney's office, Harrison quickly fell into the age-old routine Macha had seen hundreds of times from convicts. The visitor was smiling and courteous, nervous and overeager, dotting his conversations with a steady repetition of "yes sirs" and nods of agreement.

He wanted to help, he said, but wanted to make it clear that he didn't feel it would be in his best interest to give a written statement or agree to be a state's witness. "I've got plenty of troubles of my own," he said, "without getting involved in somebody else's."

"We're just here to talk," Macha acknowledged in a calming voice.

A week earlier, Harrison began, he'd been placed in a cell with Laughlin, and during the course of a conversation they discovered they had both been in the same unit while in the army. "Turned out we'd both been stationed at Fort Richardson up in Alaska. We weren't there at the same time, but we found that we both knew some of the same people."

Impatient, Macha moved the conversation along. "What did he tell you about Toni Gibbs?"

"He was telling me how he was the prime suspect in this murder . . ."

"Of Toni Gibbs?"

"Yeah, I think that was the girl's name." Harrison nodded. "He started telling me how they went out and done some cocaine and marijuana. He told me they'd gone someplace out in the country and he'd wanted to have sex with her and she'd said no. That's when he raped and killed her."

"Why did he kill her?" Macha asked.

"He said he had to because she would have been able to identify him as the person who raped her." His words were coming fast now, his sentences all run-ons. "I remember telling him 'Hey, man, you shouldn't be telling me this. You don't even know me. Hell, I could be an undercover cop or something.' He just shrugged and said that if I was he was really screwed."

Later, Harrison said, Laughlin had added a gruesome footnote to his story. "He said the next day he went back out to where he'd left the girl's body, taking this dog with him. He told me that the damn dog ate away some parts of the body.

"I didn't want to hear any more and told him so. He just looked at me for a minute and started crying. Said he understood, but that it had made him feel better to get it off his chest."

Concerned with maintaining an informal atmosphere, Macha kept his questions to a minimum despite the strong feeling that Harrison, in his rush to recap the conversation, had likely left out details that might well make the story more convincing. Somehow, the D.A. knew, he would have to convince Harrison to do two things: take a polygraph test that would determine his credibility, then, if he was telling the truth, provide a detailed witness statement that might be used in court.

It was easier than he'd thought it would be. After Harrison had finished his story, Macha had spoken of how important what he'd had to say might be to the justice that Toni Gibbs's family continued to await. Harrison listened intently, then nodded. "Yes sir," he said, "I understand what you're saying. I gotta do the right thing."

He agreed to return to Macha's office the following day to give a written and recorded statement. And, yes, he said, he would submit to a polygraph test.

Twenty-four hours later he changed his mind. His attorney had phoned to say that he would not be keeping the appointment. Angered, Macha hung up the phone and looked across the room at investigators Paul Smith and Bill Horton. "Find him," he said.

Confronted at a friend's apartment, Harrison apologized for not keeping the appointment, explaining that he was concerned over the possibility of eventually becoming a witness in the case, exposed to press coverage. "A guy in my position has to keep a low profile," he said. "I could buy myself a lotta trouble by snitching someone out." And then, with only slight prompting from the investigators, he began to retell the story of his conversation with Laughlin. "Something I forgot to say the other day," he noted, "was that he told me him and the girl had been in some bar or club that night before he took her out into the country."

In a matter of minutes he had changed his mind again. "Aw, hell," he said, "y'all go back and tell Mr. Macha that I'll give him a statement."

And then he vanished.

. . .

While resigned to more waiting, the district attorneys were confident that Harrison would soon surface. They agreed that his track record, combined with the fact he'd most likely jumped bail and would have a new warrant out for his arrest, reduced his chances of remaining in hiding for long. Putting aside their impatience, McGaughey and Macha opted to proceed to other matters. On August 14 Danny Laughlin was walked across the street from the jail to the Archer County courthouse and pled nolo contendere to charges of aggravated perjury and burglary. Later that same day he was driven to Wichita Falls where he pled guilty to two additional counts of burglary. For each crime he was sentenced to seven years in the Texas Department of Corrections.

Though still concerned that they would never have the necessary evidence to try him for the Gibbs murder, the prosecutors agreed that at least one positive finally had resulted: When and if they did finally put the case together, it was now assured they would have no difficulty locating their primary suspect.

Less than two weeks later Macha, returning to his office from lunch, stopped to gather his messages from the receptionist. One was a long-distance call from Dallas. A county jailer there had left word that he had an inmate named Harry Harrison in custody and "he says tell you he's ready to help you out on the Gibbs case."

On the seventh floor of the monolithic Dallas County Government Center, Harrison was escorted into an interview room where Macha and McGaughey sat waiting with investigator Paul Smith. Neither was surprised that the elusive Harrison, a bit thinner and the circles under his eyes now darker, had a wide smile on his face as he entered the room.

Smith had already tested the tape recorder that was placed in the middle of the only table in the room and motioned for Harrison to have a seat. There was no way the meeting would turn into a warm and fuzzy reunion. Punching the "record" button even before the inmate was seated, the investigator spoke the time and date into the machine, made note of everyone who was present, then read Harrison his Miranda rights. The preliminary formalities quickly completed, Smith wasted little time getting to the conversation Harrison said he'd had with Laughlin.

"Like I told you, when he first started talking about it I told him that for all he knew I might be a DPS agent, an undercover agent, or something like that. But he went ahead anyway.

"He told me that he'd been working as a bouncer at this place and this gal had come in there two or three times. He'd been trying to take her out and finally she agreed. He said they went out some place and smoked some weed and tooted either crank or cocaine. Then he made a move to have intercourse with her and she refused him."

Shifting in his chair, Harrison's eyes darted across the room at the three men. "When she told him no," he continued, "he put this knife to her throat. Then he got him some. And then he said he got scared and killed her. He went into all this detail about how he stabbed her, then he went to crying, saying he felt better after talking about it."

Then, he said, they had returned to reminiscences of their army days in Anchorage.

Smith knew that was not all of the story Harrison had to tell. "Harry," he asked, "did he tell you what the girl's name was?"

"Yes sir. I think the last name was Gibbs or something like that. It was that nurse that had come up missing. They had her picture all over Wichita Falls. It was the same person; he told me that. I just know from the way he told me about it that the crazy sonuvabitch killed her. But he didn't tell me how many times he stabbed her or anything like that."

The silence from Smith and the D.A.s signaled to him that they wanted to hear more.

"I think he might have said something about he fucked her in the ass. Man, I didn't want to hear any more about it because, you know, I had problems of my own."

"What did he do when he talked about stabbing her?" Smith asked.

Harrison shook his head. "He was showing me. Making this side-to-side motion when he talked about it. You could tell this dude wasn't messing with a full deck of cards."

"Anything else? Did he talk about his dog?"

"He said something about having a dog that looked like a wolf. He went back out there the next day and took it with him. Said he wanted to check on her. And the dog chewed on her or something like that. I don't know . . . see, I had a lot of problems of my own . . ."

Macha leaned forward, placing an elbow on the table. "Did he say where he took her?"

"I think it was a secluded spot somewhere out in the woods. I'm not sure. I mean, I don't recall that much about it. All I know is he told me that he did kill that gal."

"He say anything about what the girl said?"

Harrison nodded slowly, a resigned look sweeping across his face. It was becoming clear to him that he was going to be forced to tell every detail of the conversation. "She was saying 'Please don't hurt me' when he first started taking some pussy from her. He told her he wouldn't if she would just go along. She did, but afterward he got scared that she would tell the authorities on him. So he killed her."

Laughlin, he said, had not mentioned what he had done with the knife after killing Gibbs.

The questions were now coming rapidly. McGaughey asked if Laughlin had given any description of the area where the crime had occurred or if Laughlin had said where he'd left the body. "Did Laughlin give you any impression that he had told anyone else about this?" he asked.

"He said that he hadn't."

"Harry," Macha asked, "is there anything—anything—else that you can think of that Laughlin described to you?"

"When he was crying and telling me how he felt better after talking about it," Harrison replied, "he told me that since he'd been in jail he'd found God. He had him a Bible and said that God was going to help him."

"And he didn't tell you what he did with the knife?" Macha asked.

Harrison shook his head. "I didn't want to know. Damn, I'd already heard more than I wanted to."

"Did he describe the type of intercourse he had with her?"

"Yeah, yeah, he did," Harrison acknowledged. "I said he did it the regular way; you know, missionary position while he was holding the knife on her. Then after he got through he killed her. That's when he said something about fucking her in the ass. Something like that."

"Did he indicate whether the anal intercourse occurred before or after he stabbed her?"

"After," Harrison said. "You gotta understand. I'm looking at this sonuvabitch while he's talking and he's glassy-eyed. Hell, I don't know if he's going to go off on me or what. Then he starts crying and telling me how glad he was he could talk to somebody. It was pretty damn spooky."

For several seconds the room went silent. Harrison rested his head in his hands as the three men who were questioning him exchanged glances. "Okay," Macha finally said, "I want to clear the record to show that Mr. McGaughey and I haven't offered you anything like a reduction in sentences or dropping criminal charges pending against you in exchange for your giving a statement. Is that correct?"

"That's correct," Harrison replied.

Would he be willing to take a polygraph test? "Hook it up," he said. "I'm ready right now." Would he appear before a grand jury to testify to what he'd just told them? "You bet."

"Last question," Macha announced. "Would you be willing to testify in front of a jury?"

"You bet," Harrison repeated. "I've got nieces myself, and I damn sure don't want a person like that to ever get ahold of one of them. Just because a person don't want to give you no pussy, that's no reason to take their life. If you can't get pussy, boy, you've gotta be hurting 'cause there's so much of it running around out there free. You know what I'm saying?"

Neither the D.A.'s nor the investigator bothered to reply. The half-hour interview completed, each was anxious to breathe some fresh air.

A week later Paul Smith sat in his office, reading a letter sent him by Dallas Police Department polygraph operator Troy McKenzie. In testing Harrison, he had asked three pertinent questions regarding his jail cell conversation with Danny Laughlin:

Has anyone put you up to making the statement you gave? Answer: No. No deception indicated.

Did Laughlin himself tell you he killed a young lady named Gibbs? Answer: Yes. No deception indicated.

Have you lied on the statement you gave about your conversation with Laughlin? Answer: No. No deception indicated.

Smith placed calls to McGaughey and Macha. His message to both was the same: "We've got him," he said.

On the first day of December 1985, Danny Laughlin returned to Archer County on a bench warrant to again appear before a grand jury. This time, after the new evidence was presented, he was indicted for the murder of Toni Gibbs.

Still, the nightmare that hung over Wichita Falls like a shroud was far from over. The year-old question of who killed Terry Sims remained. And, even as plans to try Laughlin for Gibbs's murder got under way, the body of yet another young woman had been found.

What he'd been hearing on the news confused him. Who was this guy the police had arrested? Was it somehow possible that he had only dreamed that night of rage when he'd grabbed the woman, shaking her violently and screaming at her? Had he only imagined her aloofness, her refusal to pay even the slightest bit of attention to him? Was the picture of her lying dead that had been burned into his memory nothing more than some cruel fantasy meant to add to his pain?

Was it possible that he really hadn't done it, that his fear and sleepless nights were all for nothing? He hoped so and worked hard to convince himself. And in those fleeting moments when he was successful, it brought a welcome sense of relief.

Maybe all the lying and hiding and the aimless nighttime walking were for nothing. Maybe his secret was safe.

CHAPTER SIX

Far removed from Wichita Falls, both geographically and in mind-set, Saddle River, New Jersey, is an upscale, eye-appealing community hidden away and just an hour's drive from the frantic bustle of New York City. Mild summers offer a stark contrast to the wilting heat of north Texas, the rich autumn colors shame the brittle browns that annually spread over Wichita County. The winters, though often long and bone-chilling, are of the type that inspire the artistry of Currier & Ives. The late President Richard Nixon's homeplace is nearby, and the magnificent and meandering Hudson River is only a short drive down Interstate 87, lined with restaurants filled with intoxicating chowder smells, offering a popular and picturesque gathering spot for young and old alike.

And there was something, indefinable yet vibrantly real, in the landscape that made Ellen Blau restless. Like so many teenagers, dissatisfied with the affluent lifestyle her parents provided and distraught over the strict rules that governed her young life, she was anxious to put her bucolic home life and private boarding school upbringing behind her. Young love and an adventuresome spirit will do that.

Schoolwork had come easy to her, resulting in excellent grades, yet she lacked the fascination her brother, Andrew, had for academics. Two years older, he couldn't wait for the year of study in France his parents had promised and then to begin work toward his degree at Swarthmore College. Meanwhile, Ellen's feelings about higher education vacillated. At times she talked of one day becoming an obstetrician; then, only a short time later, she would confide to friends that she simply could not see herself in another classroom once the demands of high school were completed. There were things in the world she wanted to learn about that no professor or textbook addressed.

Though her father's financial success as the owner of a printing ink manufacturer that supplied dye used in U.S. currency gave the Blaus rare status, amenities seemed of little importance to the young woman whose lengthy list of friends knew no social boundaries. She was as comfortable on a ski trip to one of the exclusive eastern winter resorts or a week of horseback riding at an equestrian camp as she was hanging out with friends who couldn't afford to pitch in for the beer at the impromptu parties that she often organized—and knew full well her straitlaced parents would not approve of. Ellen embraced life as if starved for new experiences, her interests venturing far beyond the country club dances, dinner parties, and the traditional extracurricular activities her school had to offer. Additionally, she had inherited the stubborn assertiveness of her father, a personality trait that regularly ignited heated verbal sparring matches between the two. Murray Blau, headstrong and demanding, a man who never relinquished the strict adherence to rules he had learned as an army mapmaker during World War II, loved his daughter dearly but admitted that she was "a handful."

There had been the time he picked her up from a party,

only to realize that she was intoxicated. En route home, she threw up in the backseat of his car, prompting an angry temperance lecture and a month's grounding. On another occasion she arrived home with a radical new hairstyle, her thick dark hair braided and beaded, that her parents immediately insisted she change. Ellen knew which buttons to push to get a rise. Rebellion was as much a part of her personality as the friendly smile she offered to everyone she met.

The situation only worsened when she fell in love.

She had met Jeff, six years older, in her junior year at Choate Rosemary Hall school, which she was attending in Wallingford, Connecticut. One evening Ellen and a roommate had slipped from their dorm room after curfew for a quick trip into town. At the entrance to an all-night grocery–liquor store they happened on the part-time mechanic, still dressed in his work overalls. Though neither handsome nor particularly personable, Ellen had immediately been drawn to the quiet, moody "townie." Both, they quickly discovered, were devoted Bruce Springsteen fans. It was common enough interest for the impulsive teenager to make a date with him before heading back to the campus. In short order they were seeing each other regularly.

When school ended after the spring semester and Ellen returned home, Jeff wrote her daily for weeks, then, to Ellen's surprise, showed up at her front door. He had, he told her, moved his small trailer house to Saddle River so that he might spend the remainder of the summer near her.

The reaction of Murray and Rima Blau was predictable. The young man who had followed their daughter home from boarding school was too old, they argued. They forbade her to see him. Which, of course, only heightened the intensity and romance of the relationship. Ellen, telling her parents that she was doing charity work at the local hospital, would sneak away to spend every day with her boyfriend.

Finally, when caught, she dug her heels in and insisted that she would continue to see him, even if it meant leaving home to be able to do so. The Blau house again became a battleground.

Ellen's stubborn stance gave Jeff, who wasn't crazy about the manner in which his own parents continued to try to regulate his behavior, an idea. Ready to sample life on his own, he had been thinking of moving to Wichita Falls to live with an older brother who was stationed at Sheppard Air Force Base, Texas, with its wide open spaces and promise of new freedom, might be interesting. Why, he suggested, didn't Ellen come with him?

It was just the kind of adventure she had so often dreamed of. In midsummer, Ellen Blau ran away from home.

Angered and worried, her parents immediately contacted the local police and began making the rounds of their daughter's friends in an effort to learn where she might have gone. Despite being convinced Ellen could not have kept her plans secret, the elder Blaus found themselves dealing with the frustrating code of silence that the young generation holds to so dearly. It took almost a week for one of Ellen's friends, finally admitting concern that the young man she had accompanied might not have her best interests in mind, to share what had been told her. She reluctantly provided Murray Blau with an address that Ellen had sent to her shortly after arriving in Texas.

Hastily preparing to travel to Wichita Falls and retrieve his daughter, Blau placed a call to the police in Texas, detailing the sequence of events that had led to Ellen being in their jurisdiction. Would they please pick his runaway daughter up and hold her at the city jail until he arrived?

Twenty-four hours later, Ellen Blau was back home, safe but resentful of the police involvement her father had summoned and the new restrictions he'd outlined to her during their flight back to New Jersey. Instead of returning to boarding school in the fall, she would remain at home and enroll for her senior year at nearby Ramsey High School. Though resigned, Ellen remained defiant. She would, she promised, adhere to the rules of her parents, but only until she graduated. Once out of school, she insisted, her life would be her own.

Rima and Murray Blau, certain that distance and the passage of time would bring an end to their daughter's determination to continue the relationship with Jeff, offered a conciliatory agreement they never expected to have to keep: Stay at home and graduate; then if you still wish to return to your boyfriend in Texas, we'll not stand in your way.

Dutifully, Ellen enrolled at Ramsey High, made good grades, and earned her diploma. The morning after graduation exercises, she packed and again left for Wichita Falls.

"I'll be fine," she told her parents. "I'm not a little girl anymore."

The tearful mother and angered but resigned father she was leaving behind were not at all convinced. Confused and frightened, they watched their daughter venture into a world whose rules she viewed as clear, simple, and nonthreatening.

Back in Wichita Falls, Ellen found the maverick environment invigorating. She liked the friendliness of its people, the jangly country music they danced to, and the casualness of their lifestyle. Redneck cowboys, with their boots and oversized belt buckles, mingled with women who were more comfortable in jeans and running shoes than in designer dresses. People partied hard, worked hard, and worshiped no class distinctions. The air force base, temporary home to soldiers from throughout the world, made Wichita Falls a social melting pot of whites and blacks, Hispanics and Asians. And Ellen met them all with a warm and friendly smile that was both endearing and disarming. If ever there was someone who never met a stranger, Ellen Blau was that person.

Which is not to say that her newfound life was idyllic. The relationship with Jeff began to deteriorate soon after her return. While she worked the morning shift at a Dunkin' Donuts shop, he lounged in the living room of their rented mobile home, watching television and daily promising to find work. When it became apparent that he wasn't going to do so, Ellen declared their relationship over and moved out.

Weary of Texas and the unfulfilled adventure he'd envisioned, Jeff decided to return to the East Coast.

It was, however, the last thing the young woman he'd lured from home wanted to do. For her, the move had actually been more a declaration of independence than blind love for a boyfriend whose ambition had proved disappointing. She would move on with her life, asking help from no one. During infrequent phone calls home to assure her parents that she was okay, she routinely turned down pleas that she return and offers of financial help. No, she always said, she was doing just fine.

In truth, she was struggling daily to make ends meet. To keep a roof over her head, she first moved in with an acquaintance of her ex-boyfriend, a young man who repossessed cars for a living. When it became apparent that the latter was no longer satisfied to adhere to the platonic relationship that had been agreed on, Ellen became wary and moved into a ramshackle apartment in a less-than-desirable section of town. Though her mother had repeatedly offered to buy her a car, she relied on a secondhand bicycle she nicknamed Trigger for transportation to and from work and the Midwestern University campus where she'd enrolled as a part-time student.

When the weather was bad, she arranged for rides with friends. And sometimes strangers. After telling an adult customer of a harrowing ride home provided her one evening by a biker—"He was holding a beer in one hand and steering the motorcycle with the other," she said. "When we went across the railroad tracks, I thought I was going to be pitched off."—the listener shook his head and issued an ominous warning: "They're going to find you lying dead in some field one of these days if you don't stop that kind of crap," he said.

Ellen only laughed dismissively. She could take care of herself.

Like most young women entering the fast-food workforce, she was constantly on the lookout for a better job. In time she left the doughnut shop and took a position as a waitress at a Bennigan's restaurant. Soon two fellow waitresses invited her to move into their apartment and share the rent. That arrangement lasted only until Ellen, ever on the lookout for lost souls, invited a couple of down-on-their-luck construction workers she'd met to sleep on the living room floor for a couple of nights until they could find work and a place of their own.

Not only did the visitors' stay extend long past the "couple of nights," but they were soon eating the young women's food and arguing with them over what television shows to watch. Yet only when her roommates threatened full-scale revolt did Ellen insist that her guests, having badly abused the hospitality she had extended, seek other accommodations.

When her dog, Little Bear, another stray that had come into her life, gave birth to a litter of puppies that

Ellen insisted on keeping in her room, it was finally suggested that she either get rid of the animals or find a new place to live. Packing her few belongings into one cardboard box and Little Bear's puppies into another, she moved out.

For all her endearing qualities, even the closest of her new friends could not help but be concerned over the naïve attitude Ellen had toward strangers. How could someone so bright, so polished and well educated, not see the potential dangers of the world in which she lived?

Among those who wondered was a Bennigan's waitress named Janie Ball.

Married and expecting her first child, Janie was older than most of the Bennigan employees. With little in common with the younger women, most of whom were working their way through college, she made no attempt to establish any real friendships in her workplace. As a result, she was never invited to after-work beer and pot parties that she knew to be routine occurrences among the younger waiters and waitresses.

Another who seemed to avoid such gatherings was the young woman named Ellen, who almost daily worked a double shift. She rode her bicycle to work, wore her hair in pigtails that made Janie think of the Indian maiden Pocahontas, and had a radiance about her that was hypnotic. For weeks the older waitress watched the woman—just a girl, really, she thought—and felt an inexplicable yet growing compassion for her. That no one ever dropped her off at work or picked her up once her shift was completed made it clear she was on her own, without family or a boyfriend. Her work ethic was that of a person desperate to keep the job. She would often wear the same clothing, though always washed and pressed, several days in succession.

This girl, Janie thought, could use a friend—and a little help.

She had a number of pairs of jeans at home that she had outgrown, and agonized for days over how she might offer them to the young woman without offending her. She decided it best to get to know her better before making such a gesture. One afternoon, when it was obvious Ellen would not be staying for the night shift, Janie offered her a ride home.

Despite the eight years' difference in their ages, they hit it off immediately. "I have someone I want you to meet," Janie was soon telling her husband. "She's the neatest person I've met in a long time."

Danny Ball, then, accompanied his wife when she delivered the used jeans to Ellen's apartment. Though dismayed at the living conditions he saw, he too was immediately charmed by the young woman with the slight eastern accent. Before leaving he whispered the suggestion to his wife that she invite her new friend for dinner some evening.

As they returned to their car, Janie sensed that her husband had also recognized something special about Ellen. "Well," she asked, "what do you think?"

Danny pondered the question until he was behind the wheel. "I like her," he finally responded. "I think that she has a good heart."

His wife thought the answer a bit odd, but on target. She smiled. "I think you're right."

Soon Ellen was a regular visitor to the Balls' tiny upstairs apartment on Bell Street. She and Janie would talk for hours about a variety of subjects, from the soon-to-arrive baby, to school, work, and plans for the future. What intrigued Janie most about her new friend was her enthusiastic yet simple view of life, an uncluttered and beautiful sense of who she was and wished to be. When

Janie, concerned that her friend's schedule was too demanding, suggested that she consider taking a semester off from school, Ellen balked at the idea. To do so, she feared, would allow her mind to go fallow. She cared little for material things yet seemed driven to make her place in the world. And she spoke only generally of her family back east, never so much as hinting that her parents might be wealthy. Janie, determined not to pry, would have guessed that Ellen had been subjected to the same hard-scrabble upbringing that she had endured as a child.

She also saw much of herself in the young woman, and quickly a bond that she found pleasantly remarkable developed. In a short span of time, she and her husband began to look upon Ellen as a member of the family. And with that attitude came a growing concern for her welfare, and worry about her trusting, free-spirited ways.

When, one weekend, Ellen suddenly decided to make a trip to California with a long-haul truck driver she'd met, Janie and Danny unsuccessfully tried to talk her out of it, then spent anxious days awaiting her safe return. When she knocked on their door several days later, bringing them a soda pop bottle filled with sand she'd gathered from the beach as a gift, any irritation they had felt quickly melted away.

Though careful not to fall into the role of surrogate mother, Janie could not help but offer occasional advice, particularly about being too trusting of strangers. It was dangerous, and she had close-to-home examples to make her point. There was that pretty young nurse, Terry Sims, who had been raped and murdered just two blocks away. Then the body of another Wichita Falls woman, Toni Gibbs, had been found in a field outside of town. Their killers had still not been arrested.

"Not everyone," she warned, "is as nice as you want to think they are."

She also told Ellen of a man who lived in a downstairs apartment, suggesting that she avoid him. That's what Janie had decided to do after first meeting him. Tall and lanky, with a strange, vacant look, he had made her uneasy simply by saying hello when she'd passed him in the hallway. When he'd introduced her to his pregnant wife and his infant son, Janie still felt no inclination to get better acquainted, even if they were neighbors. It was, she knew, an attitude some would define as judgmental. Janie, however, prided herself on being able to quickly read people. What she'd read in the face of the man who had introduced himself as Faryion Wardrip had immediately sent up a red flag.

"He gives me the creeps," she told Danny. Pointing out that she'd seen cars pull up to the curb and drivers leave their motors running as they hurried to the man's apartment for brief visits, she was convinced that there was drug dealing going on.

"Just stay away from him," Danny said. "And warn Ellen."

It was just a few nights later when Ellen appeared at their door, a bright smile on her face, perspiration from her bike ride beading on her forehead. "Hey," she said, "I just met the guy you told me about. He was standing outside when I rode up. He seemed okay to me."

For the first time since their friendship had developed, Janie fought to subdue a sudden rush of anger. "Ellen, dammit, I told you the guy's a creep. Trust me on this. Avoid him. Promise me."

"Okay, if you say so."

Janie was delighted just weeks later when her husband called from work to suggest they look at a new apartment he'd found across town on Ardath Avenue. It was going to strain their budget, he admitted, but with the baby coming, they badly needed a larger place. As a bonus, he

SCREAM AT THE SKY   89

added, it was in a much nicer neighborhood than that along Bell Street.

Changes came rapidly in that spring of 1985. The Balls moved into the new apartment, their son, Kelly, was born, and Ellen moved to a better-paying job at Suds 'N Subs, a popular beer and sandwich place located near the air base. The friendship between Janie and Ellen bloomed.

In her still-infrequent calls to her parents, Ellen never failed to talk at length about the Balls. "Mom," she said, "I wish you could meet them. You would love them as much as I do."

And while Janie never pressed for information about her friend's parents, Ellen occasionally volunteered the fact that they continued to worry about her and plead that she leave Texas and return home. "They just don't think I can make it on my own," she said. "When I mentioned something to Mom the other night about riding my bike to work, she had a fit and started in again about sending me money to buy a car."

Janie gave Ellen a puzzled look, then placed a hand on her shoulder. "My God," she said, "let her. That's what parents do. You need a car."

Ellen pondered the argument silently for several seconds. "Maybe," she mused, "I could pay them back a little at a time."

"Sure, that'll work." Janie could not help but admire the fierce determination of the young woman sitting across the kitchen table. "I think that will work just fine."

What she did not express was her concern that Ellen's exhaustive struggle, however valiant, seemed to be gaining her little ground toward a comfortable life. When she and Danny had visited the latest apartment that Ellen was renting, they returned home heartbroken. It was worse than the one they'd seen before. The roof leaked, the plumbing groaned, and the kitchen was infested with insects, yet the landlord had recently informed all tenants that the cost of their leases would soon be going up. Danny expressed concern for the neighborhood, wondering aloud about her safety.

"We've got room now," he said. "Talk to her about moving in with us until she can save enough to get a decent place."

His suggestion was music to Janie's ears. A week later Ellen moved in. Soon, with money sent by her parents, she had purchased a used Volkswagen Rabbit and stored Trigger in the Balls' garage.

At last, she was making headway.

For much of his life he had silently watched from the shadows of his own miserable existence as others happily went about their lives. And he came to deeply resent their joy.

There had been the pretty girl back home who, unlike most of the others, had shown interest in him. They had become good friends, and he had thought it might even develop into something more. Then, one day, she had appeared at the front door and his father had answered. When she'd asked if he was home, his father had only laughed. Didn't invite her in, just laughed. And asked what a pretty little girl like her was doing hanging around his good-for-nothing boy. His father would deny the story, but that's how he now remembered it. Maybe it was just another invention of his tangled imagination, another lie. He'd told so many.

The fantasies were his only protection, his small comfort, his weapon for lashing out. At his parents, at those who belittled him, at women—all of whom seemed so set on putting him down. The women, they were the worst, always too good, too pretty to pay any attention to him. Even those who did lost interest quickly. When he'd first met the woman who would eventually become his wife, she had seemed so different. They sat in the bars and shared beery laughter and had good times. Then, however, no sooner had they married, she settled into a maddening routine of complaining, belittling him, telling the world of his hopeless failings. Her greatest purpose in life was to add a new level of misery to his. God, how he had grown to hate her and resent the undeserved pain she was so determined to inflict.

For his entire life the world had been deserting him, pushing him aside. His parents, at wits' end with his irresponsible behavior, stealing, and drinking, had finally ordered him from their home when he'd still been a teenager. With no place else to go, he'd dropped out of school and joined the service. Soon it too had deemed him unfit for its ranks and sent him away. Even his in-laws had turned their backs on him after his wife and children had gone to live with them. Once his father-in-law had stood at the front door with a gun in hand, threatening to kill him if he ever came around again. And he'd lost track of the jobs he'd been fired from.

All of which fueled an anger that he could no longer control. His enemy no longer even had a recognizable face. It was everywhere. It was everyone.

CHAPTER SEVEN

Early on the Friday morning of September 20, 1985, Janie Ball woke from the light sleep that had become her habit as a new mother. She had expected to immediately hear the soft cries of her newborn son, alerting her to the fact it was time for his morning feeding. Instead, it was the ringing of the phone that summoned her from bed.

"Is Ellen there?" a harried young voice demanded.

Janie stretched the phone cord into the hallway where she could look past the open bedroom door in the rear of the apartment. She was surprised to see that Ellen's bed was still made. "I don't think she came in last night," she replied.

"She was supposed to open this morning."

"What time was she supposed to be there?" Janie asked, feeling a knot suddenly growing in her stomach. Even years later she would not be sure whether her immediate reaction to the early-morning call was one of concern or anger.

The ground rules that had been established when Ellen moved in with the Balls had been few and simple. They would not act as parents, Janie had promised. But for her own peace of mind, she had asked that if Ellen was going to be late arriving home, she call. Ellen had agreed and, on the rare occasions when she did go out with friends or on a date, she had warned Janie that she might be late getting in. Never had she spent the entire night out.

If anything, their guest had shown an increased degree of responsibility during the time she had been living with the Balls. She helped with the baby, even insisting that his crib remain in her bedroom so she could watch over him during the night and allow the new parents some badly needed rest. So frugal had she been that she had quickly saved enough for the necessary deposits and advance rent payments on an apartment of her own. She'd recently found one—a vast improvement over her previous residence—that suited her needs and budget and was planning to move into it the following week.

Janie's mind raced. "This," she said, "just isn't like her. Are you sure she was supposed to open?"

"Yeah, I'm looking at the schedule right here. That's what it says."

She suggested that the caller contact Curtis Cates, manager of the Suds 'N Subs, to make sure the employee schedule was right. "There has to be some kind of mix-up. Get in touch with Curtis, then let me know what he says."

Minutes later the phone rang again. "Yeah, Curtis says she was supposed to be here an hour ago." The last anyone had seen of Ellen, she learned, was when she and several others from the Suds 'N Subs had stopped in at a nearby Pizza Hut shortly before midnight.

Janie hung up the phone, checked on her still-sleeping baby, then began pacing. She wanted to begin making calls to locate her friend, yet was numbed by the frustrating realization that she knew no one to contact except for Ellen's coworkers. And that was being done from the Suds 'N Subs. This is stupid, she told herself. Ellen's going to come walking in any minute, laughing at me for being so worried. I'll fuss at her, threaten to kick her rear end, warn her that she's probably in trouble with her boss, and she'll promise never to do it again. And it will be all over.

Still, every ten minutes she called the restaurant to see if Ellen had arrived.

It was late morning when she answered the phone to hear the voice of a man who identified himself as Farley Friday. A local bread truck driver, he said he was a friend of Ellen's and that while making his regular delivery to the restaurant had overheard the manager and one of the waitresses talking about the fact she hadn't shown up for work. He mentioned that en route to the Suds 'N Subs he thought he'd seen her car parked just a few blocks away at a convenience store where he'd stopped for coffee.

"Ellen drives a little green Volkswagen Rabbit, right?" he said.

"That's right," Janie replied.

"It was in the parking lot," he said. "The keys are in the ignition and it looks like her purse is on the seat."

"I'll be right there," Janie replied, her words spoken from a mouth gone suddenly dry.

This couldn't be happening. It made no sense. Less than twenty-four hours earlier, she had talked with Ellen when she returned to the apartment for a break during the split shift she was working. She had been upbeat, telling about the deposit she'd decided to put down on the apartment and a new boyfriend she had begun to see, a navy diver named Greg Warnock, recently transferred to Sheppard Air Force Base.

Arriving at The Country Store on Burkburnett Road, Janie could see that the parking lot, which stretched along the side of the small drive-in grocery, was empty except for Friday's delivery truck and a green Volkswagen whose front bumper was almost touching the building's cinder-block wall. Even before lifting her baby from the car seat and walking toward the car, Janie knew it was Ellen's.

"It's not locked," Friday said, pointing to the button inside the window. Janie approached slowly, dread already sweeping over her. Leaning forward, she could see Ellen's key chain dangling from the ignition and her purse on the passenger seat. In the floorboard were what appeared to be pieces of a broken beer bottle. In the backseat was the shirt Ellen wore while on duty at the restaurant. Careful not to touch the car, she squinted her eyes and focused on a small rusty-looking spot on the edge of the driver's seat. "My God," she said, turning to Friday. "I think that's blood." Clutching her infant to her breast, she was not aware that she had begun to scream. "Call the police."

As soon as Friday had spoken with a Wichita Falls Police Department dispatcher, Janie phoned her husband at work. "You've got to come out here," she pled. "Something's happened to Ellen."

The casual attitude of the patrolman who soon arrived only heightened her concern. Displaying no real urgency, he approached Ellen's car, opened its door, and began looking inside. He picked up her purse and spent a few seconds checking its contents, picked up the pieces of broken glass from the floorboard, and gave them a cursory examination.

"Ma'am," he said, "she probably just took off with her boyfriend," he said.

No longer trying to hide her frustration, Janie shot back. "Without her purse? Leaving her keys in her car? I don't think so." Then she pointed to the spot on the seat. "That's blood, isn't it?"

The patrolman ignored the question and began taking

information for the missing persons report he would file if Ellen Blau didn't show up by the end of the day.

Janie Ball had no intention of allowing the matter to vanish into a mound of wait-and-see paperwork. Contacting Curtis Cates at the Subs 'N Suds, she suggested that search parties be organized. Cates replied that he'd already been in touch with the owner, who agreed to post a $1,000 reward for information about Ellen's whereabouts. The restaurant, he said, could be used as the command post for those volunteering to look for Ellen. Danny Ball, meanwhile, was already designing a flyer that he would print at the Coors distributorship where he worked. "Make enough," his wife had urged, "for us to post one in the window of every business in Wichita Falls."

She telephoned the newspaper and local television stations to alert them of the situation and explain that volunteers were wanted for the search that would begin over the weekend. And then, with everything she could think to do done, Janie turned her attention to what she knew would be her most difficult task.

She placed a call to Shelton, Connecticut, where the Blaus had moved, to tell them their daughter was missing. Rima Blau said she would leave for Wichita Falls immediately.

The police impounded Ellen's car to process it for evidence and dispatched a surveillance helicopter to fly over the vacant pastureland near where she had last been seen. A half-dozen members of the department's SWAT team spent a morning searching the area near where the car had been located. Their attempts were as futile as that of Ellen's friends and coworkers who randomly walked back alleys, vacant lots, and through the mesquite-dotted countryside.

Meanwhile, Dennis Huff, a spokesman for the police department, was assuring members of the media that Blau's disappearance was being treated as a missing persons case and nothing more. Despite the small drop of blood that had been confirmed, there was nothing inside the car to indicate that any kind of struggle had taken place. And, in response to a reporter's question, the likelihood that there might be any link to the tragic homicide of Toni Gibbs, the young woman whose body was found earlier in the year in an Archer County field, was remote.

"I wouldn't want anyone to jump to the conclusion that something terrible has happened to this young woman," Huff suggested. "It's entirely possible that she just went away for the weekend."

"That," an angered Janie Ball said to her husband after reading the morning paper, "is bullshit. Something bad has happened. I can feel it in my gut. I know it and you know it."

Danny, who had busied himself throughout the weekend putting up the flyers, could only nod his agreement.

Janie racked her brain to come up with someone, anyone, who might have wished to harm her friend. And even as she did, her imagination could not reach into such darkness. The police had already determined that the young man whom Ellen had recently begun dating was assigned to on-base training during the time of her disappearance. The old boyfriend who three years earlier had lured her to Wichita Falls had not been back since he'd returned home. None of the friends she'd acquired and introduced to Janie seemed capable of any manner of violence. Still, somewhere out there was someone with ill feelings for Ellen, someone capable of creating this nerve-wracking nightmare.

For a time, her suspicions focused on the manager of the Subs 'N Suds. She reflected on recent conversations she'd had with Ellen in which she had complained of Curtis Cates's attempts to persuade her to go out with him. Ellen had not been interested, and Janie had suggested she explain to him that she simply didn't wish to complicate their employer–employee relationship. Once she decided to follow Janie's advice, however, Cates had apparently become increasingly difficult to work for. He constantly criticized her with no good cause, Ellen complained, and saw to it that she worked long hours and the least attractive shifts. It had, she confided, only gotten worse when he found out she was dating the navy diver from Sheppard.

Yet Cates had been instrumental in placing the reward for information on Ellen's whereabouts. He had regularly joined in the searches—though he seemed always to stray from the group to look in other places—and had been among the first to greet and console Ellen's mother when she arrived in Wichita Falls.

Still, Janie thought him strange. Finally she confided her feelings about Ellen's boss to police detective Joe Shepard, who had been assigned to the case.

As the long days crept by without word, exhaustion fell over the Ball apartment, which had become an informal clearinghouse for information. Rima Blau eagerly accepted the young couple's invitation to stay in their home and share in the vigil. Friends of Ellen's stopped in at all hours, hopeful there might be some news. The phone rang constantly. Murray Blau, advised by his doctor not to travel because of heart problems, called several times a day to speak to his wife. Ellen's cousin, *Dynasty* actress Kathleen Beller, phoned from Los Angeles to say she had contacted a detective friend in the L.A. Police Department for any suggestions he might have. And there were the cranks. Sometimes as often as three times a day a woman called, claiming psychic powers. Each time her conversation would begin with the same explanation: "I'm calling now," she would say, "because my husband's gone. He'd get really mad if he knew I was calling." Then she would describe a murky "vision" she claimed to have had: "I saw a man driving this car out on a dark road," she would always say. Never, however, could she provide a description of the driver or the road she saw him on. Another caller claimed expertise with a divining rod and strong "feelings" about where Ellen might be. Did Janie want to go on a search with him?

The call most anticipated, however—one from Detective Shepard advising them that there had been some break in the case—did not come.

Tending to the baby, spending endless hours trying to buoy Rima Blau's spirits and dealing with her own fragile fears and frustrations, Janie fought to hide her feeling that hope was slipping away. At night, while everyone else slept, she sat alone on the back porch, allowing the tears she'd fought to hide stream down her cheeks. In the darkness she whispered prayers, fearing that they would not be answered and listened for a call from her lost friend that never came.

Indeed, in time the fruitless searches ended, the media attention waned, and the authorities admitted they had no real clues to pursue. The only thing they knew for certain was that Ellen Blau had vanished. Wan and dejected, her mother decided to return home. She could, she explained, wait just as well there as in Wichita Falls. Bidding her a tearful farewell, Janie promised to call the moment she had any news.

The first hint of relief from the long and cloying north Texas summer did not come until October arrived, bringing with it cool breezes that finally lent the promise of fall. There was, however, nothing in the gentle winds to suggest that a bizarre and tragic moment in the region's history was about to repeat itself.

County worker Donald Morgan had spent the early Thursday afternoon of October 10 mowing the barrow ditches along East Road, less than four miles from where Ellen Blau's abandoned car had been found. Morgan was lost in the solitude of his work until he caught something unusual out of the corner of his eye. Backing up for a better look, he stopped and rose from his tractor seat into a standing position. "Oh dear God," he whispered.

Less than twenty feet away, just beyond the rusting barbed wire fence, lay a nude body.

It was an hour later when Janie answered the phone to hear the voice of Tom Callahan, a lieutenant with the Wichita County Sheriff's Department. During his years in law enforcement he had adopted a gentle but get-to-the-point approach with both homicide suspects and families of their victims. Bad news, he had determined, was best delivered straightforwardly and quickly. "Ma'am," he said, "we've found a body in a pasture out near the air force base."

Janie felt the air suddenly rush from her lungs as she anticipated his next sentence. "We think it may be Ellen Blau," he told her. "I'd appreciate it if you and your husband could come down here as soon as possible."

It had been twenty-one days since her friend's disappearance, and now the numbed and grieving Balls were being asked to help with the identification of a body. "I can't do it," she told Danny. "If it's Ellen, I don't want to see her."

Hugging his wife, he cradled her head against his shoulder. "We've got to know," he whispered.

In an interview room at the sheriff's department, Lieutenant Callahan laid a small evidence bag on a table. "I need to ask if you recognize any of these things," he said, first pulling a silver knot ring from the plastic bag. Janie looked at it for several seconds before shaking her head. "I've never seen that ring. If it's Ellen's, I don't remember her wearing it." For an instant, she felt a rush of relief. Maybe, she thought, there has been a mistake. Maybe the body they had found was not that of her friend.

Yet whatever glimmer of hope she might have held quickly disappeared as she saw the lieutenant pull a tiny necklace from the bag. Attached to a slim gold chain were two praying hands. Janie nodded, placing her own hands to her face. "That's hers," she acknowledged. "It was a family heirloom given to her by her grandmother. She always wore it."

Callahan gently placed the items back into the bag. "I know this is difficult," he said, "but I'd appreciate it if the two of you could drive out to the scene with me." Looking across the table at Danny, he said, "It would be helpful if you could assist us with an identification."

Minutes later they were driving down an unpaved road, their destination looming just ahead. Several police and sheriff's cars were parked near the fence line and an ambulance waited nearby, its back doors swung open. Overhead, a helicopter circled lazily. Just a few yards off the road, near a clump of mesquite trees, a half-dozen officers and the district attorney huddled in a semicircle, their heads down, each silently looking at something on the ground in front of them.

Callahan stopped his car at a distance. "If you'll just wait here for a few minutes," he told the apprehensive couple in the backseat, "I'll be right back."

"I just can't do this," Janie repeated.

"You won't have to," her husband promised.

Soon the lieutenant was back, his face drained of color.

Settling into the driver's seat, he turned to face his passengers. "It won't be necessary for you to go out there," he said. "The district attorney says he thinks we can make a positive I.D. through dental records."

What he did not tell them was that the body of twenty-one-year-old Ellen Blau, nude except for a sock that remained on one foot, had been ravaged by animal predators, her once-beautiful face now only a skeleton, her left arm torn away.

By late in the day, the remains were en route to Dallas's Southwestern Institute of Forensic Sciences where an autopsy would be performed. Police had telephoned the Blaus, asking if they would make arrangements to have their daughter's dental records sent to Texas as soon as possible.

Little in Dr. Mary Gilliland's personality or physical makeup would tip one to her chosen profession. Just over five feet tall, she moves with the quick, flighty motions of a busy wren, often talking to herself as she accompanies coworkers or visiting law enforcement officers on hurried trips through the various offices in the medical examiner's building. She has a no-nonsense air about her, accented by her blunt-cut hairstyle, her functional lace-up shoes, large-frame glasses, and her sparing use of makeup. She looks more like the stereotypical small-town librarian than a big-city forensic pathologist.

Those who know her well speak of her engaging sense of humor, her ability to pilot her own plane to cities where she is called to testify about her autopsy work, and the professional manner in which she does her job. Aware that there are those still taken aback by the idea of a female medical examiner, she signs her name "M.F.G. Gilliland" and insists that she be called that or, simply, "Dr. Gilliland." Only her closest friends know her as Mary.

Professionally, she was regarded as a thorough, conscientious pathologist. Dr. Gilliland, virtually everyone working at the Dallas County Medical Examiner's Office would agree, was good at what she did.

It was frustrating, then, that despite a lengthy examination of the body, she could not arrive at a specific cause of death. She could find no gunshot wounds, and the deterioration of the body made it difficult to locate evidence of stabbing or blunt trauma from some life-ending blow. There was no way the remains could reveal if there had been any form of sexual attack. All the doctor knew for certain was that the body that lay before her in the frigid downstairs examining room had been exposed to some kind of horrible, maniacal violence. Then discarded, it had suffered the added humiliation of wild animals roaming in search of a meal.

The best she could do was officially rule that the victim had died of an undetermined form of homicide.

Back in Wichita Falls, investigators also had little to go on. A thorough search of the desolate area where the body was found had provided no real clues. Ellen's clothing—jeans turned inside out, a shirt, a sock, and a bra—were found near a muddy stock pond a short distance from where her body lay. Her tennis shoes, the laces still tied, were located a few yards away, as was the neck from a recently broken beer bottle. Time and the elements had eliminated any footprints or fingerprints that might once have existed.

Their only suspect, Ellen's boss, was a long shot with no record of criminal behavior and only the most tenuous of motives to have committed such a horrendous crime.

By Sunday the paralysis of disbelief that had gripped Ellen's circle of friends had begun to evolve into grim acceptance that she was gone. At Janie's invitation, they gathered at the small Ardath Street apartment. It would be neither a wake nor a religious gathering, she said, but rather just an opportunity for everyone to draw strength from each other as they mourned their friend's death.

Among them was Rima Blau, in town to await word that her child's body would be released so that it might be returned home. For much of the evening, she sat stoically, listening as others talked about Ellen, telling of her generous and fun-loving nature and the lasting impact she'd had on their young lives. Eventually the somber mood evolved into occasional laughter as stories of frivolous events and reflections of happier times were shared. Even Mrs. Blau smiled occasionally as she learned what her daughter's life had been like during the past three years. That Ellen had had so many loving friends lent the first touch of warmth she had felt since the day, weeks earlier, when she had answered the phone to learn that her child was missing.

For much of the evening, Janie Ball found her attention repeatedly drawn to Ellen's former boss, Curtis Cates. He had not mingled among the others but, instead, remained close to Rima, talking to her about what a good employee her daughter had been and things he'd planned to do for her. Ellen, he repeatedly acknowledged, had a bright and promising future.

His presence made Janie uncomfortable. Since Ellen's disappearance she had found his actions strange and unsettling. During the searches, he and the Suds 'N Subs owner, Robert Wright, had routinely distanced themselves from the others, always going in a direction opposite from the group. When volunteers gathered at the restaurant for a break, Cates and his boss would sit apart from the others, talking in whispered voices. One of the troubling things investigators had shared with her was the story they'd been told that a white van, matching the description of the one Cates often drove, had been seen parked in the field where Ellen's body was found just days before the discovery. Among the rumors that had begun to circulate was that someone had gone to the crime scene and moved Ellen's body to its location beneath a tree so that searchers in the police helicopter would not be able to see it.

Janie avoided Cates as she mingled with her guests. She fought the notion that Ellen's killer might, in fact, be sitting in her apartment, but could not move beyond what she considered his strange behavior. She had not even shared with Rima Blau the fact that the police had told her they would soon be talking with Curtis Cates.

There would be time for discussion of such matters later. Mrs. Blau and her family had more immediate matters to attend. On a chilly Thursday evening, Janie and Danny Ball sat with Rima and Murray Blau in a Connecticut chapel as a memorial service was under way.

It was not until they were making their way to the cemetery that Janie began to cry. "I should have taken better care of her," she said.

Rima Blau cradled her into her arms. "Don't blame yourself," she said as the distraught young woman laid her head in her lap. "You were her friend and family in Texas, and we'll never forget that."

A few days later, on a late afternoon when a purple cloud cover hid the setting sun and hinted at the promise of rain, District Attorney Barry Macha left his office and wearily made his way toward the parking lot. Tossing his briefcase into the backseat, he decided to make a detour before going home. Driving toward the air force base, he slowed as he passed the Suds 'N Subs where Ellen Blau had once worked, then drove on to the location where her abandoned car had been found. Then he made his way through the growing traffic on Highway 270, finally turning onto East Road.

A few minutes later Macha was standing on a small rise in the pasture where Blau's body had been discovered. His tie loosened, coat discarded and back in the car, he looked out onto the still water of the stock pond. Eventually he let his eyes wander the landscape, searching out the nearby mesquite where the body had been first seen. Then the spot where the young woman's clothing was discarded. And finally to the barbed wire fence that bordered the road.

He was following a lonely ritual that he had begun in the early days of his career as a prosecutor. Revisiting the scene of a crime, Macha believed, was a vital part of the job he'd sworn to do. Thus he stood for some time, looking, silently pondering questions that still had no answers. *What manner of evil occurred here? What was the sequence of the horrible events that played out? How did the killer and the victim get over the barbed-wire fence? Was she still alive when he brought her here? And, if not, why hadn't he hidden the body farther from the road?*

His only reply was the gentle whisper of the Texas wind.

CHAPTER EIGHT

It was no surprise that Danny Laughlin's court-appointed attorney, Roger Williams, requested and was quickly granted a change of venue. In both Wichita Falls and Archer City, publicity and public awareness of the year-old crime his client was accused of would make it difficult to find a jury pool that had not formed some degree of opinion on the matter. Thus, in an effort to find a more neutral and un-biased climate, the trial was scheduled to be held 100 miles away in the Cooke County courthouse in Gainesville.

Since the crime had occurred in Archer County, Jack McGaughey would serve as the lead prosecutor while Wichita County D.A. Macha, who had spent far more time on the case, would find himself in the unusual role of second chair. Williams, being paid by the state, would be the lone attorney at the defense table.

Few in the north Texas legal community, however, felt that the two-against-one odds put Laughlin at a disadvantage. Williams, who operated out of a small storefront office in the rural community of Nocona, had a reputation for tireless preparation, regularly shunning the aid of hired investigators in favor of doing legwork and inter-views himself. A former prosecutor, the bulk of his private practice was a mixture of small-town deed transactions, divorces, and DWIs. And while he was comfortable in his self-described role of "country lawyer," he was no stranger to high-profile criminal cases. And, most colleagues, including longtime friend McGaughey, agreed that he was good. As an example, they pointed to his defense a few years earlier of a local secretary accused of the poisoning murder of her wealthy employer. Though the evidence weighed heavily in favor of the prosecution—so much so that the woman was, in fact, convicted—Williams's persuasive courtroom demeanor prevented his client from spending a single day in jail. The jury, moved by his presentation and closing argument, had opted for a ten-year probated sentence instead of the life in prison that the district attorney had sought.

Convinced that his new client was innocent, Williams had already begun drafting an opening argument that would include the suggestion that despite what investigating officials had publicly stated, there was a strong likelihood that the person who killed Toni Gibbs was responsible for the deaths of Terry Sims and, more recently, Ellen Blau. He would remind the jury that Laughlin had been in jail when Blau's murder occurred.

"At the very least," he told Danny during one of their numerous pretrial meetings, "I think I can establish reasonable doubt. What I'm planning for, though, is an outright acquittal." It was one of the few times over the course of his career that he'd spoken with such optimism to a client.

Williams was also good at sizing up his opposition. McGaughey, he knew, was a man whose interests extended well beyond the courtroom. He was an avid reader, had traveled extensively throughout Europe, and approached his duties as district attorney in a measured, conscientious manner. Though McGaughey had certainly not said as much, Williams privately felt his old friend had reservations about the quality of the case he would be presenting.

Macha, meanwhile, seemed ready to blindly bet the house on Laughlin's guilt. He, Williams felt, would be the adversary to watch.

When the trial opened on the first week in April of 1986, Judge Frank Douthitt's courtroom filled quickly with curious local residents who rarely had the opportunity to get a firsthand view of a murder trial. Elderly women, forsaking their soap operas, came, seat cushions under their arms, to watch. They shared the wooden benches and curious whispers with visiting members of the Wichita Falls media assigned to cover the proceedings. Sitting in the front row directly behind the defense chair were a middle-aged woman named Mona Brown and her twenty-year-old friend, Anita Rivas. Brown, a member of a Bible study group in nearby Olney, had met Rivas during a jail visit with Laughlin. An attractive woman with dark eyes and shiny black hair that fell to the small of her back, Rivas had known Danny for some time, having met him one afternoon at a Wichita Falls service station long before his troubles surfaced. They had talked and she reluctantly gave him her phone number. Shortly, the two developed a romantic relationship, and Laughlin was proposing marriage. Though she did not discourage the idea, Anita ultimately would have to argue that they wait until his legal problems were resolved. Meanwhile, she wrote him daily, promised to attend the trial and said that she would be waiting when he got out of prison. Through the wall of glass that had separated them during jail visits, he continued to talk of marriage and ask that she keep her promise to be in the courtroom. None of the defendant's family, however, was present. Wilma Hooker, his mother, had telephoned attorney Williams just days before the trial was scheduled to start, explaining that she had only recently opened a small restaurant near her home in Huachuca City, Arizona, and thus would not be able to travel to Texas.

In the gallery directly behind the prosecutors, the front row, reserved for the family of the victim, was empty. Toni Gibbs's still-grieving parents had spent weeks agonizing over whether to attend the trial, finally deciding that reliving the nightmare was more than they could deal with. Toni's father had phoned Barry Macha, asking that he be kept informed as the trial played out.

The victim's brothers and closest friends, scheduled to be called as witnesses, were, by the judge's order, not allowed inside the courtroom. The lawyers' opening statements, then, were heard only by strangers.

In the classic formula all prosecutors hold to, McGaughey and Macha spent the first day identifying the victim to the jury, then detailing the tragic fate that had befallen her. Hospital coworkers briefly took the stand to describe Gibbs's always-reliable work habits, and her brothers recalled organizing search parties in the frantic days and sleepless nights that followed her disappearance. Jurors heard how Wichita Falls police had found her abandoned car, then listened as Charles Hayes, the Texas Electric employee, described happening upon the body.

"At that time," asked McGaughey, "did you suspect who it might be?"

"I sure did," the nervous Hayes replied.

Shortly thereafter, Dr. Roger Fossum, the medical examiner who had performed the autopsy on Gibbs's body, took the stand to detail his findings.

Late in the afternoon, Texas Ranger Bill Gerth was called as the prosecution introduced a video and a montage of color photographs taken at the crime scene. While

the Ranger graphically described the condition of the
body and provided a gruesome inventory of items found in
the abandoned trolley, jurors sat motionless. Bombarded
by nightmarish images and bloodstained pieces of clothing that brought a new level of reality to the crime, they
chose to fix their collective gaze on Gerth. The steady
sound of his voice was, obviously, much less disturbing
than the ugly scenes playing out on the television monitor.

By the time Judge Douthitt called for a recess until the
following morning, it was as if all the air had been sucked
from his courtroom. Jurors and trial watchers alike filed
out without so much as a whisper. It was, one observer finally noted as he walked into the last rays of spring sun-
light that still bathed the courthouse steps, as if he had
just attended a funeral.

It was the effect prosecutors had hoped for. What the
jury now knew was that a beautiful young woman, talented and well liked, had been the victim of an indescrib-
ably savage assault. The next order of business would be
to convince them that the person who had committed the
unspeakable crime was the young man seated at the defense table.

The following morning, as Gerth returned to the witness stand, he stared silently at Danny Laughlin for several seconds before replying to Macha's first question.
Acknowledging the D.A.'s request that he recount his first
meeting with the defendant, Gerth said that Laughlin had
told him of having met Toni Gibbs at the Stardust Club
and of the nickname—Georgy Girl—he had given her.

And he had said that he'd been in the field only days
before her body had been found.

"At any time," Macha asked, "did Mr. Laughlin say
anything about the condition of the body?"

Gerth nodded. "He mentioned something about an arm
and a leg being eaten off."

"Had that information been released to the media?"

"No," the Ranger said.

Only when Nikkie Standifer took the stand to testify that she had seen Laughlin and his dog in the field was defense attorney Williams visibly eager for the opportunity to cross-examine a witness. She retold her story of her weekend drive by the pasture and seeing the defendant in the area near the old trolley car. No longer unsure about the date, she testified that it had, in fact, been on the afternoon of February ninth. "Is the man you saw in the field on that day seated in the courtroom today?" McGaughey asked.

"Yes," the woman replied, pointing toward Laughlin.

She told of her trip past the Wichita Falls home of Laughlin's girlfriend with Bill Gerth and of identifying the gray Monte Carlo parked there. It was, she told the prosecutor, the same car she had seen parked near the entrance to the field that day. She again described the dog she had seen in the backyard. "It looked like the same dog that was in the field," she said.

For the first time since the trial had begun, Danny Laughlin was agitated. As Standifer testified, he wrote furiously on a legal pad in front of him and leaned to whisper in the ear of his attorney.

Williams was on his feet as soon as the prosecution passed the witness. "Your memory seems to have cleared up considerably since you first gave a statement to the police back in January," he said, before pointing out that she had not been able to recall whether it had been on a Saturday or Sunday that she had driven past the field. "Could you tell us what you used to refresh your memory?"

Far less comfortable than she'd been addressing McGaughey's questions, Standifer's answer was terse. "My own mind," she said.

Williams also quizzed her on the fact that she had remembered the man she saw had short hair when, in fact, Laughlin had worn his hair at shoulder length at the time. And how, after only seeing the accused at a distance, was she now able to positively identify him today?

"I just know," she answered.

"Going back to that February weekend," Williams continued, "do you recall working overtime on either of those days? Saturday? Sunday? Perhaps both?"

"I'm not certain," she replied.

The first hint of sarcasm began to creep into Williams's voice. "You might have worked overtime that weekend but you don't recall?"

"Yes."

"But you do recall seeing the man in the field that same weekend?"

"Yes."

The defense attorney silently examined his notepad for several seconds, allowing the jury time to ponder the answers of the witness.

"Just one more question," he finally said. "Why did you wait so long after Miss Gibbs's body was found to come forward with your information?"

"I didn't think it was important," she replied. Even as she was speaking, Williams had turned his back on the witness and was walking toward the defense table. "No further questions," he said.

In less than ten minutes the defense attorney had raised doubt as to the witness's credibility. Before trial's end, he knew, he would inflict even worse damage. If the prosecution was going to make a convincing case that Danny Laughlin had visited the pasture, he was certain, it would need a much stronger witness than Nikkie Standifer.

McGaughey then called three of Laughlin's coworkers to the stand, each of whom stated that he had told them he was in the field with his wolf on the February weekend before Gibbs's body was discovered. Cecelia Smith and Anna Guerieri both testified that Laughlin had, in fact, also described unsuccessful sexual advances he'd made to Gibbs at the Stardust.

While Gibbs was still missing, Anna's husband added, Laughlin had told him that "they would never find her." "He said if they did, she'd be cut up in a bunch of pieces in a box somewhere."

A young man who had once been a neighbor of Laughlin's testified that sometime in January of 1985 he recalled seeing Laughlin in a car similar to the one owned by Gibbs; another remembered hearing the defendant brag of being a suspect in the murder investigation.

Just a few nights before Gibbs disappeared, her friend Barbara Foster testified, they had been in the Stardust and Toni had introduced her to Laughlin. Later the women had discussed the unsolved murder of Terry Sims. "Toni said she dreaded the thought of ever being attacked with a knife," Foster told the jury. Laughlin, she was certain, had overheard the conversation.

For a time after Gibbs's body was found, she continued, he had followed her home from work on several occasions. She'd also received several threatening phone calls that she was certain were from Laughlin. After threatening to call the police, she said, "He told me that if I didn't keep my mouth shut, I'd be joining Toni."

Williams lent no subtlety to his cross-examination. "You're here to try and fit missing pieces into this puzzle, aren't you? You had to help make sure there was a connection between Danny and Toni. That's what you're here to supply, isn't it?"

The young woman immediately broke into tears. "I don't know if Danny killed Toni," she said. "I don't have the pieces to this puzzle. All I want is for the person who killed my friend to be found." She paused, composing herself with a deep breath, and looked squarely at the defense attorney. "Lying wouldn't help Toni. And it won't help me," she said.

"That," Williams shot back, "is something we can both agree on."

At best, the parade of witnesses had, with a litany of bits-and-pieces testimony, positioned Danny Laughlin somewhere on the outer fringes of the crime for which he was standing trial. Still, the jury had yet to hear or see any evidence that suggested he was the person who murdered Toni Gibbs.

The responsibility for that would fall to the first person scheduled to testify the following day. The state's star witness would be Harry Harrison, a lifelong criminal currently serving a fifty-year prison term for assault.

On the day the prosecution planned to rest its case, Harrison, head shaved, wearing a polyester suit and a pair of boots, took the stand. Macha carefully led him through his recollection of the breakfast conversation he'd had with Laughlin while they were both in the Archer County jail. No longer attempting to hold back details, Harrison related that Laughlin told him of the date he'd finally gotten Gibbs to agree on, of her refusal to have sex, then the knife-point rape, and finally the detailed account of the murder. "After he told me about it," Harrison told the jury, "he started crying. He said he'd found the Lord and that God was going to forgive him."

"Mr. Harrison," Macha asked, "what do you hope to gain by testifying here today?"

The convict pondered the question briefly, then turned to face the jury. "I've got a sister and nieces," he said. "What I hope to gain is that the person who did this doesn't ever get back on the streets."

"No deals?" Williams asked as he began his cross-examination.

Harrison shook his head. "There ain't nobody cutting any deals," he said.

"Sir," the defense attorney said, "can you tell us where you currently reside?"

"The Texas Department of Corrections."

"And can you tell us what crime you committed that has caused you to be there?"

Macha was quickly on his feet, objecting.

"Maiming," the convict said even before the judge could overrule the prosecutor.

"I'm afraid I'm not familiar with that particular charge," Williams said. "Could you explain it?"

Again Macha unsuccessfully objected.

"Maiming," Harrison said, "is when you mutilate or disfigure someone."

There were murmurs of surprise throughout the courtroom when the defense attorney ended his cross-examination after so few questions.

The state's final witness was an inmate who had been in jail with Laughlin in the week preceding the trial. Glen Lowrance said they had been discussing their respective cases.

"And what did Mr. Laughlin tell you?" Macha asked.

"He told me, 'I know I'm guilty but I've got this case beat. I'll be out in two weeks and write to you.' "

Williams chose not to cross-examine the prosecution's final witness.

"Your honor," McGaughey said, "the state rests."

Williams's defense was as carefully orchestrated as that of the prosecution. He called friends and coworkers of Laughlin's who offered detailed accounts of his whereabouts on the weekend of Toni Gibbs's disappearance. They told of a mundane Saturday during which the defendant had stopped in to visit friends and later helped them

move several large pieces of furniture into Dana Gearardo's apartment, delivering a rent check to his new landlord, and doing laundry. Then he'd routinely reported for
work at the Stardust. Witnesses came forward to testify
they had seen Gibbs alive at a Wichita Falls shopping
mall as late as nine o'clock on the evening prior to her being reported missing.

The subtle message the defense attorney was sending to
the jury was that the crime in question had never been fully
investigated. Had it been, the evidence he was providing
should have given investigators reason to keep looking
rather than seek the premature indictment of his client.

With each witness, he demonstrated the weakness of
the circumstantial case.

To convince the jury of the possibility that Nikkie
Standifer had, in fact, learned elsewhere that his client
had said he visited the pasture near her home, he introduced a televised news report, aired on a Wichita Falls
station, that had included a reenactment of the abduction,
the crime, and a visit to the rural murder scene by the suspect and his dog. By calling Standifer's employer to the
stand to introduce records showing that she had, in fact,
worked overtime on the weekend she said she'd seen
Laughlin and his wolf, he raised further doubt about the
validity of her testimony.

And, like McGaughey and Macha, he saved his best
shot for last.

When Danny Laughlin took the stand, wearing jeans and a
dress shirt, the tension inside the crowded courtroom was
almost palpable. Members of the Wichita Falls media,
which had been daily traveling to Gainesville, arrived early
in anticipation of the drama that was certain to unfold. Even
the weary jurors seemed suddenly eager to hear Judge
Douthitt call the proceedings to order. Finally, after almost

two weeks of testimony, they would hear the defendant's version of the circumstances that had brought them there.

While the only evidence they'd heard connecting the young man to the murder were the accounts of Harry Harrison and Glen Lowrance, the prosecution's assertion that Laughlin had been in the pasture only a few days before discovery of the body had raised troubling questions in their mind. Why would someone apparently so consumed with the details of Toni Gibbs's disappearance and death wind up in that field, even claiming that he had climbed onto the old trolley car in which she had been murdered? And while she might have seemed a bit confused about dates, what motive would Nikki Standifer have had to lie about seeing Laughlin there?

They were not prepared for the explanation Laughlin had to offer.

Seated at the defense table, Williams quickly led his client through a detailed account of his actions and whereabouts on the day and evening of Gibbs's disappearance, then moved to Laughlin's alleged trip to the pasture to allow Diablo to run.

"Had you, in fact, been at that field on February tenth?" the attorney asked.

"No."

"What did you do on that day?"

Leaning forward, Laughlin glanced in the direction of the jury box. He told of getting up at about seven, going jogging, then stopping at a convenience store to pick up a newspaper. Then he had returned to his apartment. "Later," he said, "I did something."

"And what was that?"

"I went to the Southwest Bell Building on the corner of Ninth and Lamar in Wichita Falls," the defendant answered.

And with that he confessed to a crime for which he'd not even been suspected.

There had been a time, prior to his taking the job at the Stardust, when he had worked for a janitorial service that cleaned downtown office buildings. Among them, he explained, was the Southwest Bell Building. In its cafeteria were numerous coin-operated vending machines and a large money changer mounted on a wall.

On a Saturday afternoon, he said, he'd driven downtown to visit with a friend he knew would be working in the building. With Valentine's Day approaching, Laughlin had designed a card for a girlfriend and planned to ask the friend, whose penmanship was far superior to his, to do the lettering. "Since it was the weekend, the building was locked, so I knocked on the glass door. Luckily, he was working on the first floor at the time and saw me. He let me in and we talked for a while. I told him I might drop by again later, and he wrote down the four-digit code number that would unlock the door for me."

The following morning, Laughlin testified, he returned, aware that his friend would not be there. "He plays the organ in his church, so I knew he wouldn't be working until sometime in the afternoon."

"What did you do when you went into the building that Sunday morning?"

Laughlin described taking the back stairs into the basement, then making a thorough search of all nine floors to be sure there was no one else in the building. Then he had returned to the eighth floor where the cafeteria was located.

Using a screwdriver he'd hidden beneath his jacket, he removed the chrome-plated money changer from the wall. It had been far heavier than he'd anticipated, he recalled, forcing him to push it across the cafeteria floor and along the hallway to an elevator. "I hated to do that," he pointed out, "since I'd polished that floor many times in the past. I knew it was going to leave scratches." Once back on the first floor, he'd pushed the metal box out a doorway that led onto a porch in the alley.

"What," Williams asked, "did you do with it once you got it into the alley?"

"At first, I couldn't figure out how I was going to get it into my truck. Finally I drove around to the alley and backed my pickup as close as I could get it to the landing. Then I just pushed the box as hard as I could and put my hands over my ears."

The money changer, he recalled, landed in the bed of his pickup with a loud bang that echoed along the deserted alley.

Then, he remembered, no sooner had he driven onto a downtown street, than a police patrol car pulled in behind him, following closely for several blocks. "I got really nervous," Laughlin told the jury. "I drove around for a long time, watching to see if it was still behind me."

Finally he drove several miles beyond the city limits before turning off the highway onto a dirt road. "I followed that road for a ways until I was on top of this hill," he remembered. He parked his truck there, feeling that the elevated location provided a good vantage point from which to see anyone who might be driving along the road.

Then, using the screwdriver and a crow bar, he managed to pry open the money changer. "It took me about an hour to get it open," he said. "At one point I got so cold that I stopped and sat in the truck with the heater on."

His efforts were finally rewarded with ninety-nine one-dollar bills and two trays filled with quarters. Then he managed to flip the machine over the tailgate, into a nearby barrow ditch. "When it hit the ground a lot more change—nickels, dimes, and quarters—began spilling out, so I jumped down there, took off my gloves, and started picking them up."

It was then that he became aware that someone was

headed in his direction. He managed to get into his pickup and start the engine before a truck, driven by a woman, passed. While watching her drive past in his rearview mirror, he saw a car backing out of a nearby farmhouse. "I took off," Laughlin said.

Again fearful that he might be followed, Laughlin drove back into downtown Wichita Falls, making numerous turns into alleys, driving down side streets, and circling blocks before finally returning to his home.

Inside his apartment, he poured the stolen quarters into a box, then knocked on the door of a neighbor. "I told him if anybody happened to ask about where I was, he should tell them we'd been here, playing dominoes and gin rummy all day. He asked me why and I told him 'I don't want to tell you.'"

En route to work that evening, Laughlin said he had stopped at a Dumpster behind a Braum's Ice Cream store and discarded the metal trays that had contained the stolen change. "I just pitched them out of my pickup as I drove by," he said. "One missed, bouncing back onto the parking lot, and I ran over it. I remember thinking to myself, 'Oh, great, now I'm going to get a flat tire.'"

That evening, he said, he arrived at the Stardust five minutes late.

Several jurors shook their heads as they listened to his story. Even the judge seemed fascinated by the testimony of the young man sitting on the witness stand. He could not, over the course of his lengthy career on the bench, ever recall a defendant using a confession to a crime as an alibi to prove he'd not been involved in another.

By day's end, Laughlin had also disputed Harry Harrison's testimony. The only things they had discussed while eating breakfast in his jail cell, he said, were their army days in Alaska and a restaurant where Harrison had eaten shortly before his arrest.

"Danny," Williams said, rising from his seat to walk in the direction of the witness stand, "did you tell Harry Harrison that you killed Toni Gibbs?"

"No, I didn't tell him that."

"Did you describe stabbing her?"

"No, I did not."

"Did you describe having sex with her?"

"No. Harry was too nervous to talk about much of anything that morning." Laughlin said that he had, in fact, briefly read from the Bible in an attempt to calm the agitated inmate.

Now standing in front of his client, looking in the direction of the jury box, Williams had but one final question. "Danny, did you kill Toni Gibbs?"

"I not only did not kill her," Laughlin replied, "I had nothing to do with it."

Despite a vigorous cross-examination during which he was admonished by the judge at one point for badgering the witness, Barry Macha made little headway in debunking the story of the telephone building burglary. The fact that the very man whom Laughlin had seen backing from his driveway that afternoon had discovered the discarded money changer and telephoned the police eliminated the possibility that the crime described to the jury had not actually taken place. Nor did the defendant budge from the detailed account of his actions and whereabouts on the day and evening when Toni Gibbs had disappeared. Masking his frustration at the calm demeanor Laughlin had displayed since he'd begun his questioning, the visiting district attorney remained convinced that he had Gibbs's killer on the stand. But would a jury, not having seen or heard a single bit of physical evidence that put the defendant at the scene of the crime, collectively share his conviction?

There was no question that Roger Williams had presented a strong case on behalf of his client.

To discredit Harry Harrison, the defense attorney even called Prosecutor Macha as a witness, asking what, if any, deal might have been struck with Harrison's bail bondsman, Kenneth Knowles, in exchange for the damaging testimony. Though the D.A. vehemently denied any arrangement with Harrison or the owner of Central Bail Bonds, he left the stand knowing full well that Williams had added more cause for doubt in the minds of the jurors.

That doubt was reinforced when Knowles begrudgingly took the stand.

"Isn't it true," Williams asked, "that shortly after your client Harry Harrison agreed to testify, you were cleared of seventeen criminal charges on your record?"

"Yes sir," Knowles answered.

Members of the media, who had been kept in the dark for months about the evidence the state had planned to present, had fallen into a routine of comparing notes during midmorning coffee breaks and over quick lunches, whispering their concern that the prosecution's case seemed weak, and exchanging guesses about the mind-set of the seven women and five men in the jury box.

Soon they would find out. On a Thursday afternoon, following closing arguments, the jury began its deliberations. Among those pacing the halls in hopes of a quick verdict was Bill Gerth. Finally he entered the vacant courtroom and walked to a corner where the bailiff sat near the door leading to the jury room.

"How's it going?" the Ranger asked.

The bailiff smiled and nodded in the direction of the door. "Just listen."

From inside they could hear the muffled sound of shrill exchanges between what sounded like two women.

Soon an angry male voice joined in. "Sounds like there's a fistfight going on," Gerth observed.

When told what the Ranger had overheard, Roger Williams lifted his palms in a shrug. "Maybe," he joked, "they're making nomination speeches for foreman."

What was transpiring behind closed doors, in fact, bordered on the comical.

What it all signaled would have been welcome news to Williams. The twelve people charged with deciding his client's fate were definitely not in agreement.

Such would still be the case shortly after midnight when the judge received a note saying they were deadlocked, hungry, and tired. They were sent home with instructions to return the following morning to continue deliberations.

What neither Judge Douthitt nor the attorneys knew at the time was that on the only vote taken, seven jurors felt the state had failed to make its case against Laughlin. Five had voted for a guilty verdict.

The grinding wait continued through Friday. While the prosecutors remained in McGaughey's office, reporters and trial watchers sat on hall benches outside the courtroom, passing the time reading newspapers or paperbacks, and wondering among themselves if their weekend would be interrupted if a verdict had still not been reached by day's end.

By midafternoon a rumor began to circulate that the vote of the jurors was split, 10 to 2. If true, the prosecutors realized, their case had been lost. When, just after five in the afternoon, the judge received a handwritten note from the foreman stating that the jury was, after almost fifteen hours of deliberation, unable to reach a verdict, McGaughey and Macha decided on a legal move neither had hoped would be necessary. If deliberations continued and the jury came back with an acquittal, they

knew, the double-jeopardy rule would become applicable
and Laughlin could never again be retried for Toni
Gibbs's murder.

Told that the foreman had underlined the word "unable" in his message to the judge, the prosecutors knew it
was unlikely that any decision would be reached. "Your
honor," Macha said as court was called back into session,
"we move for a mistrial." It was the only way to preserve
the opportunity to retry Laughlin if new evidence was
discovered at some later date.

Despite defense attorney Williams's objection, the
judge granted Macha's request. Only later would the
lawyers learn that the last vote taken inside the jury room
had been eleven to one in favor of a not-guilty verdict.
The lone holdout had been the woman whose angry voice
had filtered through the jury room door shortly after deliberations began.

"When all was said and done," one juror told a reporter,
"we just didn't think the prosecution proved its case."

Laughlin, clutching the Bible he'd brought to the courtroom every day, stood at the railing near the defense table
and smiled at Anita Rivas. "I was hoping for an acquittal,"
he told members of the press, "but I respect the jury's decision." He was then led away by sheriff's deputies.

Standing nearby, his arms folded, Williams had watched
as his smiling client once again insisted that he'd had
nothing to do with the abduction and murder of Gibbs.
His newfound faith in God, he said, had provided him
strength throughout the trial. The attorney listened but
said nothing. Members of the media, he hoped, had not
caught him shaking his head as Laughlin spoke. Nor, he
hoped, could they read what he was thinking: Because of
some need that he could not comprehend, his client had
literally talked himself into all the trouble that had finally
crashed down on him. Had he not talked so much of a

young woman he had not even known, there would never have been a reason even to consider him a suspect. The perjured testimony before a grand jury would never have happened. And had he not called so much attention to himself, it was likely that he would never have been connected to the robberies he'd committed. If not for the jailhouse boasting, there would not have been enough evidence for a murder indictment, much less a trial that was going to cost the Archer County taxpayers in the neighborhood of $50,000. And now, only because the justice system had worked in his favor, Laughlin had managed to avoid being convicted.

Danny, the attorney thought, you should have just kept your damn mouth shut. If you had, you probably would be walking out of here instead of returning to the Texas Department of Corrections to continue serving your sentences for the perjury and burglaries.

And now there was a new postscript to Laughlin's troubles. In all likelihood his prison time would be extended when charges of the burglary he had confessed to from the witness stand were filed. "More than likely," Williams said, "they're going to file charges on the telephone company burglary. I don't think there's much we can do about that. On the other hand, I don't think they'll want to retry you for murder—unless they're able to come up with some new evidence."

Laughlin shook his head. "They aren't going to find any more evidence," he said, "because I didn't do it."

Stuffing his hands into the pockets of his trousers, the lawyer walked from the courtroom, knowing he should be feeling good about the mistrial. Instead, he couldn't shake the darkening feeling that there was no real victory to claim.

In Clayton, New Mexico, W. L. Gibbs reacted to the news that a mistrial had been declared with numbed silence. Finally, after listening to Macha's explanation of what had transpired, Toni Gibbs's father thanked him for calling. "I hope," he said, "that this case isn't over."

Aware that his call had rekindled old griefs, the Wichita County D.A. replied, "We'll continue to work on it, I'll promise you."

Gibbs detected no optimism, no declaration of real hope, in his caller's voice.

In the months following the trial, Laughlin's name faded from public consciousness. Aside from an occasional question from reporters about any new evidence that might have been discovered and the possibility of a retrial, he had become the same faint memory Toni Gibbs had. In prison, Danny Laughlin was out of sight, out of mind. If anyone did talk of him, it was to portray him as one of those rare criminals who had somehow managed to beat the system—a murderer who would never answer for his crime.

It wasn't until December of 1986 that he was back in the same Cooke County courtroom, this time to attend a hearing on a motion filed by a new attorney. Bill Brotherton, appointed by the court to replace Roger Williams, was prepared to request dismissal of the murder charges.

Again Laughlin found himself looking across the courtroom at District Attorneys McGaughey and Macha. What he heard from the prosecution's side of the room, however, was unexpected.

Rather than mount an argument against Brotherton's motion, McGaughey rose to tell the judge, "We are not seeking retrial at this time." He had, he told Judge Douthitt, already prepared the necessary papers to have the case dismissed.

Unaware that the Archer County D.A. had reached such a decision, an obviously angered Macha sprang to his feet and asked permission to address the court. "Your honor," he said, "if Mr. McGaughey would care to step aside, I'd be more than willing to prosecute this case."

The judge, surprised that the prosecutors were in disagreement over the matter, asked Macha if he was aware of some new evidence that would make conviction in a new trial a more real possibility.

"I've talked to a couple of potential witnesses," the unnerved prosecutor replied. "But I honestly don't know how much weight their testimony might carry with a jury." Pausing for a moment, there was genuine passion in his voice as he added, "I just think that this defendant ought to be retried. I feel just as strongly about this case now as I did last April."

The judge turned to McGaughey. "Are you aware of any new evidence?"

"No, your honor. I've talked with Mr. Macha and I'm not aware of anything new."

"Motion to dismiss is granted," Douthitt said. The words were barely out of his mouth when Macha stormed from the almost empty courtroom.

Any chance that Danny Laughlin would ever be retried for the murder of Toni Gibbs, he knew, had all but vanished.

In Olney, Anita Rivas had begun to number the daily letters she was receiving from the man she planned to one day marry, lovingly placing them in a box for safekeeping. In time the number would grow to almost 300. In one she had recently received, Danny had written of a strong desire to contact Toni Gibbs's family and assure them he had nothing to do with her death.

It would have been a fruitless effort. The Gibbses, like so many others who had long followed the case, remained convinced that Danny Laughlin was a murderer.

*He was running out of places to hide, his grip on the real-
ities of the dismal world in which he lived slipping. Con-
ning people was becoming increasingly difficult as he
found it harder and harder to remember the lies he'd told.
The one thing he had managed to hold to, grasping it as if
it were his lifeline, was the belief that the endless tribula-
tions of his miserable existence were the fault of others.
The causes of his failures were not his own. Hell no, that
responsibility fell squarely on the shoulders of a world
that refused to give him a fair shake. A dark, ugly, unfor-
giving world that he despised.*

*His family knew him as the failure he was, saw through
the lies and false promises. That's why he'd gone away
that night, never to return. His wife had stood at the front
door, screaming at him as he waited for the two-bit drug
dealer to arrive. If he left, she warned, going away into
the night to again spend what little money they had on
dope and booze, she didn't want to ever see him again.
His only response was to glare at her, fighting the rage
that was again building, and walk away. For good. She
had threatened him for the last time.*

Walking away, hiding, was what he did best. When the

pressures overwhelmed him, when the shadows of night were no longer a satisfactory escape, he would check himself into a rehab clinic. The story he would tell—of his hatred for his addiction and the genuine desire to rebuild his life and return to his family—was just another of his lies. He was looking for neither rehabilitation or redemption. He was looking for a place to hide. There were, he knew, people in the world who were looking for him. They would never think to look in a hospital.

He was smart, so much smarter than they were. As long as he kept up the lies, he had the upper hand. The truth was a secret he couldn't share with anyone. But it had become increasingly difficult. He'd begun to lose track of time, unable to remember where he'd been and what he'd done. Blackouts, the doctor at the clinic had called them.

Still, he'd managed to continue from one minimum-wage job to another, each less rewarding than the one before, providing him barely enough to pay rent and get high. Without a car, he bummed rides. When the landlord complained, he simply packed his meager belongings and fled into the night. There was always some good-hearted coworker or drug-culture friend to whom he could give a hard-luck story in exchange for a place to stay for a couple of days.

And then he met her. She was so pretty, her auburn hair always shining, her melting smile his long-awaited signal that there were good people in the world. She wasn't like the others. She had talked to him, listened to him.

CHAPTER NINE

In the days before she had finally decided to check into the Bethania Regional Health Care Center for the surgery she hoped would correct the debilitating back problems she'd long suffered, Elaine Kimbrew had paid little attention to the news. Despite the fact the trial of Danny Laughlin had been a fixture on the front page of the Wichita Falls paper that was delivered daily to her home in nearby Vernon, she had made no attempt to keep up with it. Though, like everyone in the region, she was generally aware of the string of murders that had occurred, Elaine was one of those who chose not to fixate on the tragedies of the world. Life, she would say, was hard enough without depressing morning headlines.

She had separated from her husband when their daughter, Tina, was a high school sophomore and had moved from the tiny farming community of Oklaunion to Odessa, back to the west Texas roots she'd known as a child. Though troubled by the end of her parents' marriage, Tina had accompanied her mother and, despite the fact she badly missed her dad, quickly adapted to her new surroundings and later graduated from Permian High School.

Robert Kimbrew, who owned and operated a successful seed-cleaning business, had remained in Oklaunion, forty-five miles to the west of Wichita Falls, and was pleased that he and his ex-wife had managed to emerge from the divorce process as friends. There had been no custody battle, no threats or long-lasting fits of anger. While the binds that had kept their marriage together had unraveled, a mutual respect and shared love for Tina had remained intact, allowing him carefree access to his daughter. She had spent time with him during school vacations, and it was not unusual for him to make a spur-of-the-moment decision to drive to Odessa and visit for a few days. When, late in 1985, Elaine phoned to tell him of her plans to return to nearby Vernon, there to care for her aging mother in the wake of her stepfather's death, Robert was delighted. She had indicated that Tina would also be moving. "She wants to get her a job and an apartment up in Wichita Falls," Elaine explained. "Lately she's been talking a lot about the nursing field and is thinking about taking some classes at Midwestern."

Proud and independent, their soon-to-be-twenty-one-year-old daughter had made it clear she wanted to make her own way. Still, Robert Kimbrew had immediately volunteered to join in the search for an apartment in a Wichita Falls neighborhood he and his ex-wife would feel confident was safe for a young woman living on her own.

Tina had been delighted the minute they drove her into the parking lot of the Park Regency Apartments located on Seymour Road. She immediately warmed to the small, newly painted dwelling, hurrying through the downstairs living room and kitchen, then up the stairs to the loft where the bedroom was located. She was almost giddy as she talked of decorating plans, where she would hang her growing collection of rainbow artwork. Since childhood, rainbows had fascinated her. "There's nothing happier," she had explained to her mother.

As if some bonus were needed, Robert said he had spoken to the manager and had been assured Tina's black toy poodle, Nichole, a gift from a friend in Odessa when it was only a puppy, would also be welcome.

Tina made the move to Wichita Falls just days after saying her good-byes to friends at a round of New Year parties.

And soon both parents were making excuses for quick visits. Elaine would bring with her the necessities of housekeeping—bath towels, detergent, staples for her daughter's pantry—while Robert arrived with new speakers for Tina's stereo system. The mother routinely expressed concern that her daughter wasn't eating properly; the father would subtly inquire about her financial well-being. "It's what parents do," Robert had explained. Mostly, however, they simply enjoyed seeing her, watching as she continued her advance into adulthood, taking control of and enjoying her life. She continued to talk of enrolling in college, but only, she insisted, after she'd saved some money. To accomplish that end, she had taken a job as a bartender-waitress at an upscale lounge located in the Sheraton Hotel.

When her mother checked into the hospital for surgery during the first week of May 1986, Tina persuaded her boss to allow her to rearrange her schedule so that she might be on hand. After working a day shift, she had driven directly to Bethania.

That evening the pain Elaine was experiencing was masked by lighthearted conversation with her daughter. The mother recounted her own days as a waitress following her high school graduation and watched as Tina counted out the tips she had earned earlier in the day. She talked of her plans for the future. Tina explained that she enjoyed the work she was doing, had a nice boss and was meeting new friends, but bartending was not something she wished to make a lifetime career. She was more convinced than ever that she would soon be enrolling in nursing school. The plan pleased her mother, and they spoke of grants and financial aid programs that were available. "And, you know," Elaine added, "your daddy will help."

"I know," Tina replied as she moved from a nearby chair to the foot of her mother's bed, "but I'd like to see if I can make it on my own." Robert Kimbrew, she knew, would understand. He'd been the person from whom she'd inherited her independent nature.

They talked late into the evening, until a nurse entered to give Elaine a sedative to help her sleep. "I'll be back tomorrow," Tina whispered as she leaned forward to kiss her mother's cheek.

The following afternoon, the first person Elaine saw as she woke in the recovery room was her daughter. Blurred at first, Tina's smiling face finally came into full view as the anesthetic began to wear off. She was holding a spoon filled with Jell-O. "They want you to eat something as soon as you feel like it," she said, waving the spoon in a manner that caused the unappetizing red gel to jiggle near her mother's face. "Doesn't it look yummy?"

Though still groggy and feeling discomfort, Elaine laughed.

Tina did not leave her side that day. Friends and family members stopped in, some bringing flowers or cards that urged Elaine to get well soon, but their stays were brief, limited by the doctors' orders. Only Tina was allowed to remain. Her mother had requested that she be allowed to do so.

It was after ten that night when Tina left for home. She again leaned over the bed to kiss her mother. "I love you," she said. "See you tomorrow."

Elaine nodded weakly and smiled. "Get some rest,"

she said as she watched her daughter disappear into the hallway.

Though still heavily sedated, Elaine Kimbrew slept little during the night and was awake when her former mother-in-law, Mildred, and niece, Shelley Kelley, arrived from Vernon. It was when Shelley, eager to see Tina, asked when she was coming to the hospital that Elaine suggested they phone her apartment.

Mildred dialed the number and spoke briefly with her granddaughter. "She said she's going to shower and take her dog out for a little walk," she reported. "Then she'll be here." Privately, she expected that it might be a little longer than Tina promised. She had heard the soap opera *Days of Our Lives* playing on the television in the background and assumed her granddaughter might remain home until it was over.

Elaine smiled and closed her eyes. In just a few minutes she was asleep for the first time since she'd been moved from the recovery room. Her visitors tiptoed away to search for the hospital cafeteria so Shelley's two-year-old daughter could have lunch.

It was while they were gone that Elaine woke suddenly, a strange and frightening feeling sweeping through her body. Something, she instinctively knew, was terribly wrong. Her heart was pounding furiously and she rose to look around the empty room. Frantically summoning a nurse, she asked that Mildred Kimbrew and her niece be located immediately.

As they rushed into the room just minutes later, Elaine was sitting up, her pained body shaking, tears streaming down her ashen face. "Something has happened to Tina," she cried out. "You've got to go over to her apartment and check on her."

Shelley stepped toward the bed, hoping to calm her

aunt. "Hey, everything's okay," she whispered, gently placing a hand on Elaine's shoulder. "Everything's fine. We'll go get Tina and bring her here."

Elaine could only nod. "Hurry," she finally said. What she could not bring herself to share with her concerned relatives was a feeling that defied logical explanation, a feeling unlike any she had ever experienced.

She had felt her daughter's life going out of her own body.

Shelley, just thirteen months older than her cousin, had grown up with Tina and was thrilled when she'd moved to Wichita Falls. The two had seen each other regularly in recent months, and Tina had even given Shelley a key to her apartment.

When there was no reply after she had rung the doorbell and knocked at apartment 105, Shelley became concerned. She had seen that Tina's car was still in the parking lot. Perhaps, her grandmother suggested, someone had given her a ride to the hospital. Then, looking over at Shelley's daughter, the grandmother suggested they go inside and wash the child's face before returning to the hospital.

Even before she made the suggestion, Shelley was fumbling through her purse for the key.

As she slowly opened the door, she saw her cousin's dog standing in the hallway. "Hey, Nichole," she said, "where's Tina?"

The small dog barked, then quickly disappeared into the living room.

Her daughter in her arms, Shelley followed the few steps down the hallway before she had a view of the apartment's living area. What she saw caused her to gasp, then turn away in hopes her child had not seen what she had. Tina lay on the floor near the sofa, one leg bent at a

strange angle. Her nightgown and robe were gathered
around her waist, her unblinking eyes staring toward the
ceiling. As the young mother shielded her child's face,
she hurried toward the kitchen. Summoning a firm voice,
she told the toddler to remain there until she returned.
Back in the living room, Mildred Kimbrew was already
on the floor, kneeling beside Tina's body, trying to wake
her. Turning to Shelley as she entered the room, the
grandmother slowly shook her head as tears began form-
ing in the corners of her eyes. "She's dead."

Shelley felt herself try to scream, but no sound came.

For several seconds the two women knelt on the car-
peted floor, frozen in place by the scene they had happened onto. The poodle, whining softly, moved near
Tina's lifeless body and lay down, awaiting a miracle that
wasn't to happen.

It was Shelley who finally got to her feet, walked back
into the kitchen to check on her child, and dialed 911.
When she returned to the living room, she found her
grandmother sobbing uncontrollably. "I can't look at her
like this," she said. "We need to cover her before anyone
gets here." Too distraught to give thought to the fact that
she might be disturbing a crime scene or fouling evidence, Shelley hurried upstairs to the bedroom, found a
sheet, and returned to cover her cousin's body.

Back at the hospital, Elaine Kimbrew had become so
agitated that doctors suggested another sedative. No, she
told them, she wanted to be awake when her daughter
arrived.

Wichita Falls Police Detective Steve Pruitt, summoned to
the crime scene while en route home, stood at the entryway to the living room, allowing his eyes to slowly take
everything in. The patrolman who had initially responded
to the 911 call had greeted him at the doorway and

quickly explained how the two women who found the body had been responsible for it being covered by the sheet. The detective gently pulled the cover away and knelt by the victim. *So young, so pretty*, he thought. It was a process he'd been through more times than he cared to remember. But it had never gotten easier.

While there was no evidence of forced entry, it was obvious that a struggle had taken place. An end table near the sofa was overturned, one of its legs broken. Books and magazines splayed across the floor and pillows from the sofa were scattered about. Near the young woman's body lay a pair of ripped panties. The detective methodically moved through the remainder of the apartment, making note of the fact the victim's purse lay open on the kitchen table. It didn't appear that any money had been taken from it. For that matter, it did not look as if any other part of the apartment had been disturbed. Whatever had happened had occurred quickly. And, from the bruises he'd seen on the young woman's face and legs, violently.

Though responsibility for determining the cause of death would ultimately fall to the medical examiner's office, Detective Pruitt was reasonably sure the victim had died from either strangulation or suffocation. If there was a weapon left behind, he thought, it had to be one of the sofa pillows that lay near the body.

He was still studying the crime scene when a fellow officer entered to tell him that a canvass of the complex had yielded a potential witness. A teenage resident named Ellery Lambert said he had briefly seen Tina outside with her dog earlier in the day. Shortly after she'd returned to her apartment, he'd seen a skinny white male, well over six feet tall and wearing a baseball cap, approach her door and knock. It had been sometime between eleven-twenty and noon, he said.

"Did she let him in?" the detective asked.

Lambert shrugged. "I guess she must have," he replied, "because I didn't see him again." He had no recollection of the man arriving in a car, nor had he noticed any unfamiliar vehicles in the parking lot near the apartment until police cars began pulling up.

"She knew the guy," Pruitt whispered to himself.

Robert Kimbrew was working later than usual when his sister-in-law phoned to relay a confusing message she'd just received from his mother. His mother, she said, had been crying when she called, barely able to explain that she urgently needed to reach her son but was unable to remember his number. The message that reached Tina's father was that she had been robbed and beaten badly. The sister-in-law hesitated for a second before adding a final sentence. "Robert," she said, "she might even be dead."

In moments he was in his pickup, speeding toward Wichita Falls. Suddenly swallowed into a world of unreality, numbed by the fractured message he'd received, he made a quick stop at a convenience store and hurried to a pay phone. Calling a friend who was a Department of Public Safety dispatcher, he quickly explained that his daughter had been injured and he was on his way to Wichita Falls to check on her. "Tell your guys that if they see me speeding," Robert said, "to just let me go."

By the time he reached the city limits, he realized the scant information he'd received afforded him no real plan. Assuming that his daughter would have been rushed to a hospital, he stopped first at the emergency room of Wichita Falls General, then Bethania, only to learn that Tina had not been admitted to either. Soon he was speeding in the direction of Tina's apartment. The scene he soon encountered sent a chill through his body.

Police cars and a van from a local television station were in the parking lot. A ribbon of yellow crime scene tape blocked the entrance to his daughter's apartment. As he stepped from his pickup he saw his mother and Shelley walking toward him. Escorting them through the growing crowd was a police sergeant named Wyle Hopson.

"Let's go over to the manager's office where we can talk," the officer suggested.

Kimbrew stood his ground. "I need to check on my daughter first," he argued. "I went by the hospitals and she wasn't there. Where is she?"

"Sir," the sergeant said, "she's still in the apartment."

"Well, I need to go see her."

"No," Sergeant Hopson said firmly. "I don't think you want to see her." A father himself and one who had too often seen the reaction of loved ones to crime scenes, he placed a hand on Kimbrew's shoulder and guided him toward the office. Only when they were inside, hidden from the frenzied activity of investigators, reporters, and onlookers, did the officer tell the distraught father that Tina was dead.

He explained that since the investigation had just begun, he had few definitive answers to questions he knew Robert would have. The cause of death had not yet been determined. There was no evidence of a break-in or robbery. He was relieved when Kimbrew didn't question him about the condition in which the victim had been discovered.

"I've spoken with your mother and Mrs. Kelley," he continued, "and they've told me that Tina's mother is currently in the hospital."

Robert nodded.

"They both feel you should be the one to tell her what has happened."

Robert Kimbrew felt all energy drain from his body. How was he going to do it? How do you tell someone who had devoted her every waking hour to her daughter for over two decades that the most important thing in her life was suddenly gone?

Haunting memories began racing through his mind: that exact moment when he'd learned that his wife was pregnant, despite doctors' repeated warnings that it was unlikely she would ever bear children; then the long late-night discussions about the physical dangers likely to accompany the pregnancy. But Elaine had been so determined, so eager to have a child. It hadn't been an easy nine months in her life, but she had remained optimistic even when the doctor had requested that her husband sign an agreement that, should problems develop during childbirth, the first priority would be to save her life, not the child's. And, finally, from all the worry and anxiety and pain had come a healthy, beautiful child who had stolen their hearts from the first minute she entered the world.

With great effort, Robert stood and buried his trembling hands deep into the pockets of his jeans. Looking out into the busy courtyard, he watched as reporters mingled. As if reading his mind, Sergeant Hopson told him that Shelley was on her way to the hospital to instruct nurses to be sure that the television and radio in Elaine Kimbrew's room were removed.

The moment Robert entered the hospital room, Elaine could tell something was terribly wrong. For as long as Elaine had known him, he had never gone out in public before changing out of his work clothes into a pair of creased jeans and a starched western shirt. The boots he wore were always polished.

He had been dressed that way the previous evening when he'd briefly stopped in to see how she was feeling.

Now, however, he looked different, the grime of work still ground into his clothing, his hair slightly disheveled. As he entered the dimly lit room, he leaned against the wall for several seconds, saying nothing. Elaine had tried to sit up in her bed when she thought she'd heard crying in the hallway before Robert gently closed the door.

He had begun slowly moving toward her when she broke the discomforting silence. "What's the matter?" she asked. "What's wrong?"

On his drive to the hospital Robert had tried to think of what he would say, how he would relay the message that was certain to break his ex-wife's heart. He had come up with nothing satisfactory.

"It's Tina, isn't it?" Elaine finally said in a frightened whisper. "Something's happened."

Robert was quickly at her bedside, his eyes stinging as he nodded and reached for her hand. "She's been killed," he said.

Family members waiting anxiously in the hallway were jolted by the painful scream that came from behind the closed door.

The following day in Dallas, Dr. Mary Gilliland found herself conducting an autopsy on yet another body delivered to her from Wichita Falls. For a time she studied the contusions and abrasions visible on the young woman's face and quickly concluded that they had likely been caused by blows from a fist. The bruise patterns on her arms and legs spoke of a violent struggle. The examiner was mildly surprised when she found no indication that the victim had been sexually molested. It was, however, not until the examination yielded small traces of colored fibers in the victim's lungs that she was able to determine the cause of death.

The fibers matched the material used to cover one of the sofa pillows that had been found lying near the victim and delivered to the medical examiner's office along with the body. The pillow, Dr. Gilliland determined, had been held over the victim's mouth and nose until she had stopped breathing.

Tina Kimbrew, her report would indicate, had been suffocated.

Just three days after her surgery, Elaine Kimbrew was demanding her release. The doctors argued, pointing out that they had not yet even felt comfortable having her attempt to get out of bed and walk the halls of the hospital. It was still too soon, they insisted.

"I can walk," the weak and bereaved mother told them. "I have to. I've got to bury my daughter." With that she climbed from her bed and slowly made her way across the room toward a small closet where the clothes she'd worn to the hospital hung. After painfully reaching her destination, she turned toward the doctors, a look of sad defiance on her face. "I've got to go tell my baby good-bye," she said.

Already, thanks to her ex-husband's efforts, arrangements had been made for a Dallas funeral home to deliver Tina's body to Vernon. Together, the grieving parents had selected the casket, picked her gravesite, and talked of the design they wanted for their daughter's headstone. On one side, they had decided, a bouquet of roses should be carved—symbolic of the beauty of their child—and on the other a shock of wheat—a symbol of the heartland where she'd grown up.

The service was scheduled for Mother's Day.

It was less than two hours before the afternoon funeral was to take place when the phone rang at Mildred Kimbrew's home. On the other end of the line, Sergeant Hopson asked to speak with Robert.

"I thought I might find you there," the officer said. "I

know this is a terrible time to be calling, but I thought you would want to know that we've got the guy."

For a second Robert didn't understand. "What are you saying?"

"The guy who killed your daughter is in custody. In Galveston. He's confessed, Robert. I've got two officers on the way down there now to pick him up. Come on in tomorrow and we'll talk about it."

Standing in the living room of his mother's house, Kimbrew had hung up the phone without even asking the name of the man who had been arrested. All he could remember the sergeant saying was that he'd told the authorities that he'd murdered a woman in Wichita Falls. She'd been a friend, he'd apparently said, and he'd killed her by suffocating her with a pillow.

Already dressed for the funeral, Robert fought the urge to race to his pickup and drive immediately to Wichita Falls. Instead, he said nothing to his mother about the message he'd just received. He suddenly craved fresh air and decided to wait outside as she finished dressing. Standing alone, the spring air filling his nostrils, he thought back to an observation the police officer had made to him just a day after his daughter had been killed. *I've talked to a lot of people about Tina,* he had said, *and she didn't seem to know any bad people. Everyone she knew and worked with—people who we might normally have had to track down to talk with—has come to us, volunteering to help in any way they can. Your daughter associated with some very nice people. I don't think she knew anyone who didn't have a conscience. I'm still convinced that she was murdered by someone who knew her and that person won't be able to live with what he's done for long. Trust me: He'll confess sooner or later.*

Robert wondered if Sergeant Hopson's prophecy had come true.

He also found himself wondering about a forgotten conversation he'd had with Tina several weeks earlier.

He'd driven into Wichita Falls to take her to dinner one evening, and as they were eating, she had surprised him with a question. "Daddy," she had said, "I know that in the five or six years since you and Mother divorced you've gone out with a lot of women. How do you get rid of somebody whose feelings you don't want to hurt but who you don't want to be around?"

There was this man, she explained, whom she had met when he'd come into the club. She'd been friendly with him, as she was with all her customers, and soon he was a regular, finally asking her out. "I don't want to get involved with him," she said, "but he just won't leave me alone."

At that point Robert had made a suggestion that he knew would be unacceptable. "Let me talk to him," he'd offered.

Just as he'd expected, Tina had made it clear she wanted to deal with the problem herself.

"You ever gone out with this guy?" her father asked.

"Once," she said. "He overheard my boss telling me I could take off early one evening and suggested we go have dinner. I couldn't see any way out of it."

Even then she had been careful, telling another waitress where she was going, asking the man to show her coworker his driver's license, and then having her accompany them into the parking lot so she could copy down the license plate number of his car. "All the girls that work there do that," she explained. "That's the way we look after each other."

She said that they'd gone to a nearby restaurant for dinner, then the man had delivered her back to the club. By then she'd been comfortable enough to allow him to follow her home, making sure she arrived safely.

"He didn't come in or anything," Tina had said, "but from that point he knew where I lived. After that he came by a few times and started calling. He seems nice enough—bashful, really—but I just don't want to give him the impression I'm interested."

The situation, Robert had judged, did not seem out of hand. And so he had suggested that she simply find something else that she had to be doing any time the man phoned or came by.

"I don't want to lie to him," his daughter replied.

"Then don't. Just tell him he's called or come at a bad time, that you were just on your way to the grocery store or you've got to meet someone. Then just go ahead and do it. Go shopping. Go see a friend. That way you're telling the truth."

Tina had smiled at his plan. "Is that what you do?"

Slightly embarrassed by the personal nature of the conversation, her father nodded. "It works," he said.

"Then I'll give it a try," she'd promised.

"What's this guy's name?"

"I don't even know," she'd said. "He calls himself Gonzo."

On a warm and cloudless day when the blue Texas skies seemed to stretch endlessly over the plains country, the smell of dozens of floral arrangements wafted through the parlor of the Sullivan Funeral Home. The large chapel was filled to capacity with friends and relatives who had arrived from as far away as Colorado. One of Tina's uncles, stationed in Okinawa, had been granted an emergency leave and arrived just hours before the service was scheduled to get under way.

For Robert and Elaine, it was a painful blur of faces and scripture, hymns and heartfelt hugs and handshakes. And private memories of a daughter who had been so filled with life and promise only days earlier. Both were near exhaustion by the time the pastor said a brief prayer that brought the graveside service in East Wilbarger Memorial Park to a close.

Robert waited until he and Elaine were alone, the last people standing alongside the freshly covered grave, before telling her of his conversation with Sergeant Hopson.

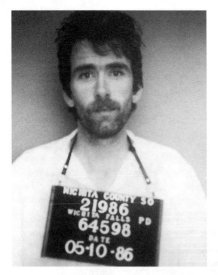

Faryion Wardrip, 1986. He said he had gone to Galveston, where he planned to see the ocean before taking his own life. Instead, he called police and confessed to the killing of his friend, Tina Kimbrew. No one connected him with the earlier murders of Toni Gibbs, Terry Sims, and Ellen Blau. He was paroled in 1997. *(Wichita County District Attorney's Office)*

Danny Laughlin had met victim Toni Gibbs at a bar she frequented, and admitted to police that he'd been in the field where she was killed only days before her body was found. Prosecutors were rightfully suspicious and eventually charged Laughlin with murder. *(Wichita Falls Record)*

Terry Sims, 20. On the night of December 21, 1984, the demure EKG technician became Faryion Wardrip's first known victim. *(Catie Reid)*

Sims's mother, Marsha Bridgens and her daughters, Catie Reid and Vickie Grimes, who saw Terry's case through to the end. *(both Pat Stowers)*

Toni Gibbs, 24. She became Wardrip's second known victim in January 1985. *(Jeff Gibbs)*

Authorities found her 1984 Camaro abandoned only two blocks from the apartment where Terry Sims had been murdered a month earlier. *(Wichita County District Attorney's Office)*

The trolley car where Wardrip stabbed Toni Gibbs. Her body was found 100 feet away. *(Wichita County District Attorney's Office)*

Ellen Blau, 21, disappeared on the night of
September 19, 1985, after meeting with
friends at a Wichita Falls restaurant. Her
remains were found in a rural field 21 days
later. Her father, Murray Blau, offered a
$10,000 reward for information leading to
the killer. *(Murray Blau)*

Blau's friend and roommate, Janie Ball,
would be on hand 14 years later to see
Wardrip convicted of the murder.
(Pat Stowers)

Faryion Wardrip admitted to killing college student Tina Kimbrew, 21, in May 1986. *(Robert Kimbrew)*

Kimbrew's mother, Elaine Thornhill *(Pat Stowers)*, and father, Robert Kimbrew. *(Pat Stowers)*

ABOVE: Wichita County District Attorney Barry Machak, who in 1997 turned his attention to the 12-year-old murders after DNA analysis proved that Terry Sims and Toni Gibbs had been assaulted by the same man. *(Carlton Stowers)*

ABOVE: Detective John Little, seen here with Catie Reid and Barry Macha *(Dee Dee Bridgens)*, staked out Wardrip's work from this Olney, TX, laundromat (BELOW). *(Pat Stowers)* When the moment arrived, Little's quick thinking would allow him to obtain the critical piece of evidence in the Wardrip case.

After Wardrip drank coffee out of this cup *(Wichita County District Attorney's Office)*, John Little asked the suspect if he could use it as a makeshift spittoon. Instead, he took it back to Dallas forensic lab technician Judy Floyd, who matched Wardrip's DNA to that of the man who killed Sims and Gibbs. *(Pat Stowers)*

Under arrest, Wardrip *(Wichita County District Attorney's Office)* confessed to the murders of Sims, Gibbs, and Blau, along with the unsolved 1985 murder of Debra Taylor, a Fort Worth wife and mother.

Wardrip and Defense Attorney John Curry in court. On the first day of his trial, he pled guilty to the killing of Terry Sims. He was sentenced to die by lethal injection, and to three more life sentences for the other murders. *(Pat Stowers)*

CHAPTER TEN

The historic old city of Galveston, located on a skinny Gulf of Mexico island just a short drive south from Houston, is a vacationer's paradise, beckoning with warm sun, pristine beaches, and cool, blue ocean waters. Annually, it is the destination of thousands of college students on their spring break, the partying that occurs during that two-week stretch legendary. For the remainder of the year, however, a more subdued tourist crowd arrives from the north to bask in the city's warmth and enjoy its shops, its seafood specialties, and charming hospitality.

Though not without its share of crime, the misdeeds that routinely occur do not compare with those daily recorded in most Texas cities of similar size. Galveston, with its antebellum architecture, its old wealth and its proud sense of history, generally moves at a slow and easy pace.

Such was the atmosphere on the afternoon of May 9, 1986, when a strange call came in to the Galveston Police Department. A man staying at the Driftwood, one of the aging, low-budget motels located near the sea wall, phoned to announce that he was planning to commit suicide.

Within minutes, police officers were knocking on the door of Room 201. They were greeted by a tall, disheveled man, dressed in jeans and a T-shirt, holding a knife he'd purchased just hours earlier at a nearby Wal-Mart. Without a threatening word, he handed it to one of the officers, then began to sob. "I couldn't do it," he said.

Assuming he was dealing with someone who was either mentally ill or on drugs, Officer William May quickly assumed a friendly, nonthreatening demeanor. "Hey, fella, everything's going to be okay," he said. "What's your name?"

"Wardrip . . . Faryion Wardrip." He was already shaking his head before he replied. "And everything's *not* going to be okay. I just came here to see the ocean before I killed myself. That's all I wanted: to see the ocean and die. I wish I could have done it."

"Why would you want to kill yourself?"

The answer the officer received was hardly what he had expected. "Because I murdered this woman back in Wichita Falls. She was my friend and I killed her. I hit her and I strangled her . . . and I killed her."

May immediately turned businesslike, his thought process speeding into high gear. He needed to get in touch with authorities in Wichita Falls immediately to see if a homicide like Wardrip was vaguely describing had, in fact, occurred. In the meantime, the officer pulled handcuffs from his belt and began to recite the Miranda warning. "You have the right to remain silent . . . ," he said as the distraught man placed his hands behind his back.

The officer immediately noticed that the knuckles on Wardrip's hands were badly bruised.

Even before they arrived at the police station, a call had been placed to Wichita Falls. It was confirmed that the homicide of a young woman named Tina Kimbrew was under investigation.

"I'm ready to give a statement," Wardrip said.

"You want a lawyer?" May asked.

"No, I'm ready to just get this over with."

And for the next half hour he sat in a small cinderblock room, hundreds of miles from home, reliving the nightmare he'd created just days earlier.

He had first met Tina, he said, during a brief period when he'd worked as a doorman at a western dance place called the Stardust Club. Then he'd begun to frequent the lounge where she worked. They had talked and become friends. "Acquaintances, really," he corrected. "I went over to her place to see her a couple of times," he said in a voice that was barely a whisper, "even took her out for coffee one night. She was a really nice person."

Then, on the previous Tuesday, he'd walked to her apartment after having a dream about her the night before. "I was coming down off a high—been doing a lot of heroin and crank—and needed more drugs," he said. "I went over to her place to see if maybe she had anything."

The minute she opened the door, still dressed in her robe, he had gone into an inexplicable rage, hitting her in the face.

"I don't remember her saying anything that set me off," he continued, "but after I knocked her down I just kept on hitting her and hitting her. I don't know why, but I couldn't stop. I didn't mean to kill her. I was just angry and wanted to hurt her."

The next thing he remembered was closing the door to her apartment and walking back home.

"It all came back to me when I saw on television how Tina had been found, beaten and strangled to death. They said the police had a description of someone seen going into her apartment and it sounded like me. That's when it occurred to me that I was probably the one who killed her."

From that moment on, he said, all he could think about was ending his own life. Before doing so, however, he wanted to fulfill a wish he'd entertained since boyhood. He wanted to see the ocean. "So, I bought me a bus ticket and here I am," Wardrip said with a resigned shrug.

Though convinced that the man seated across from him was being truthful, William May felt certain there was some motive that Wardrip was hiding. If the detective were a betting man, he'd put money on the woman's death being triggered by some kind of drug deal that had gone bad.

Even as the interview was under way, Wichita Falls police officers Steve Pruitt and Bob Geurin were driving toward the coast to take the suspect into custody.

It was almost eight in the evening when they arrived and read the statement Wardrip had given. "Want me to bring him back into the interview room?" May asked.

In just a matter of hours, Wardrip's bizarre story had already begun to change. Now, as he spoke with the Wichita Falls officers, all he could remember was going to Tina's apartment in search of drugs, then returning home. He had no real recollection of killing her.

Pruitt reached over and took the prisoner's hands, forcing them flat on the table. He said nothing as he carefully examined the bruised knuckles.

"I don't know how that happened," Wardrip said, shaking his head wildly. "All I know is it happened the day she was killed, and that's what really scared me."

"You're admitting that you were at her apartment the day she was murdered?"

Wardrip nodded. "I'd smoked some dope that day," he says, "and needed some more. Crank, heroin, weed—anything I could get my hands on. First, I thought about breaking into this house down the street from where I was living and stealing the air conditioner so I could sell it. But somehow I wound up at Tina's instead.

"See, I just went there to get drugs, not to kill anybody. It was an accident. She was my friend." He'd begun crying again. "I don't know why or how, but I feel in my heart that I killed her. Sometimes I have these blackouts and can't remember things. But, yeah, I'm thinking that's what happened."

"You're thinking that you killed her but don't know how or why?"

"Yeah," Wardrip acknowledged. And then he was off on another ramble about his wish to view the ocean before dying. "I just couldn't live with myself, thinking I'd taken someone else's life."

On the drive back to Wichita Falls the following morning, Wardrip had nothing more to say about the crime. Instead, he talked endlessly of the fact that his wife had left him and was planning to file for divorce. His life had been one giant mess from the day he met her. And now she wouldn't even let him see his two children. Most of the other women he'd known weren't much better. Did they know he'd admitted himself to the state mental hospital twice? Women and drugs will do that to you, he said.

Eventually the officers seated in front wearied of his self-pity and the monotone cadence of his voice and tried to tune him out. It barely registered with them when, while talking of people he'd known, he offhandedly included the name of Ellen Blau, victim of a homicide being investigated by the sheriff's department. Pruitt thought little about it but made a mental note to mention it to his sergeant.

It was one of those rare truths that, in years to come, Faryion Edward Wardrip would regret having uttered.

In the weeks that followed the arrest of the man who had killed their daughter, things got no easier for Elaine and

Robert Kimbrew. Her days were shrouded in pain and depression as she tried to deal with the lingering effects of her operation and the loss of her only child. His were spent battling a growing, bitter anger he'd never before experienced and a dark guilt over not having listened more carefully when his daughter had told him of the man she was attempting to exclude from her life. He could not get the strange nickname he'd been told Faryion Wardrip used—Gonzo—out of his mind. It echoed in his thoughts like some vile obscenity. There was no place to escape, even for a few peaceful minutes, the tragedy that had so scarred his life.

For days after the arrest, the Wichita Falls television station had repeatedly run footage of Tina's body being removed from her apartment, stretched on a gurney and hidden away in a black body bag. Finally Robert had called the news director and said he was bringing him a photograph of his daughter. "If you're going to keep talking about her," he said, "I want people to see how young and beautiful she was."

For the mourning parents, the most trivial of responsibilities became mountainous chores. Aware of the need to retrieve Tina's belongings from her apartment, they had postponed the inevitable visit to the scene of her death by arranging with the manager to pay an additional month's rent.

Finally it could be put off no longer. Five weeks after Tina's funeral, Elaine, summoning every ounce of strength she had, arrived at the door of the apartment on a cold and gray day just as a light drizzle began turning to sleet. Jo Lynn Coates, a longtime friend, had volunteered to accompany her.

In truth, there was little Elaine wanted to retrieve. She would collect some of her daughter's personal items— photographs, a few books, some of her rainbow figurines—

but little else. Only at the last minute did she gather up a small blanket that was neatly folded in a corner of the bedroom. It had been the favorite sleeping place of Tina's dog. Perhaps, Elaine thought, Nichole would like to have it in her new home.

A friend of Jo Lynn's, she had learned, was moving into a new residence, and Elaine had phoned to say he was welcome to Tina's furniture if he would come and haul it away. Her only mission, then, was to clean away the reminders of her daughter's too-brief life.

Already she had come into possession of the single most treasured item she could imagine. When the police had returned Tina's purse to her weeks earlier, she had found a poem tucked inside a billfold.

Deeply religious, Elaine had often discussed the importance of faith with her daughter. And as she had read the words of the verse, titled "The Cross in My Pocket," a great calm had come over her.

I carry a cross in my pocket, it read in part, *A simple reminder to me, Of the fact that I am a Christian, No matter where I may be. . . .*

For much of the day the women silently wandered through the small apartment, unsuccessful in their efforts to ignore the remnants of the violence that had occurred and the investigation that had followed. They watched as the furniture was removed, then cleared items from cabinets and closets. By the time the rooms had been emptied and the floors vacuumed, only a small cardboard box filled with things Elaine wished to keep remained.

At one point her friend had tried to lighten the mood by pointing out that Tina had, as usual, gotten the last word. "Here you are, once again, cleaning her room," she'd said. Elaine had only smiled faintly and nodded.

At day's end, Jo Lynn carried the box to the car while Elaine walked to the office of the apartment manager to return the key. It was when she approached the parking lot in the gloom of the late afternoon that she noticed her friend looking skyward. The rain and sleet had ended and the gray cloud cover was finally beginning to peel away. Across the horizon, a beautiful rainbow arched.

And Elaine smiled. "I guess she did get the last word," she said.

The legal system into which Tina Kimbrew's parents had been so unwittingly thrust was a strange and cold world neither could grasp. Everything, it seemed, moved glacially slow. Phone calls to learn what might be happening went unanswered. Both were angered by the exclusion they were feeling. When the parents of Faryion Wardrip had phoned the police in an effort to contact Elaine and pass along their condolences, it was arbitrarily decided that she would not be interested. She and Robert shared a frustrating sense that those handling the case would prefer that they simply went away. It was as if their daughter were being taken from them again.

For several weeks their only source of information was Sergeant Hopson, and he rarely had any new information. "It's in the hands of the D.A. now," he would explain to Robert, "but if I do hear anything, I'll let you know."

For the Kimbrews it all seemed so cut and dried, so simple. Faryion Wardrip had confessed to the crime. The young man who had watched someone knock on the door of Tina's apartment that morning had reviewed a photo line-up and said that it was Wardrip he'd seen. The indictment had only been a formality. So why was it taking so long for punishment to be dealt?

Elaine, in particular, had taken an immediate dislike to the district attorney when she and Robert had finally met with him. When, during the course of their conversation, he had told her that he "knew how she was feeling," she had erupted. "No, sir," she'd spat back, "you don't." Robert's reaction had not been much better. When Barry Macha began explaining the law that would allow a maximum life sentence—not the death penalty—for the accused, he'd felt insulted. "To qualify as a death penalty case," Macha had said, "it would be necessary to prove that more than one crime had occurred inside Tina's apartment." Since there was no evidence of rape or robbery, nothing even to indicate that he had broken in, the only charge possible was murder.

It was at a later meeting in Macha's office that the frayed emotions of Tina's parents erupted. After discussions with Wardrip's court-appointed attorney, Macha explained, the most logical approach to disposing of the case appeared to be a plea bargain instead of a court trial. Explaining that a defense attorney could argue that there was no physical evidence linking Wardrip to the crime and that the scene had been contaminated by the innocent decision of Tina's grandmother to cover the body before police arrived, he suggested that a conviction would not be as easy as they assumed. Yes, there was an eyewitness who said he'd seen Wardrip knocking at the apartment, and, yes, there was the confession. But a good attorney could still make a strong case for reasonable doubt. "He will agree to a thirty-five-year sentence," the district attorney said.

Robert was immediately on his feet, angrily pacing the office. "What, are you worried about how much it's going to cost to take him to trial?" he asked. "Is this about saving the county some money? Or just taking the easy way out?"

The young D.A. was taken aback by the challenging tone of Kimbrew's voice. Since his earliest days as an assistant prosecutor, he had found it difficult to deal with the families of victims. Their fragile emotions, suspicions

of the judicial system, and constant pressuring just made
his job more difficult. Right or not, he had determined
that keeping them at a distance was the only way he could
properly perform his duties. His responsibility, he believed, was to focus only on the evidence of the case and
do his very best to see that justice was done. The responsibility of mending broken hearts and playing the mes-
senger of vengeance were not his to carry out. The only
real contribution he could make to anyone's healing process was to do his best to put those who had caused their
pain behind bars.

It would take yet another angry assault from Robert
Kimbrew to convince him differently.

Wyle Hopson had phoned Robert to be sure he knew
that the hearing on Wardrip's plea bargain had been
scheduled for October 27. "They can't do that," Kimbrew
had replied. "The twenty-seventh," he explained, "is
Tina's birthday. Elaine is determined to be in the courtroom anytime something is done on this case, and it just
isn't right that she should have to do that on her daughter's birthday. They just can't do that."

"Robert," Hopson said, "all I can suggest is that you
talk to Barry about it."

"And say what?"

"Just stress the importance of that particular day to
you and Elaine and explain how difficult it would be to
have to go to court on that date and see the guy who killed
your daughter."

Macha's response was hardly what Kimbrew had
hoped for. "I really don't see what difference that would
make," he argued, "but I'll speak with the judge and see if
he'd consider moving the date. I have to tell you, though,
my guess is that he isn't likely to do it."

Kimbrew leaned forward, bracing himself on the edge
of the D.A.'s desk. For several seconds he silently stared

into Macha's face. His voice was even and measured when he finally spoke. "Barry," he asked, "do you have any children?"

"No, I just recently married."

"So, how could you possibly know how I feel? How Tina's mother feels? You keep saying that you do, but you don't. There's no way. Everytime you tell someone whose child has been murdered that you 'understand what they're going through,' you're insulting them. I want you to think about that."

And with that he turned to leave.

For the first time since his visitor had entered, Macha rose from his desk, then followed Kimbrew to the door. He watched the agonized father disappear down the hallway, then closed his door.

The pain and anger he'd witnessed had unsettled him. Robert Kimbrew, he knew, was right. He didn't understand. How could he? He and his wife, Jane, had just begun talking of starting a family. What, God forbid, if something were to one day happen to the child they were planning? How would he feel? How could anyone else be expected to understand? Since the day he'd passed the bar, he'd made a vow to pursue justice, to right the wrongs that defiled his world. To do so effectively and efficiently, he'd felt it necessary to focus only on those things over which he had control. Given the proper evidence, he could get the conviction necessary to rid the streets of those who threatened his community. That was the job he'd sworn to do.

But, as he sat alone at his desk, his hands locked behind his head, staring out the window, he began to realize it wasn't enough. Robert Kimbrew, with his frustrated rage and strained face that mirrored unspeakable pain, had made his case well.

He's right, the district attorney thought. Reaching for the phone, he dialed Judge Ashley's number.

. . .

Anger drove Robert Kimbrew. Discomforting though it was to a man who had spent most of his adult life being friendly and outgoing, the new emotion was an easy choice over the aching sadness that had virtually disabled him in the days after his daughter's death. Months after the murder the bitterness had not subsided.

When he received a $350 bill from the ambulance service that had transported Tina's body to Dallas for the autopsy, he was immediately on the phone to Wyle Hopson.

"Don't pay it," the sergeant said. "That's the county's responsibility. I'm sure it's already been paid. I'll check on it. Meanwhile, just ignore it."

He did until a second notice arrived the following month, this time accompanied by a letter advising him that payment was overdue. Kimbrew phoned the ambulance service.

"I'm not paying this," he told the business manager.

"But, sir—"

"I said I'm not paying it," Robert repeated. "I'm told that it has already been taken care of."

The young woman on the other end of the line was taken aback by the determination in the caller's voice. "Sir," she finally said, "if you aren't responsible for payment, who should I send the bill to?"

"Send it to the man who murdered my daughter."

"Excuse me?"

"Send the bill to Faryion Wardrip in care of the Wichita County jail."

For a moment there was a silence, then the woman responded. She, like most, had read about the case in the newspapers. "Sir," she said, "I would be more than happy to do that. Would you mind spelling Mr. Wardrip's name? And do you happen to have the street address of the jail?"

The following day Kimbrew placed a call to a friend at the Vernon funeral home that had handled arrangements for his child's service and burial. Though he'd already paid the bills, he asked that copies for everything involved in the funeral costs be made. He requested that they be mailed to Wardrip.

Later, explaining to Elaine what he had done, Robert acknowledged that it had been a really ridiculous thing to do. "But," he said, "it really felt good."

Days later, when Sergeant Hopson called, he made an effort to hide his amusement at what Robert had done. "Look," he said, "Barry wanted me to call you and ask that you not send any more bills to the jail. He's about got this plea bargain thing worked out and is afraid that if you continue this, Wardrip might back out. Might even sue you for harassment."

Kimbrew exploded. "Sue me? For harassment? Maybe I should sue him for the harassment he's brought into my life. I think he ought to know what a funeral costs. Let him sit there thinking he's got debts to pay. Do you think he has any idea what it's like to have to walk in a room and pick out a casket? Has he ever buried anyone in his family?"

The officer, who had come to greatly admire the man posing the questions, waited until his railing ended. "Robert," he finally said, "just do me a favor. Don't send any more bills."

Kimbrew, regaining his composure, sighed deeply. "Okay," he said, "but can you do something for me?"

"What's that?"

"See if you can find out what his reaction was when he got the bills."

"I already did," Hopson said. "He went crazy, thinking he's not only in jail but deeply in debt."

"Good," Robert said.

On the second day of December 1986, Wardrip was sentenced to serve thirty-five years in the Texas prison system. Charlotte Harris, the public defender representing him, noted to the judge that she had never seen a defendant with a better attitude. "From the outset," she said, "he has been willing to take full responsibility for Miss Kimbrew's death."

Neither Robert nor Elaine Kimbrew had been advised of the new date for the proceedings. Thus they were not in the courtroom.

Robert, feeling the need to get away for a while, had traveled to Las Vegas for the annual National Rodeo Finals. Elaine, meanwhile, had begun to visit Tina's gravesite regularly and was making plans to decorate it for Christmas.

One sun-splayed morning as she arrived, the toy poodle she'd adopted after her daughter's death leapt from the car the minute she had opened the door. By the time Elaine made the short walk to the headstone, little Nichole, her head resting on her front paws, lay across the grave.

The dog's faint whine brought tears to her new master's eyes. When, she wondered, would the pain ever ease?

CHAPTER ELEVEN

Though they knew the identity of their daughter's killer and could find some solace in the fact he had been convicted of the crime, the longed-for peace sought by Robert and Elaine Kimbrew remained elusive. Just as it did for the families of Terry Sims, Toni Gibbs, and Ellen Blau. Time passed, lives moved on, and the murders and their devastating aftermath all but faded from public thought. Except, however, for those who had been directly affected.

Every year on his daughter's birthday, Murray Blau placed an ad in the Wichita Falls paper, reminding that the long-promised reward was still available to anyone who could provide information that led to the arrest of Ellen's killer. In the years that followed her death, he always paused at the large photo of her that hung in the hallway leading to his bedroom. "Good night, El" were his last words of the evening. Toni Gibbs's brother occasionally phoned the Archer County Sheriff's Office to see if there had been any progress in the investigation, never with any real hope. Terry Sims's sisters grew into young women, married, and began planning families of their own. Aside from regular visits to her gravesite and the occasional urge to reread some of the poetry she had written, they tried to avoid dwelling on the dark days.

There would, as the passage of time dictates, be changes: marriages and divorces, job promotions and retirements, moves from one location to another. Life advanced, dimming the past to a point where several days might go by without conscious thought of the horror that once visited. But then it would all come rushing back, triggered by a simple sight or smell, the melody of a long-forgotten song or a stranger's laughter that sounded, just for a moment, exactly like Terry. Or Toni. Or Ellen.

It was at such times that the families of the victims, while strangers, were bonded in a manner they could not be expected to realize. They were united by their endless and unresolved grief. And, collectively, they were convinced that the legal system had grandly failed them.

Certainly that was the case with Robert Kimbrew, despite the fact his child's killer had been caught. With little knowledge of the workings of the judicial system, he had assumed that when Faryion Wardrip pled guilty and was sentenced to serve thirty-five years in prison, it meant he would remain behind bars for at least a third of that time before parole was even considered.

When, just thirteen months after his incarceration, Wardrip made his first visit to the parole board, Kimbrew was livid. And despite the board's denial, he launched a campaign that would become his life's work in the years to come.

The dismal overcrowding of the Texas prison system had given rise to a new definition of the "good time" an inmate could accrue while serving his sentence. Participation in rehabilitation programs, attending chapel regularly, joining the workforce, and, most important, causing no trouble for attending guards could shave years from one's sentence. On average, a prisoner could get credit for as much as a year in only thirty-five days. The bitter joke shared among prison officials and legislators who fought to have the Faryion Wardrips of the world do their actual time was that convicts went in the front door of Texas's prisons, were processed, and then proceeded straight out the back door. Hello, good-bye, and, oh, by the way, on your way home please don't murder, rape, or rob anyone else, okay?

Robert was determined to see to it that Wardrip remained in prison for as long as possible. Elaine, remarried and living with her new husband in the Houston suburb of Pearland, quickly joined his cause. Immediately she began placing petitions in local businesses, urging friends and strangers alike to sign them and make the parole board aware of the community's desire to see Wardrip's next request for parole denied.

Robert spoke at length with a close friend of a parole board member. "The petitions aren't the best way to go," he was told. "You need letters. Get everyone you know to write a personal letter to the board, asking them to deny the parole. The more the better."

And then he had added a warning. "People will pat you on the back and tell you they'll do it, that they'd be glad to help out. But without a little prodding, a lot of them don't ever get around to it. Ask them to send you copies of the letters they write. If you don't hear from them, call them, hound them a little." Such pressuring went against Robert's personality, but he agreed to follow the advice.

So while Elaine routinely made her rounds, gathering the petitions bearing hundreds of signatures, he sought out those who would write letters—friends, neighbors, state and local politicians, total strangers, anyone willing to listen and help. Among those who promised to do so was Barry Macha, who now had a young daughter of his own.

When, less than a year later, another review of

Wardrip's status was scheduled, the letters and signed petitions were delivered to the twelve-man parole board in an overflowing grocery cart.

And parole was denied.

Each victory, however, was short-lived. Within months a new letter of notification from Austin would appear in Kimbrew's mail. He could recite the tired message from memory: "This is to inform you that the case of Faryion Edward Wardrip, Texas Department of Corrections inmate number 439572, is scheduled for review on . . ." Only the date would change. And again the anger and depression would return as Robert searched for new strength to continue his fight.

The battle lasted for over six years.

Finally, early in 1995, he received notice from the parole board that Wardrip, a model prisoner throughout his incarceration, would soon be released. Though the decision had already been reached, he was told, family members of the victim would be allowed to attend the parole hearing and speak out against the vote.

Feeling a new level of desperation, Kimbrew placed a call directly to one of the board members. Identifying himself and referring to the notification he'd received, he told the official, "I'd like to schedule a meeting with you."

"And why is that?"

Robert responded with a question of his own. "You're going to let the man who murdered my daughter out and you want to know why I want to meet with you?"

"Sir, it would be a waste of your time," the board member replied. "I sympathize with your situation, but I'm not going to change my mind."

He told Robert that he had spoken at length with Wardrip about the crime. "He told me that he went to your daughter's apartment and she had let him in. He was going through her purse, looking for some kind of drug—

speed, I think—when she'd seen him from the balcony of her bedroom. He said she had come downstairs and became quite violent. He fought back and the next thing he knew, she was dead. This terrible thing that happened resulted from what he considered a justified effort to defend himself."

The word "justified" seemed to explode through the receiver. Robert choked back the curses he so desperately wanted to shout. "And you're willing to take the word of a murderer, a drug addict?" he asked. "How can you believe anything he says? How can you think, even for a minute, a second, that what this guy did was . . . justified?"

"Sir, I'm not saying that it was, in fact—"

Robert cut him off. "Look, what I called you about was to set up a date and time to meet with you and, believe me, I want to do it. Regardless of what you have already decided or what you think, it isn't going to be a waste of my time. Time's all I've had for the last six years."

"I'll have to check my schedule and get back to you," the man finally said.

"When? I don't want to sit by this phone for days, wondering if and when I'll hear from you."

"I'll call tomorrow," the board member promised.

During the course of his tiresome battles against the system, one of Robert's strongest advocates and sounding boards has been Raven Kazen, a determined and energetic woman who had been appointed as director of the Department of Corrections' Victim Service Division. On numerous occasions Kimbrew had phoned her Austin office for advice or to ask a legal question. Once he had even driven to Austin to meet her and personally thank her for the genuine concern she had shown.

"I've reached a point in my life," he'd told her, "where there aren't many people I trust. You're one of them."

And as he sat at his kitchen table, mentally replaying

what had just transpired, certain that he had alienated one of the few who had the power to help him, Robert dialed Kazen's number.

"I think I just messed things up pretty badly," he told her. He recounted his conversation, including his angry reaction to the suggestion that Wardrip's actions might have somehow been justified.

Soon Kazen shared his anger. "This man," she said, "has no right talking to you that way," she said. "No one is going to talk to my people like that." Suddenly anxious to get off the phone, she told Kimbrew that she had some other calls to make. "I'm going to fix this . . . right now."

Robert was smiling when he hung up, feeling better for having talked with her. *You don't mess with that lady*, he thought.

The following day he received a call from the secretary of the board member he'd lashed out at. "Mr. Kimbrew," the woman said, "I was asked to call and tell you that Faryion Wardrip's parole application has been reconsidered and denied."

Robert couldn't believe what he was hearing. "Did you say it has been denied?"

"Yes sir."

He asked to speak with her boss.

"I'm sorry," she said, "he's not in the office."

For all the empathy and compassion she felt for the frustrated father's plight, Raven Kazen knew that Kimbrew's success in battling Wardrip's release would end soon. Ultimately a mandatory release date would arrive, and she wondered how Robert would deal with the reality of his daughter's killer being set free.

She'd liked him from the first time he'd contacted her. Over the years, it had been her experience that when a child was murdered, the mother initially took the active role, reaching out to her for counsel. She had, then, been surprised when Robert had called. In time she would also get to know Elaine, but it was the haunting pain she heard in Robert's voice that had stayed with her. And when they had finally met on his first impromptu visit to her office, she had been moved by the hurt she saw on his face, the suppressed rage in his body language. Unfortunately, Robert Kimbrew desperately needed answers she could not offer. He could not understand how anyone, regardless of the evil that blackened his soul or the drugs that might have clouded his judgment, could kill his daughter. To prevent anyone else experiencing the same agony, he wanted to know everything he could do to see that Wardrip remained in prison, unable to inflict additional harm.

And Raven Kazen had told him everything she knew to do. But now time was running out. Like it or not, Wardrip would soon be a free man.

It was shortly after yet another parole request had been reconsidered and denied that she mentioned one final thing Robert might consider. It was a new program called Victim Offender Mediation/Dialogue, a revolutionary experiment recently initiated by her office. "What we do," she explained, "is put the inmate and a family member of his victim together for a mediated discussion. It happens only if both parties are agreeable and only after both have gone through a rather intensive preparation for the face-to-face meeting." There had already been a half-dozen such encounters, she said, each coordinated by her young associate David Doerfler, a former minister, and the results she had seen were impressive. "A lot of questions were answered for all concerned. The people who have gone through it have told us that it helped them get on with their lives."

Robert told her he would have to think about it.

Wardrip, contacted by Doerfler, initially said he was willing to participate. Just days later, however, he'd written to the coordinator to say he'd changed his mind. When Doerfler visited him again to ask why, he said, "Fear, I guess. I'm just too afraid to face Tina's father."

"Think about it," Doerfler had suggested. "It might be your first step toward a new start."

For Kimbrew, the idea held merit only if he would be allowed to ask Wardrip specific questions about what had transpired in his daughter's apartment, of what kind of relationship—if any—he had had with Tina. "I'm not looking for an apology," he explained. "I want answers." Though he made no specific mention of it, the suggestion that his daughter might have been involved in drugs had long torn at him. It had been there since the early stages of the investigation, always subtly alluded to, but there nonetheless. Then, in the wake of Wardrip's arrest and confession, it had become a part of the news reports of Tina's death. It was always pointed out that he had gone to her apartment "looking for drugs." In his heart, Robert knew it was a lie; he was convinced that his daughter had not been involved in drugs. And he wanted to hear it from Wardrip.

Yes, he finally told Doerfler, he was willing to participate in the program. Soon he received a rambling, scripture-laden letter from Wardrip. He had thought and prayed about it, he wrote, and had decided to decline.

Again the old angers surfaced. Kimbrew sat at the desk in his office for most of a day, composing a reply. "You are the piece of shit I thought you were," he wrote. He criticized what he perceived as Wardrip's hiding behind Bible verses and "God's will" as nothing more than an excuse for not facing up to his responsibility. "I'm offering you a chance to do something right, if you're man enough to do it. If not, you'll never be anything more than the coward who killed my daughter."

Instead of sending the letter directly to Wardrip, Robert mailed it to David Doerfler, asking that it be delivered on May 6.

The date didn't immediately register. "That," Kimbrew reminded him, "was the day he killed Tina."

"I'll hand-deliver it myself," Doerfler promised.

It was after reading the letter that Wardrip agreed to the meeting. "It's something I know I have to do," he said.

Neither of the men anticipated the lengthy preparation that would be required.

For the next several months Doerfler held meetings with both parties individually, outlining the ground rules. The meeting would be conducted in the privacy of one of the prison visiting rooms with parties seated facing each other across a table. Well before they met, each would have submitted written questions and topics to be addressed. Repeatedly he stressed that only from an honest exchange could anything positive be derived. He would serve as the moderator, making certain the conversation stayed on track and that emotions were held in check. It would, he warned, not be an easy day for anyone.

As part of his preparation, Robert viewed a videotape of an earlier meeting between a young man whose brother had been murdered and his sister-in-law, who had hired the killer. He'd watched as the man's anger seemed to melt away during the course of the highly emotional conversation. The young woman, meanwhile, had shown genuine remorse over the destruction she had brought on the family. "I could see," Kimbrew told Doerfler, "that they got something out of it."

Elaine, meanwhile, was stunned when Robert told her of his plans. "Have you lost your mind?" she yelled. In the first disagreement they'd had over matters related to their daughter's death, Elaine had vehemently argued that

Robert's plan to meet with Faryion Wardrip was an insult to Tina's memory.

"You might be right," Robert admitted. "At this point I don't know. All I do know is I've got to make some sense out of all this. I'm tired of wallowing in pain and misery. If doing this helps, great. And if it doesn't, what the hell—things can't get any worse than they already are."

The meeting was finally scheduled for October.

Arriving a day early, Kimbrew had accompanied Doerfler to the prison, where he was given a tour and shown where the meeting would be held. That evening Robert sat in his motel room, pondering the grim prison lifestyle he'd observed during the visit and nervously anticipating what the next day would hold, when the phone rang.

It was Elaine. "Are you going to go through with it?" she asked.

"I am," he replied.

Resigned, she wished him well. "What are the rules?" she asked.

Robert forced a strained laugh. "I can't hit him or cuss him," he said. "Beyond that, anything goes."

For all the mental images that had played in his mind, the montage of imagined scenarios, seeing Faryion Wardrip in person for the first time was not at all what the apprehensive Kimbrew expected.

Instead of the unkempt, shaggy-haired man he'd seen in newspaper photographs and on television reports, the Wardrip who entered the room was well groomed and clean shaven, wearing slacks, a short-sleeved sport shirt, and running shoes. In one arm he cradled a worn Bible.

His eyes immediately met those of the man already seated at the table, then quickly strayed to examine the surroundings. In one corner a man he didn't know stood silently behind a video camera mounted on a tripod. He had been told that a video record of the encounter would be made. David Doerfler sat near the table, nodding in the direction of the empty chair. The guard who had escorted him into the room had stationed himself by the door. Only a few feet away, Robert Kimbrew waited.

Taking his seat, Wardrip continued to glance around the spartan room, avoiding the stare of the man across from him. After several silent seconds, it was Robert who initiated the conversation. "I don't want there to be any question about how I feel about you . . . about what you did," he said. "I've done everything in my power to keep you in here for as long as possible. And if there was something else I could do, believe me, I'd be doing it instead of sitting here. The fact is, I hate your guts."

Wardrip only nodded in response, still avoiding eye contact.

"What I don't understand," Robert continued, "is how my daughter could have even known someone capable of committing murder."

"That's not the person she knew," Wardrip responded. "The person she knew was a high school graduate, someone who had gone to college for three years and made straight As, played football, liked people, stuff like that. She didn't know the person who had messed up his life with drugs."

And with that Wardrip was telling his life story, pleading his case in a halting, nervous voice. His father, he said, had been an alcoholic. Wardrip described himself as the youngest member of the family. "I was the baby," he said, showing the first hint of a smile.

"I've been writing to my dad since I've been in here," he said, "and we've put a lot of bad things behind us. I've told him that I love him. Since we got things straightened out he's quit drinking and smoking. He told me that the letter I wrote him, reminding him of all the terrible things he'd done when I was a kid, changed everything for him. Said that after he read it he made up his mind to straighten out his life."

Wardrip paused for a moment, lightly running a finger across the cover of the Bible sitting on the table in front of him. "One of the main reasons I want to get out," he finally continued, "is so I can go back home and take care of him. He's dying."

For the first time since he'd entered the room, Robert felt a tinge of compassion.

"How did you know Tina?" he asked.

"She was such a pretty girl, such a nice person," Wardrip replied. "I met her back when I was checking I.D.'s at the door at the Stardust Club. She would come in there sometimes. We just started talking and became friends." For the first time, he looked directly into Robert's eyes. "She talked about you all the time," he said. "She was so proud of you.

"Sometimes I'd go over to her place and we'd just talk. She was a nice person, a good friend. I was wearing my hair real long back then and she would sit and comb it while we talked."

Robert felt himself breathe deeply for composure as a forgotten memory suddenly played. He could remember Tina as a child, standing behind his chair, combing his hair and asking, "Daddy, does that feel good?"

Sensing Kimbrew's uneasiness, Wardrip changed the subject. Knowing that the primary reason for Tina's father's visit was to learn the details of her death, he was soon trying to broach the subject—to get things said and over with—and every time, Robert had quickly changed the course of the conversation.

For all the strength he'd gathered to reach this point, Robert was not yet ready for the moment of hoped-for truth that had drawn him there. Despite occasional suggestions from Doerfler that an explanation of what had happened years earlier at the Park Regency Apartments might be in order, the conversation continued along a biographical line. "I want to know who this man is," Robert said.

It had been drugs, Wardrip volunteered, that ruined his life. "Nobody knew, though," he said. "I was able to con everybody. And I never stole to buy them. I always worked hard, sometimes as many as three jobs at the same time. Nobody in my family ever knew I was a drug addict. The people I worked for didn't know. Somehow I managed to keep it hidden, even from my wife. But then, finally, it got out of control. That's when I went to see Tina . . ."

As Robert prepared to change the subject once more, Doerfler interrupted to suggest that it might be a good time to take a short break. As the two men rose, Robert extended a hand across the table, a gesture he had neither planned nor anticipated. "I want you to know," he heard himself say, "that I appreciate what you're doing here."

Surprised, Wardrip shook his hand.

After the guard had escorted his prisoner from the room, Kimbrew looked toward the mediator as if anticipating what he was about to say. "I know," he said. "I'm getting there."

"You're doing fine," Doerfler replied.

It was a far more relaxed Wardrip who returned to the room in the afternoon. "Mr. Kimbrew," he began, "I don't know why I did it. She was my friend.

"I went over to her apartment that day. I'd been doing a lot of drugs and wanted to get straightened out and asked her if she could let me stay at her place for a few days until I got myself dried out.

"And you know what the first thing she said was? She

said, 'No, my daddy would kill me if I let you stay here.'
But she told me that if I was serious about getting
straightened out, all I had to do was call you and you
would help me. That you would know who to get in touch
with. She said you were always ready to help people. She
offered to call you. Like I said, she was proud of you.

"She still had on her robe and told me she had to go to
the hospital. Then she went upstairs to get dressed. I kept
asking her if I could just stay for a couple of days, and she
said, 'No, you're not staying here,' and told me to leave.
When I didn't, she came downstairs and starting yelling
at me. Then she started hitting on me. And that's when I
started hitting her. I just lost control."

Robert listened silently as Wardrip described how he
had spun her body around so her back was facing him,
then locked his arm across her face to silence her
screams. "The next thing I knew," he said, "she was
dead."

As if trying to relate the entire horrific tale before being interrupted, he described his decision to flee to Galveston and his aborted suicide plan. The only reason he had
finally decided to phone the local police, he said, was so
he could tell them that he was the person who had killed
Tina. "There hasn't been a day gone by since that I
haven't thought about her and what I did. I'd never hurt
anybody in my life before that day. I'm so sorry for what
I did."

There were tears in his eyes as he spoke. "Since I've
been here," he continued, "I've tried to get right with
God. I've gone to AA meetings, Narcotics Anonymous
meetings. I've tried to help other inmates. I haven't been
in one day's trouble.

"I've still got all of those bills you sent me," he added.
"When I get out of here I'm going to start paying them.

"And," he concluded, "there's something I'd like your permission to do."

Robert, who had been staring down at the table, looked up. "What's that?"

"Someday," Wardrip said, "I'd like to visit Tina's grave."

For the remainder of the afternoon, Kimbrew listened as Wardrip responded to his questions about life in prison, his relationship with his family, and what plans he had once he was released. The inmate talked openly of the stormy years he'd spent with his wife. They had lived together for quite some time. After they had married and had children he came to hate her. In his drug-induced paranoia, he said, it was his wife he was killing that day, not Tina. "I thought it was my wife that I was hitting," he said.

He expressed hope that he would be able to reestablish a relationship with his children once free.

And then Doerfler said that it was time to wrap things up. The five-hour ordeal, having passed more quickly than any of the parties had anticipated, was at an end.

Wardrip looked across the table at Robert. "I want to thank you for forcing me to do this. I had no idea how much it would help."

"We both need to understand as much as we can," Kimbrew replied.

"Will you ever be able to forgive me?"

Robert pondered the question for some time. "I'll let you know if I ever do," he finally said. "Before I go, there's one other thing I want you to do."

Wardrip nodded.

"If she's up to it, I want you to meet like this with Tina's mother."

"She's written to me . . ."

"What you've been through today is nothing compared to what you're going to face when you meet her. You're going to be in for a tongue-lashing like nothing you've ever experienced. It won't be easy, believe me. But it might help both of you."

"You tell her I'd like to talk with her," Wardrip said.

Standing, Kimbrew looked across the table one last time. "You're going to be getting out of here soon," he said. "In spite of how I feel and everything I can do. That's just the way it is. So, I can only hope you're going to be able to stay out of the kind of trouble you got yourself into before." He paused and drew a deep breath, as if preparing himself to finish his thought. "If things do go bad again someday, if you have a problem and you've gone to everybody you can think of for help and they've turned you down, I want you to call me. Anytime, day or night. I'll do whatever I can to help you."

David Doerfler was stunned by what he heard. As they prepared to leave, he took Robert's arm. "I don't think you understand what you just said," he whispered.

"Oh, I understand it," Robert replied. "If I can help prevent what happened to Tina happening to anyone else, I've got to be ready to do it. I may not like it, but I've got to do it."

In nearby Pearland, Larry Thornhill had watched as Elaine nervously paced the house. "He'll call when its over," he told his wife.

Years earlier he and his first wife had been close friends with Elaine and Robert, then, following a divorce, he'd left Vernon and lost touch. He'd just returned from a hunting trip when he learned that Tina had been murdered. Phoning Elaine to express his sympathy, he'd learned that she and Robert were no longer married.

Their friendship was renewed and gradually developed into something more. Even before they decided to marry, Larry had understood that he would have to accept the fact that a bond remained between his new wife and her ex-husband. That bond was their murdered daughter. That, Elaine had warned him, would never change.

"I need to be there," she had finally said. "He's going to need to talk to someone when it's over."

Her husband argued against the idea, worried about the emotional toll it promised. "Just wait until he calls," he said.

"No," she said, "I'm going. Just give me directions."

Though he offered to drive her, Larry knew she would prefer to go alone.

The sun was beginning to set as Robert, drained yet feeling oddly at ease, walked from the prison's main gate into the parking lot. He was surprised to see his ex-wife step from her car and hurry toward him.

Even from a distance, Elaine recognized a change in the man she had known most of her adult life. The weariness seemed gone from his walk, the air of defiance and anger replaced by a look of renewed peace.

"I didn't do anything that showed disrespect for Tina" were the first words he spoke. "I don't want you to stay angry with me for doing this. I can't explain it right now—I may never be able to—but I feel better than I have in a long, long time."

It was time, he suggested, that she, too, begin looking for a way to escape her grief. Introducing her to Doerfler, who was standing nearby, he said, "This man right here can help you if you'll let him."

With that David handed her his card.

Later, as they sat in an almost deserted restaurant, Robert quietly detailed the intense experience he'd just left behind.

"Robert," Elaine finally said, disbelief creeping into her voice, "it almost sounds like you're apologizing for him. How can you feel the slightest bit of compassion for someone who did what he did to Tina, to us?"

"It's hard to explain," he acknowledged. "I didn't forgive him or anything like that. I'll never be able to bring myself to do that. I can't even say how much of what he said I really believe. But, yes, I guess I did feel some compassion before it was all over. His life was out of control. He made a terrible mistake."

Elaine stared silently, shaking her head. "I can't believe you shook his hand."

"All I really know," Robert replied, "is that what happened in that room today was one of the hardest things I've ever been through. And that I feel a lot better for having done it. I'm not going to try and tell you how to live your life, but if you'll let it, talking to him could help you, too."

That evening as she drove home, Elaine calmed herself by listening to the soft gospel music that played on her car radio. And wondered how she would tell Larry that someday, maybe in the very near future, she would pay a visit to the man who had murdered her daughter.

For weeks after the encounter, Robert found himself replaying the conversation with Wardrip until it had been committed to memory. The part he had vainly tried to shut out, to erase, was the description of how his daughter had died. Then, one evening, in the midst of a restless sleep, it came rushing back and he found himself suddenly sitting upright in bed.

For months after Tina's murder, one of the things that had haunted him was the suffering she had experienced before dying. Finally he had contacted the medical examiner's office. Hesitant at first, Dr. Gilliland had located

the report and explained her findings. From the fact that
his daughter's saliva was found on the pillow she had examined and that particles of fabric had been lodged in her
lungs, she had no doubt that the victim had been suffocated by having the pillow pressed tightly to her face.

"How long did it take her to die?" Kimbrew asked.

Anywhere from seven to fifteen minutes, the pathologist said. Then, hoping to soften the image she knew she
was creating in the distraught caller's mind, she had
added that one being suffocated in such a manner would
likely lose consciousness in no more than two minutes.

When Wardrip had described placing Tina in a head-
lock, using his arm to cover her mouth, Robert had interrupted him, explaining his conversation with Dr. Gilliland
that had suggested a far different scenario. Rather than
argue the fact, Wardrip had simply reminded him that
much of what had occurred remained a blur and continued with his story.

In the darkness of his bedroom, Robert felt suddenly
chilled as he wrestled with a question he would share
with no one:

Was it possible, he silently wondered, that Faryion
Wardrip had described to him the murder of someone
other than his daughter?

CHAPTER TWELVE

Elaine had been secretly writing to Faryion Wardrip for years. She had, in fact, been doing so since his incarceration in the Wichita County jail. At first her letters had pleaded with him to see her and offer some explanation for the nightmare she was being put through. Several times she had acted on impulse, arriving unannounced at the jail to request that the sheriff allow her to see the man who had murdered her daughter. That Wardrip had refused to see her or answer her letters had only increased her resolve. Once he'd agreed to a plea bargain and was moved to prison, Elaine began sending cards on every holiday—Christmas, Easter, Valentine's Day—each bearing the same message: I just wanted you to know that I'm thinking of you and that I hope you are rotting.

In time, though, her anger had subsided and she found a certain degree of comfort in the simple fact that Wardrip was locked away, at arm's length. Then all that changed with the dreaded realization that soon he was to be paroled. And Robert, seeking relief from the darkness that had surrounded his own life, had complicated everything with his determination actually to sit and talk with him.

And now she, too, was going to give it a try. When her

husband and family members expressed skepticism, she did not attempt an explanation. "I had trouble understanding why Robert chose to do it. But, in time, I accepted it. You'll just have to do the same," she said.

Having become an increasingly spiritual person in the years following Tina's death, she prayed often for guidance as she prepared for her visit to the prison. Finally she confided her purpose to Doerfler: She wanted Faryion Wardrip to promise her that he would fully explore the possibilities of becoming a Christian.

Only when Wardrip pointed out to the coordinator that he was already working toward that goal, that one of the first things he planned to do upon his release was to be baptized, did plans for the meeting move forward. "She's not going to be satisfied with promises," Doerfler warned. "She wants proof. She wants to help you with Bible studies, to know that you have a job and are attending church once you're out, that you're doing everything possible to make something of yourself."

Wardrip assured him that the goals he'd set for himself were the same as the demands of the woman he was soon to meet.

If Larry Thornhill had doubts about his wife's resolve to move ahead, they were erased as he sat with her in the hospital on the evening before yet another back surgery. Despite her pain and the drowsiness brought on by her medication, she sat up in bed, filling out the final bit of paperwork Doerfler required.

"It's your decision," her husband had finally told her, "and I respect and support it. I have only one request."

"What's that?"

"Let me go to the prison with you."

Wardrip had been transferred to a unit near Beaumont, a facility that processed inmates soon to be paroled. It was there that Larry delivered his wife to the warden's office where David Doerfler was already waiting. "Do you want to be in the room when he arrives?" the coordinator asked. "Or would you rather he go in first?"

Nervously, Elaine said she wanted to be taken in first. "I want him to have to look at me the moment he comes in," she said. She felt a sudden need to be in control, if at all possible, of what was about to take place.

What she'd not been prepared for were Wardrip's eyes. She saw no evil in them. They were beautiful.

Advancing toward the table, Bible again in hand, he politely asked if he might sit down.

Nodding, Elaine spoke her first words, not to Wardrip but to Doerfler. "I'd like for you to begin this meeting with a prayer," she said.

Wardrip placed his hands on his Bible as Doerfler prayed.

Even years later the former minister would recall the meeting between Wardrip and Elaine as the most intense he'd ever presided over. Methodical and organized, Elaine repeatedly referred to a written list of subjects she wished to cover. Wardrip, meanwhile, responded with articulate and sincere answers that pleased her.

"No," he insisted, "Tina never did drugs. She didn't even know I did drugs until that day I went over to ask for her help. If she'd seen the needle tracks on my arms, she'd never have had anything to do with me. She did tell me once that you were concerned about her smoking cigarettes and was trying to quit. I was trying to help her with that. In fact, she never smoked in front of me."

Elaine could only nod, remembering her daughter's teenage days when she would sneak away to smoke, thinking her secret was safe.

"She didn't want to do anything that would upset you or her daddy," Wardrip continued. "Tina was the kindest, most caring person I ever met."

There were things Elaine already knew—bits of conversation that Robert had already shared with her—but wanted to hear for herself. "What, exactly, was your relationship with Tina?" she asked. "Did you and my daughter date?"

"No, we didn't date. Oh, we went out for coffee one time after she got off work, but some other girls were with her. We were just friends." He again described how they had met when he was working as a doorman at the Stardust.

While Wardrip had found it difficult to look at Robert, his eyes never strayed from Elaine. She was pleased by the humility in his voice and his willingness to accept blame for his past. Though he reiterated the problems he'd had with his father, he'd assured her that "I'm not blaming him for anything I've done." His wife, he said, had made life miserable for him, but she could not be held responsible for his behavior. When she had divorced him, he could not hold it against her.

The drugs had been his downfall and the reason for all the heartache he'd caused. "I let them ruin my life," he said. "And I let them ruin the life of everyone I loved." With that he began to describe the last time he'd seen his children. "These two drug dealers I knew pulled up in front of the house," he said, "and I couldn't wait to get out the door and into the car with them. My wife was standing on the porch, one of the kids in her arms, the other standing next to her, and she was begging me not to go. As I walked away she told me that if I left she didn't want me to come back."

His eyes began to mist as he continued. "But I went anyway. I just walked away and rode off with a couple of good-for-nothing guys who didn't want anything but my money. That was the last time I saw my children."

It was not until he again described Tina's death that Elaine's control slipped away. She began to cry. "I'd never hurt anybody in my life," he said. "It was like I just went blank all of a sudden. It wasn't Tina anymore. I saw my wife's face, not Tina's. She wouldn't stop screaming and I just kept hitting her and hitting her."

A guttural moan came from deep inside as he spoke, and he, too, was in tears, his shoulders slumping, his hands shaking. Then, in a plaintive whisper, he asked, "Will you please forgive me for what I've done? Please . . . please . . . don't hate me."

Elaine closed her eyes, fighting to regain her composure. Taking a deep breath, she finally responded. "Faryion," she said, "I hate what you did. But I don't hate you. If I'm to be a Christian, forgiven of my own sins, I have to be able to forgive others."

Wardrip's sobs only grew louder.

"I forgive you," Elaine said.

She explained that she wanted him to work at the Bible study material she had already begun sending to him and to keep her updated on his progress. And, once back in the free world, she wanted him to make every effort to reestablish a relationship with his children. "I really want you to see them again, to be with them," she said. "And if you do get to hold them and put your arms around them, I want you to think of me when you do. Because, Faryion, that's what you took from me. I don't want you to ever forget that. You took away any grandchildren I might have had. And if you one day have grandchildren, I don't want you to ever hold one on your knee without thinking about Tina and me."

"I think about Tina every day," Wardrip assured her.

For five hours, Larry Thornhill had paced along a nearby hallway, eager for his wife's return so he might take her home. Relief swept over him as he saw her walking toward him. Though obviously exhausted, she was smiling faintly. "Before we go," she said, "I wish you would come inside and meet him."

Though he'd done everything in his power to be supportive, Thornhill had not prepared himself actually to meet the man who had caused his wife so much pain and suffering. "I don't know if I—"

"I'm going to be corresponding with him," Elaine explained. "It might be easier for you to understand if you met him."

Larry followed her inside where Wardrip and Doerfler waited. The two men were introduced and stood silently for several seconds before Larry finally extended his hand.

Wardrip shook it and looked over at Elaine. "Thank you," he said.

"I'm expecting you to follow through on what we've talked about," she said as she prepared to leave. "Don't let me down."

"I won't," Wardrip said. "I promise I won't."

Once back in Pearland, she telephoned Robert. "I did it," she said, "and I've never seen such pain and shame in a person. He begged and begged me to forgive him."

"And what did you say?" Robert asked.

"I told him that I could no longer hate him. I forgave him."

Robert responded with a long silence. For so long, his ex-wife had been angry with him, unable to accept his decision to meet with Wardrip, and he'd never fully understood her reaction. Now, however, it was Robert who could not understand, who was feeling a sudden rise of frustration.

"God, Elaine," he said, "how could you do that?"

Her voice was filled with exhaustion as she answered. "I'm his last chance, Robert. I could be some other mother's last chance."

It wasn't long before she received her first letter from Wardrip. In it, he insisted that his religious conversion had changed his life. He pointed out that Faryion Wardrip, the drug addict, the selfish, manipulative human being, no longer existed.

Accompanying it was a Bible study questionnaire with each answer carefully handwritten. What Elaine had no way of knowing, however, was that Wardrip had persuaded a fellow inmate to fill in the blanks.

While Robert and Elaine revisited the old agonies that had haunted their lives, Barry Macha wrestled with demons of his own. That the murders of three young women—Terry Sims, Toni Gibbs, and Ellen Blau—had remained unsolved throughout his tenure as district attorney was far more than a blot on his office's record. Though other crimes had demanded immediate attention, his thoughts rarely strayed far from the brutal homicides he had privately vowed to see solved. In the years that passed, it had not been unusual for him to react to a sudden urge to pick up the phone and call police and sheriff's department investigators to see if they had developed any new leads. He'd always known the answer before he called. His purpose was really to remind others that he'd not forgotten about the brutal murders.

As he matured into the job, Macha had gained a new understanding of his responsibility to the families of crime victims. Robert and Elaine had helped that along. So had Murray Blau and Jeff Gibbs, Catie Reid and Vickie Grimes, people whom he'd come to know on a first-name basis, people whose lingering grief had become his own.

Despite the distance in time, his resolve had not diminished.

In the decade that had passed since the murders, the technology of DNA analysis had advanced dramatically. Where once a microscopic or degraded sample was judged to be useless, updated equipment and techniques used in the mid-1990s had made successful results possible with only trace amounts of evidence.

When the samples of spermatozoa found in the bodies of Toni Gibbs and Terry Sims had been frozen and stored away at the Department of Public Safety crime lab in Austin, there was little hope they might ever aid in the investigation. There had simply been too little on the vaginal and anal smears to test.

Such was no longer the case in January of 1996 when Macha and Archer County D.A. Tim Cole met and decided to see if science could get their respective investigations off high center. Their first order of business was to see if it was possible to determine if DNA samples taken from Danny Laughlin while in custody could be matched to the samples recovered from Toni Gibbs's body.

By March the tests had been completed and Laughlin was excluded.

In the ten years that had passed since he'd been tried for murder, Danny Laughlin's life had continued on a downward spiral.

Paroled from prison in July of 1987, he had briefly lived in a rural area of the Texas Panhandle, engaged to Anita Rivas, the woman who had corresponded with him throughout his incarceration. There, near the town of Levelland, Danny had worked in the oil fields with the man he expected to one day be his father-in-law and attended Sunday church services with Anita. In time, however, new pressures surfaced. The whisper of local residents, aware of the fact he'd been accused of murder, grew louder and more disconcerting. Worried for Anita's safety, Laughlin left for Huachuca City, Arizona, a small community of 1,800. There he moved in with his mother, helping out in the restaurant she had opened.

And it wasn't long before he was back in trouble.

In the spring of 1989, Laughlin was charged with sexual abuse and aggravated assault of a local high school student he had briefly dated. On the night of the senior prom, a jealous Laughlin had followed the girl and her date, threatening to harm them both if she did not agree to leave with him immediately. The young couple had refused and, instead, called the local authorities. At the police station, the eighteen-year-old girl related an even more frightening experience.

After she'd tried to end their relationship a month earlier, Laughlin had forced her to drive to a secluded area outside of town where he had made unwanted sexual advances. When she had tried to get out of the car, he grabbed her by the hair, pulled her down into the seat, and waved a knife in front of her face.

The girl, by then hysterical, had told Laughlin that he "might as well go ahead and kill" her. His response, she said, was "I'm not going to kill you. I'm just going to cut up your beautiful face. When I get through nobody is going to have anything to do with you."

Arrested, Laughlin pled guilty to aggravated assault, kidnapping, and sexual abuse and spent six months in jail.

Once released, he moved on, this time to Colorado. And it was there, in the fall of 1993, that his misspent life had ended. Danny Laughlin, at age twenty-eight, was killed in a head-on car collision near Cripple Creek.

Just days before his death, he'd expressed to his mother a growing weariness with his life and the constant reminders that he remained the primary suspect in the death of Toni Gibbs. "If anything ever happens to me," he told Wilma Hooker, "I want you to continue doing whatever you can to clear my name."

Three years would pass before Laughlin's embittered mother received a letter from attorney Roger Williams, explaining that the DNA testing had finally exonerated her son. Wrote Williams: "I know that this information is ironic, coming only after Danny's death and in light of the grief law enforcement officers gave him during his lifetime. I can only hope it will make law enforcement officers hesitate before jumping to conclusions that can ruin a persons life based on a mistaken assumption. May God grant you peace."

Soon Donnie Ray Goodson was also cleared. After voluntarily providing a blood sample to be tested against the DNA left on the body of Terry Sims, it was concluded that he was not responsible for her rape and murder.

Thus, by attempting to move the case forward, it seemed the frustrated district attorneys had succeeded only in moving it in the wrong direction, back to square one.

Searching for some new avenue of investigation, Macha contacted the Wichita Falls police and requested that all evidence in the Sims case be turned over to one of his investigators. At the same time he ordered an additional test from the Department of Public Safety lab. Would they test to see if the DNA found on the bodies of Sims and Gibbs had come from the same person?

When he received word that it appeared likely that the two women had been attacked by the same perpetrator, Macha felt a twinge of renewed encouragement. The hunch he'd had for a long time—that they were looking for one person, not two or three—grew stronger.

As a bonus, investigator Patrick Sullivan, after examining the evidence he'd retrieved from the police, noticed what appeared to be a bloody fingerprint on the heel of one of Terry Sims's tennis shoes. Expressing disbelief that it had never been tested, Macha immediately had it sent to the lab, where a forensic expert soon acknowledged that it was, in fact, a partial print.

But where did they go to find a suspect to match it to?

In the summer of 1997, Roy Hazelwood, a pleasant, easy-going man who had spent sixteen years as a member of the FBI's Behavorial Science Unit before retiring to join an independent forensic consulting firm, left his Virginia home for his first-ever trip to Wichita Falls. Contacted by Macha, he had agreed to review the unsolved cases and attempt to develop a profile of the person who had murdered the young women.

For several days he read the files, spoke with investigators, visited family members of the victims, and traveled to the crime scenes. Before returning home, he warned the district attorney not to expect miracles from his report. "A profile," he said, "rarely solves a case. It's something law enforcement usually resorts to after all else has failed. If it provides you and your investigators with a fresh idea or suggests some overlooked way of viewing the case, then I'll consider it a success." What he would prepare, he said, was a profile of the killer as he was during the time his crimes were committed.

Even with the warning, Macha eagerly read the famed profiler's report.

The following information was developed specifically to describe the murderer of Terry Sims and Toni Gibbs. Recognizing that the same person may be responsible for the death of Ellen Blau, investigators may consider using this information in that crime as well.

The offender was known to Ms. Sims and/or Ms. Boone. However, it is believed that although he knew Ms. Gibbs, she didn't know him.

The offender was a white male between 24 and 30 years of age. Age is the most difficult characteristic to ascertain in unsolved crimes and while he is believed to have been the chronological age stated, it is almost certain that he was less mature emotionally and would have been known to react with anger when he experienced or perceived rejection. He was a very selfish person who exhibited a lack of concern for the welfare or safety of others.

The killer would have projected a "macho" image to friends and associates. Outwardly, he was a "man's man" and he worked at maintaining this image. Therefore, he would have operated a pick-up truck, motorcycle, or four-wheel drive vehicle and he would have worn jeans, boots or sneakers and t-shirts when not working.

It is obvious from the crimes that he was not uncomfortable getting blood on himself or killing in a very personal manner with a knife and yet rage was not evidenced in his crimes. It is therefore reasonable to suggest that, if he was working, he would have been employed in a job requiring physical exertion and working with his hands in a skilled or semi-skilled position. He exercised and participated in pick-up games such as football or basketball, but was not a good loser. He drank excessively and his alcoholic drink of choice was beer.

If he served in the armed forces in any capacity, this type of offender classically would have preferred being in the ground forces. However, given the influence of the Air Force in Wichita Falls, it is possible that he served in that branch. It is unlikely that he would have successfully completed any military obligation in that he has a dislike for authority figures.

Even though he had relationships with women and was probably married at least once, he was incapable of being loyal and "cheated" on his wife or other women in his life. Women with whom he had a relationship would advise that regardless of the image he projected, he had low self-esteem and was hypersensitive to criticism. He was a suspicious person who didn't trust others.

Women frightened him, but because of the masculine image he projected, he was able to conceal this fact from all but those women who lived with him or had relationships with him. He was known to resent and denigrate women in positions of authority, such as law enforcement, politics, and television commentators.

He would have been particularly intimidated by the physical beauty, intelligence, socio-economic status and sophistication of Ms. Gibbs and the stabbing of the victim prior to the sexual assault negated that fear. The anal assault of Ms. Gibbs was an indication of his underlying anger toward women. He experienced difficulties in his relationships with women and may have physically and sexually abused them to establish and/or maintain a position of "superiority." Women would have re-

ported him to be irresponsible and having a lack of concern with obligations of any type.

He had a high school education and may have augmented that education with some technical or trade courses. Nothing about his crimes suggests an investment of time and energy in planning and therefore it is believed that he possessed average intelligence. He would have been known as being pseudo-intelligent and trying to impress others with his imagined intellect. He would have been described as being a very opinionated person and one who irritated people with his inflexibility on seemingly unimportant matters.

At the time of the murders, he was socio-economically in the upper-lower to lower-middle class and resided in close proximity to the residence of Ms. Boone. His lack of planning and his inability to consider the consequences of his acts, combined with the fact that Ms. Boone's residence is within walking distance of the disposal site of Ms. Gibbs' car, strongly indicate this is an area with which he is familiar and geographically comfortable.

He was a highly impulsive person who acted without considering the consequences and would have been in debt beyond his abilities to pay. This impulsivity would have been reflected in a variety of ways to include the impulsive purchase of items, repeatedly changing jobs or residences, or becoming seriously involved in relationships after a very short period of time.

It is probable that he engaged in activities without reasonable concern for the danger to himself or others. He would do so to "show off." Examples of such activities may have included dangerous driv-

ing habits, engaging in illegal acts, or diving into unknown bodies of water.

At the time of the murder of Ms. Sims, he was experiencing stress. The stress could have been related to one or more of the following: occupational, health, financial, relational, family, or legal problems. He would have been known for reacting with temper and possibly violence when under stress. He drank excessively when he was depressed, frustrated or felt he had been slighted. When he drank, he became more profane and emotional, later expressing regret and remorse, but not taking any long-lasting corrective action.

He would have had difficulties with the law since he was a teenager and his arrest history would have reflected a variety of offenses ranging from misdemeanors up to and including felonies. It is probable that he would have been charged with resisting arrest because of his disrespect for authority.

People who knew him would advise that he was superficially charming but emotionally cold and distant. He was not affected by the emotional or physical sufferings of others and was known as a person who repeatedly exaggerated and lied about his accomplishments and other things.

Following the murders, or any other crime, he would not have exhibited any behavioral changes. He was not impacted by the crimes and consequently would not have experienced remorse or guilt. He would have continued life as though nothing had happened. This lack of concern for his crimes or his victims was demonstrated by the fact that within a month of the death of Ms. Sims, he abducted and killed Ms. Gibbs.

. . . AND NOW

CHAPTER THIRTEEN

On that long-ago winter day when he had joined his brother in search of the missing Toni Gibbs, bricklayer John Little was a young man content with the course of his life. Married and the father of a newborn son, he and his family lived in a suburban home he'd built. The construction work he'd been doing since schoolboy summers had always fascinated him. He liked earning his living in the outdoors, enjoyed the unique feeling that came from watching something evolve from blueprint to completion.

The youngest of seven children, he'd been born in Wichita Falls after his parents had moved from Biloxi, Mississippi, when his father accepted a position as a mechanics' instructor at Sheppard Air Force Base. Life had been carefree then, filled with the idyllic promises of youth. John had breezed through high school, making good grades and participating in athletics. Following graduation, he enrolled in Midwestern. Then the tornado came.

In the spring of 1979, a monstrous funnel cloud tore through Wichita Falls, leveling homes and businesses, claiming forty-five lives. The Littles' home was among those demolished. And everything changed. The devasta-

tion caused his older brother's construction business to
flourish. John, feeling the need to help his family get back
on its feet, dropped out of school and went to work.

It would be two years before he considered getting
back to college. And, no sooner had he returned than he
met with another distraction—a pretty blonde named Lisa
who was working toward a social sciences degree. They
fell in love and soon were talking of marriage. His enthusiasm for academics having waned considerably, John
proposed a plan whereby he would return to construction
work while Lisa completed the requirements of her degree. Her father, a successful realtor, briefly attempted to
convince his new son-in-law to consider earning a real es-
tate license, which he did, but John soon realized that he
preferred building houses to selling them.

By the time their first child, Coleton, was born in
1985, they were living in their new house and earning a
good living. Like many young couples of the time, the
Littles had settled into a routine that was both comfortable and promising. They gathered with neighbors for
backyard cookouts and boated on the lake on summer
weekends. Eager to participate in community activities,
John joined the Lakeside City volunteer fire department.

And then, in the late 1980s, the once-booming market
for new homes began to falter. Building dropped off dramatically. And Lisa was again expecting. This time the
sonogram showed twins. And her husband began to consider a career change. To care for his growing family
properly, he realized that he needed a job that offered
more stability than the get-paid-when-you-work routine
of bricklaying. Steady income and benefits he'd not previously considered a necessity became his new goal.

Among the new friends Little had acquired was a
neighbor who worked as an officer for the Department of
Public Safety. Occasionally he would invite John to ride

along as he patrolled the highways, and as they talked an idea began to take shape. Law enforcement, Little decided, might be a career he would enjoy.

He discussed it with Lisa and was soon planning to enroll in the police academy. If things went as planned, he would eventually become a member of the Wichita Falls Police Department.

The rigors of the academy drills and testing energized him, and his enthusiasm for his new career grew daily. Then, however, came a devastating blow. He would, he was told, not be considered by the police department because he had failed his eye examination. Little was told that his test had revealed that he was nearsighted and thus had problems with depth perception. He argued that if such a condition existed, it had never affected him. As a bricklayer, he had spent years looking down a plumb line that indicated the location of the wall he was building without any problems. If he did, in fact, have such a problem, wouldn't it have adversely affected him as he was fielding fly balls and line drives on the softball field? His argument fell on deaf ears. Rules were rules, he was told.

Checking with a local optometrist, he was told that a simple surgery could correct the troublesome problem. Could he reapply once the nearsightedness was corrected? Yes, he was told, but policy demanded that he wait two years.

Little returned to construction work, determined to try again.

The two-year waiting period was almost at an end when he learned that the district attorney's office had an opening for an investigator. It was not a line of law enforcement work he'd ever considered, not one that he even knew anything about, but Little decided to look into it just the same. While he and D.A. Barry Macha were not close friends, they had crossed paths numerous times

while both were students at Midwestern. They attended
the same church and had played against each other in
adult softball leagues in the summers. Little had followed
Macha's career since he'd been elected and was impressed by the vigor and enthusiasm he displayed.

Taking a long shot, he placed a call to the D.A. and in-
quired about the qualifications and responsibilities of the
position. He was surprised when Macha suggested that he
stop by the office and fill out an application.

What Little did not know at the time was that the D.A.
had a unique philosophy about the function of an investigator. Traditionally, the role was filled by a former sheriff's deputy or ex–police officer in search of a place to
complete his career before retirement. Often, Macha had
observed, they arrived on the job firmly set in the ways
they believed investigations should be conducted and re-
luctant to embrace new ideas and techniques. Ready to
test a theory that someone straight out of the academy
might quickly grow into the job, Macha hired Little.

Thus in 1993, at age thirty-one, the bricklayer began a
new career.

He had adapted to the job quickly, dealing with everything from hot check complaints to tracking down witnesses and arranging for their court appearances. Like his
boss, he was soon a familiar face at crime scenes. And he
displayed an unusual knack for organizing evidence that
prosecutors planned to put on at trial. One of his first assignments, in fact, had been to help organize the prosecution of a rapist who had attacked sixteen victims.
Assistant D.A.s, sensing his ability to judge the mind-set
of potential jurors, were soon seeking his opinion during
the *voir dire* process. In the fast-paced world of criminal
justice, Little was thrown into the deep end of the learn-
as-you-go pool. In time, even veteran detectives and

deputies, at first wary of the lack of experience he'd brought to his job, warmed to the newcomer with the quick smile and country twang.

John Little had found his calling.

It was in the second week of December 1998, when Macha called Little into his office to first talk about the unsolved murders that had haunted him since he'd taken office. Though generally aware that Patrick Sullivan, another investigator in the office, had continued to work with Archer County investigator Paul Smith in an effort to find some new lead that would breathe life back into the investigation, the only firsthand knowledge Little had of the cases had come from news reports in the immediate aftermath of the crimes.

He knew nothing of the lengthy list of suspects Sullivan and Smith had considered, including a highly publicized serial killer named Danny Harold Rolling who was awaiting execution while on Death Row in a Florida prison.

Macha slid three folders across his desk toward Little. "Pat has resigned," he said, "so you're going to have to pick up the ball. Someday, somehow, we're going to solve these cases." The tone of his voice left no doubt about his resolve. "We've done too much to just let them slide. I want you to read over these case files as soon as you have the time—maybe you'll see something we've all missed— then let me know what you think."

With that he rose and reached for his jacket. "Let's go for a ride," he said. "I want to show you something."

Despite the insistence of the agencies that initially investigated the murders of Terry Sims, Toni Gibbs, and Ellen Blau that they were unrelated, Macha had had a gut feeling that all three had been victims of the same killer, even

before the DNA testing had finally linked the Sims and
Gibbs cases. Though he had no proof to support his
hunch, he felt it highly possible that Blau had been murdered by the same person. That feeling had only grown
stronger after reading the profile Roy Hazelwood had
submitted.

As he drove toward the small frame house on Bell
Street where Sims's body had been found, Macha confided his thoughts to his investigator. Slowing as he
passed, he said, "That's where Terry Sims was murdered." He then turned onto Van Buren Street, slowing as
he neared an intersection. Pointing to the curb, he said,
"That's where Toni Gibbs's car was found after she was
reported missing." The locations were less than a half-
mile apart.

There was something in this neighborhood, he suggested, that linked the murders. "I don't know what it is,
but I want you to help me find it," the grim-faced district
attorney said as he turned back into the traffic.

There was an urgency in his boss's voice that Little
had never before heard, a signal that was equal parts frustration and determination. Clearly the unsolved cases,
now a decade and a half old, remained fresh on his mind.

Back at the courthouse, the investigator gathered the
files from Macha's desk. "As soon as we finish up this
trial we've got going," he said, "I'll get to work."

Macha nodded. "Christmas is coming," he said. "I
guess after the holidays will be soon enough."

The excitement of Santa's arrival, then the passage into
the new year had been an enjoyable time in the Little
home. Now, however, Lisa had stored away the holiday
decorations and announced that she was ready for a return
to a normal, less hectic, routine.

It was on an evening in the second week in January

when her husband waited until the children were in bed to spread the file folders Macha had given him across the dining room table. In the days after being assigned to look over the cases, Little had made a concerted effort not to discuss them further with his boss. What he wanted to do was review them with an open mind, uncluttered by the tangled history of the investigations. The less he knew, the better. A fresh, unbiased approach, he felt, would provide him the best opportunity to see if anything might have been overlooked.

Privately, he approached his task with little optimism, doubtful that over a fifteen-year period there was anything new to be discovered.

His plan was simple: He would review the cases in the order the murders had occurred, making a list of names—friends, witnesses, suspects—included in each, then see if there were any instances in which the same name appeared in more than one of the investigations, if there was any signpost that pointed to an entry back into the cases.

He had just opened the Terry Sims folder when his wife walked into the room, leaned over his shoulder, and gave him a good-night peck on the cheek. She stood silently for a second, looking down on the paperwork in front of him. "You going to stay up until you solve these cases?" she asked.

Little recognized the jesting tone in his wife's voice. "Yeah." He smiled. "It shouldn't take long."

Methodically, he read the crime scene report that mentally took him back to the small frame house on Bell Street that Macha had showed him. The savagery that had occurred that night chilled him. He read the speculation that Sims might have been involved in drugs and quickly dismissed the idea as he reviewed the background information that had been gathered on the victim. Only as he continued reading did he realize he had known Terry's

uncle. His sister's husband had once been close friends
with Pete Sims. Both had an interest in restoring old cars
and riding motorcycles. Pete, Little recalled, had been in
the car the night Terry's father had crashed into the bridge
and died. It was not Little's only "small world" encounter.

As he began to review the list of possible suspects, he
found himself thinking back to the days when he and
Donnie Ray Goodson had been friends and schoolmates.
Over the years he'd heard the rumors that Goodson had
been a suspect, how he'd known and worked with Sims.
Only as he read the files, however, did he learn the link
that had caused the police to focus their suspicion on
Goodson. Leza Boone, the reports indicated, had recalled
seeing a man speeding down Bell Street on a motorcycle
as she arrived home that morning. The rider had been
wearing a helmet, so she could not make a positive identification. But, she had noted, Goodson owned a motorcycle similar to the one she had seen. The rider, she had told
the police, could have been him.

For a moment Little's thoughts wandered from the
documents spread before him. Now married, Donnie
lived just blocks away, yet they had never reestablished
the friendship they had enjoyed during their school days.
Even when Goodson began to lend his services as an
EMT on the volunteer fire department, Little had kept his
distance. The whisper he had heard for years, long before
developing an interest in law enforcement, was that
Goodson was most likely the person responsible for the
murder of Terry Sims. With no reason to believe differently, he'd opted not to reopen their friendship.

As he read into the night it quickly occurred to him
that those investigating the cases had been quick to fixate on prime suspects: While there was indication that
others who Terry Sims had attended college classes with
or worked with at the hospital had been interviewed,

they had been quickly dismissed. Always the investigation returned to Goodson despite the fact there was no physical evidence that connected him to the crime. Danny Laughlin had foolishly made himself the prime—and only—suspect in the murder of Toni Gibbs. The DNA tests ordered by Barry Macha years earlier had eliminated both. It was clear that Curtis Cates, Ellen Blau's boss at the Suds 'N Subs, was the only viable suspect ever developed in that case. But since there had been no DNA evidence taken from her body, there had been no chance of linking him to her abduction and death.

The list that Little had hoped to compile was not going to be long. Or, he feared, very productive.

Nothing he read indicated that the investigating agencies—the Wichita Falls Police Department, Wichita County Sheriff's Department, and Archer County Sheriff's Department—had ever combined efforts or shared information on the cases. It was obvious that no one had shared Barry Macha's hunch that the murders had somehow been related.

It was well past midnight when he began to read the final pages of the file on the Ellen Blau murder. In the back of the folder, a one-page report filed in October of 1986, a year after the crime had occurred, caught his attention.

Written by Lieutenant Thomas Callahan of the Wichita County Sheriff's Department it described his contact with Wichita Falls Police Sergeant Wyle Hopson about a conversation two of his officers had with a confessed killer named Faryion Wardrip. Callahan had been told that when officers Steve Pruitt and Bob Geurin were transporting Wardrip from Galveston to Wichita Falls after he had confessed to the murder of Tina Kimbrew, he had offhandedly mentioned that he had known Ellen Blau.

Little reread the notation several times, letting the sudden thread of a connection sink in: *En route to Wichita Falls, prisoner Wardrip mentioned that he had known a woman named Ellen Blau.* Had *known* Blau. And maybe killed her? The investigator added Wardrip's name to his list and underlined it. Alone, with no one to share his discovery, Little began to smile. Barry Macha's right, he thought.

Lieutenant Callahan's report indicated that he had taken a mug shot of Wardrip by the home of Janie Ball, who immediately remembered him as a weird person who had made her uneasy when she and her husband were living in the same apartment building at 1711 Bell Street. She said that Wardrip and his family had lived there at a time when Ellen regularly visited them. It was even possible, the report indicated, that Ellen might have met Wardrip during that time period.

What drew Little's attention was the address. The Bell Street apartment building where Wardrip had lived with his wife and small child was just a couple of blocks south of where Sims had been murdered and less than a half mile from where Gibbs's abandoned car had been found.

"Damn," Little said as he began writing furiously, making notes of things he would need to do the following day. Sitting alone in the early-morning quiet, he considered waking Lisa to share his strong feeling that he'd found the link that Macha believed existed, that he just might have stumbled on something that would finally solve the cases. Instead, he decided to wait until he'd checked some things.

After gathering the files and stacking them neatly into his briefcase, he showered and prepared for bed, knowing full well that sleep would be impossible.

In the days that immediately followed his discovery, Little resisted the urge to burst into Macha's office and tell him what he had learned. Having checked records at the city water department, he'd been able to confirm that Faryion Wardrip and his wife were living at the Bell Street address when Sims was murdered. Reading a copy of the police file on the Kimbrew murder, Little found a brief statement given by a former employer who had stated that Wardrip once worked at Wichita Falls General Hospital. The dates he gave police included the time frame when Sims and Gibbs were killed. During the interview, the employer described the marital problems that had caused Wardrip to move into an apartment on Airport Drive. The address, Little noted, was almost directly across the street from the Suds 'N Subs where Blau was working at the time of her death. It was, in fact, that address that Wardrip had used when registering at the Galveston motel following the Kimbrew murder.

Examining work records at Wichita Falls General, Little discovered that Wardrip had quit his job just four days after Terry Sims was reported missing. He checked to make sure that his suspect was neither in jail nor hospitalized on the dates the murders occurred. If there was fault with the storyline he'd begun to develop, he could not find it.

The information he'd gathered in just a matter of days had already taken him well beyond the coincidental. A new and legitimate suspect, he was convinced, had emerged. Contacting the Texas prison system, he was surprised to learn that Wardrip had been released on parole in December of 1997 after serving eleven years of his thirty-five-year sentence. Since then he had been living in the nearby community of Olney, ordered to wear an ankle monitor and leave his residence only to go to work and church, and to report to his parole officer once a week.

It was time to share what he'd found with his boss.

•   •   •

Barry Macha looked up from his cluttered desk to see Little standing in the doorway, the file folders cradled under his arm. Entering the room, he laid the folders in front of the D.A. "What would you say if I told you that I believe I've got the guy who killed these women?" the investigator asked. He unsuccessfully tried to hide a smile.

"You've got someone you want to look at?" Macha responded.

Little shook his head. "No," he said, briefly pausing for emphasis. "I've got the guy."

This time it was the investigator who suggested a drive. As they rode toward the residential area first pointed out to him by Macha, Little began reviewing the information he had collected in the past few days. As he talked, he drove through the intersection where Gibbs's car had been found, then past the house where Sims had died. A few blocks later he pulled to the curb and pointed to a two-story brick building. "There are four apartments in there," he said. "Janie Ball, Ellen Blau's friend, lived on the second floor. Ellen even stayed there for a while." Then he pointed to a corner downstairs window. "That's Apartment A," he said, "where Faryion Wardrip was living when Sims was killed." It was when he placed Wardrip and all three victims in the same small geographic area that he had so often been drawn to that Macha began to nod his enthusiasm.

"We need to get a DNA sample," he said.

"He shouldn't be too hard to find," Little responded.

The D.A. shook his head. "I'd rather get it without alerting him to what we're doing and what we know," he said. "See if there are blood samples on file from the Kimbrew case."

The investigator, convinced that such a sample would match those taken from the bodies of Sims and Gibbs and stored away for so long, contacted Dennis Lockerman, supervisor of the Texas Department of Public Safety's DNA database. It would have been routine procedure, he knew, for a blood sample to have been taken from Wardrip when he was arrested and charged with the Kimbrew murder. What he didn't know was that it was also routine to dispose of such samples once a conviction in a case was secured.

No DNA sample from Faryion Edward Wardrip existed, locally or in state and national data banks.

Sitting in Macha's office, the two men talked of the disappointing setback and alternate ways to see that the suddenly revitalized investigation move forward. If they approached Wardrip and attempted to persuade him to consent to giving a blood sample, only bad things were likely to happen. If he was, in fact, the killer, he would most certainly decline. And would be tipped to the fact he was being investigated. "On the other hand," Macha said, "if he says okay, that would pretty well mean that he didn't have anything to do with these cases."

Little immediately discounted the possibility of the latter. "Let's just get a warrant," he suggested.

"I'm not sure we have enough for one," Macha said. He was silent for several seconds, then said, "Abandoned interest. Let's go that route."

What he was referring to was a method by which law enforcement, attempting to get a DNA sample, managed to retrieve a saliva sample from a coffee cup, drinking glass, or cigarette butt left behind or discarded by a suspect, then had it tested. Once such items were no longer in possession of a person, they were considered "abandoned" and not his property.

"I don't care how you go about doing it," Macha said, "just get a sample."

CHAPTER FOURTEEN

L isa Little stood in her laundry room, perplexed by the disappearance of a load of clothes she had put into the washing machine the previous evening. Among the scenarios that she considered, none came close to what had actually occurred with the damp collection of children's jeans, T-shirts, and towels.

For several days her husband had been rising early and traveling south to Olney, where he had begun following Faryion Wardrip through his daily routine. On this day, in an effort to blend into the small community of 3,400, he needed a load of clothes to wash and dry—perhaps several times. The outpost he'd chosen from which to watch his suspect was the front window of a small cinderblock Laundromat located just across the highway from Wardrip's workplace. If he was going to blend into the landscape successfully, Little had decided, he needed to appear to be tending to the chores associated with the location. Thus, before leaving home, he'd tossed his wife's washing into a plastic basket. He would be just another weary bachelor tending to the mundane duty of making sure he had clean clothes.

The surveillance had become more difficult than he'd anticipated.

Having located the address to which Wardrip had been paroled, a small duplex just a couple of blocks off a winding Farm-to-Market highway, he had spent much of a Monday afternoon watching the house that had been listed on Wardrip's parole papers. Only after a considerable amount of wasted time did he realize that the house was, in fact, the home of Wardrip's parents. Finally, late in the day, a tall, lanky man appeared on the front porch of a nearby residence. Checking the arrest mug shot he'd borrowed from the police department, he saw Faryion Wardrip for the first time. Peering through binoculars, Little watched as a man dressed in jeans, running shoes, and a T-shirt casually talked with neighbors. From a distance of 300 yards, Wardrip didn't look like a killer.

Phoning a state trooper whom he knew was working an undercover narcotics investigation in the area, Little asked if he would quietly run a check on Wardrip. "All I really need," he explained, "is his address, vehicle registration information, current place of employment, stuff like that."

Before heading back home, the investigator had confirmed the duplex was the home of Wardrip and his new wife and that he worked a 7:00 A.M. to 3:30 P.M. shift at Olney Door & Screen, a small manufacturing company located on the highway that served as the town's main street. What he didn't know was that Wardrip's father had persuaded the owner, a longtime friend, to give his paroled son the job. Or that Wardrip's limited movements, the strict condition of his parole, which included that he wear an ankle monitor, was going to make obtaining a sample more difficult than he'd anticipated.

Still, he was back in Olney early the next morning, watching as Wardrip and his wife got into a green Honda and drove the short distance to his workplace. She let him out, then quickly drove away as he walked through a large double gate and disappeared into the warehouse.

For much of the morning, Little attempted to blend into the movements of those in the community, stopping into a local café for coffee, sitting in his pickup, reading the morning paper, driving aimlessly through neighborhoods. Making his way back to the neighborhood where Wardrip lived, he watched as several cars stopped out front and mothers delivered young children to the front door. Wardrip's wife appeared to supplement her husband's income by baby-sitting during the day. At regular intervals Little made his way from the downtown area out toward Olney Door & Screen. Several times he saw Wardrip out in the fenced-in yard, operating a forklift or talking with fellow workers. It quickly became clear to him that access to Wardrip's workplace without raising suspicion wasn't going to be possible. Perhaps, the investigator thought, his suspect would visit one of the local restaurants for lunch and leave behind a glass he had drunk from, a napkin he'd wiped his mouth with, or maybe a discarded cigarette butt.

Soon, however, he realized that the small container Wardrip had in his hand when he stepped from the car earlier in the day held a homemade lunch. He would not emerge from inside the yard until his wife arrived to pick him up at the end of his shift.

Inexperienced at the task he'd set out to accomplish, Little waited until Wardrip's wife picked him up and followed at a distance as she drove him directly home. When his suspect disappeared through the front door, Little headed back to Wichita Falls.

The "discarded property" idea, he told Barry Macha, wasn't working. "This is the guy," he said. "I know it. But I don't know how I'm going to get the sample."

Macha smiled at his investigator's impatience. "Just stay with him," he advised. "It's only been a couple of days. Something will happen."

Little didn't share his boss's confidence. By midweek, all he had done was watch Wardrip go to work, remain there throughout the day, then return home. The only time the routine had varied in the slightest was on Wednesday evening when he, his wife, and his mother attended services at the local Church of Christ. Hopeful that there might be some kind of cookies-and-punch social gathering after the sermon, Little had waited in the parking lot until the Wardrips emerged. Faryion had nothing in his hand. No cigarette dangling from his mouth. His wife got behind the wheel and drove straight home. No stop at the Dairy Queen for coffee, no drop-in at the 7-Eleven for a late snack. Nothing.

As the frustrated Little drove home that evening he lectured to himself: *You're pressing. There's no deadline. And it is pretty obvious this guy's not going anywhere. Just be patient.*

By the time he pulled into his driveway, he had already begun to formulate a new plan.

It was still dark when he dressed, took the load of clothes, and placed it into a car he'd borrowed from a fellow investigator. His pickup, he feared, might have become too familiar. For almost a week he had wandered in and around Olney, repeatedly driving past where Wardrip worked, occasionally parking across the street in front of the Laundromat, following Wardrip's wife to and from the grocery store for no good reason, all the while attempting not to draw attention to himself. He had begun to worry that soon someone would begin to wonder what this seemingly aimless stranger was doing in town. The curiosity of small towns, he knew, was legendary.

Thus on Friday, he planned to settle in one place. The plate-glass window that fronted the Laundromat afforded him an unobstructed view of the Olney Door & Screen lot where Wardrip worked. He would remain inside the little building to watch and wait. For what, he had no real idea.

Placing the clothes into one of the washing machines, he began a routine he was prepared to repeat throughout the day. If a customer came in, he'd remove the clothes from the washer and toss them into a dryer. If necessary, he would go through the motions of folding them. Then, should another patron appear, he would do the wash again. And again.

He wouldn't have to follow the routine for long.

It was midmorning when he saw Glenda Wardrip turn off the highway and pull up in front of the gate leading into the yard. She had come to share Faryion's midmorning break with him. Moments later he appeared, holding a cardboard cup of coffee in one hand as he unlocked the gate with the other. In his mouth was an unwrapped package of vending machine cheese crackers. As he approached the car, a youngster whom his wife was baby-sitting got out of the front seat and climbed into the back. Wardrip folded his frame into the passenger seat and leaned over to kiss his wife on the cheek.

Feeling a sudden rush, Little watched as the couple talked for several minutes. To get a closer look, he hurriedly tossed the clothing into his basket and carried it out into the parking lot. Climbing into his car, he adjusted his rearview mirror and watched the couple for a fifteen-minute time span that seemed an eternity. Finally he saw Wardrip finish the last of his crackers and emerge from the car. He placed the coffee cup on the roof as he stood at the open passenger door, saying his good-byes.

There, less than a hundred feet away, was the sample that Little so badly wanted. Stepping out of his car, his mind was abuzz. For a moment he considered the less-than-subtle tactic of simply running across the street, grabbing the cup from the top of the car, then racing back across the highway. He wondered if Wardrip would give chase, then dismissed the idea.

The more pressing question was what Wardrip would do with the cup when he was finished. There was a large Dumpster outside the fence that he might toss it into. Or perhaps he would simply drop it in the driveway where wind-blown trash had already collected. The investigator also noticed a small blue barrel just inside the fence. In all likelihood, that was where Wardrip would deposit his trash. And if he did so after locking the gate behind him, any opportunity would be lost.

Little stepped from the car as he saw Wardrip begin to walk back toward the gate, the coffee cup in hand. Unsure that he would be able to accomplish his mission, the investigator began walking across the highway, stuffing a large dip of snuff into one cheek as he approached.

Unbelievably, Wardrip left the gate open as he entered and walked directly to the driver's door of a truck that was loaded and preparing to leave the yard. Once the brief conversation with the driver inside the truck had ended, Wardrip walked to the blue barrel and tossed his cup away. Little quickened his pace, arriving at the gate just seconds later.

"How ya doing?" he called out, waving as he approached.

Wardrip, still standing near the barrel, nodded and smiled.

"Listen," the nervous visitor said, "I was wondering if you've got a cup or something I can get from you."

"A cup?"

Little grinned and gestured toward his bulging jaw. "Yeah, a spit cup."

"Oh, yeah, sure. Help yourself." Wardrip nodded in the direction of the barrel and stepped aside.

The investigator hoped that the anxiety he was feeling was not outwardly visible as he leaned over the half-filled trash barrel. Inside were dozens of discarded cardboard cups. Little quickly scanned the contents of the barrel, not wishing to linger at the task and thus raise suspicion. His eyes focused on a cup with playing card symbols printed on the side and remnants of cheese and cracker crumbs on its rim. He reached in and retrieved it.

"This'll work," he said. "Thanks."

Wardrip did not reply. He was already walking toward the warehouse as Little hurried back across the highway. Inside the car, he took a deep breath, carefully placed the cup into a clear plastic evidence bag, then sat looking at it for several seconds. Finally, a sense of relief fell over him and he began to smile as he placed the key in the ignition.

He was still on the highway when he phoned Macha. "I got it," he said, making no effort to conceal his excitement. "I got a cup he was drinking coffee from."

As Little explained how Wardrip had discarded the cup, then even verbally allowed him to take it from the trash, the D.A. laughed. Having often chided Little about his snuff-dipping, he said, "Well, I guess your bad habits are finally paying off." Then, on a more serious note, he added, "It couldn't have been any better. The fact that he tossed it, then allowed you to take it is the classic example of discarded property. You did good, John."

"I'm going to Dallas," Little replied. If he fudged on the speed limit and didn't run into any traffic problems in Fort Worth, he could be there by midafternoon.

Judy Floyd, the lab supervisor at GeneScreen, was also amused by Little's description of how he had come into possession of the cup. Having grown up in the tiny west Texas town of Munday, she had no trouble visualizing the scene Little had re-created for her. "Only in Texas," she said, thinking back to her girlhood days, watching old men sitting on town square benches, spitting their tobacco juice into their cups.

Having done over a dozen tests on the same case over the years, she stopped short of expressing optimism. More than once, in fact, she had offered her own theory that the person they continued to search for was most likely in prison or perhaps even dead. Still, she promised to begin the testing procedure first thing the following Monday. That the cup was made of wax-covered cardboard instead of Styrofoam, she said, greatly enhanced the chances of getting a usable sample of saliva to match against the swabs taken from the bodies of Terry Sims and Toni Gibbs. "I'll do my best," she said.

Little stopped himself before asking if it might be possible to work on it over the weekend. His impatience was again showing. So was his confidence. "If you get a sample and it doesn't match," he said, "the only explanation will be that I pulled the wrong cup out of that trash barrel."

"I'll call you as soon as I know something," Floyd assured. "Go home and get some rest."

Doing so was impossible. He spent Saturday pacing the house, then on Sunday found himself traveling back to Olney. On the off-chance that another sample might be necessary, he decided to follow Wardrip to and from church in the event he discarded a soda can or decided to defy his parole regulations and take his wife out for lunch. Or maybe he would put trash out front that the investigator could steal away with. The trip, however, proved futile except for passing the time that had begun to weigh so heavily.

On Monday, Little busied himself double-checking Wardrip's work records and the addresses of his residences during the time of the murders, and writing reports on his days of surveillance. By Tuesday, the urge to place a call to GeneScreen became so great that he finally opted to get away from his desk and out of the office.

He'd not actually seen where Wardrip had been living when arrested for the murder of Tina Kimbrew and went in search of it and other landmarks from the old cases. He found that in recent years the area had changed drastically. The Pizza Hut where Ellen Blau had been last seen had closed and been converted into a television repair shop. The Suds 'N Subs where she had worked had changed hands and been renamed. The street signs had been transformed into a confusing maze with the building of new access roads and Highway 240.

Little was still searching for Wardrip's old address that afternoon when his cell phone rang.

"You in your car?" Judy Floyd asked.

"Yeah," Little replied, "I'm riding around, getting lost in my own hometown."

"You might want to pull over," Floyd said.

Little's heart was racing as he pulled to the side of the road.

Quickly and clinically, Floyd told him that she had not only been able to lift a DNA sample from the cup but, after running a preliminary test, had not been able to exclude Faryion Wardrip as the person whose DNA was found on the bodies of Terry Sims and Toni Gibbs.

"I've still got some other tests to run," she said, "but I think you've got your man."

When, after several seconds, she got no response, she began to yell into the phone. "John . . . John, can you hear me? Where are you?"

It was a breathless Little who finally responded. "I was out running around the car," he said. "People passing by probably think I've gone nuts. I can't believe this. You've got it?"

"Yes," she replied, "I think I've got it. But I'm going to run it through a couple of other systems to be sure. I'll get back to you tomorrow."

Little appreciated her thoroughness. He'd seen it exercised in other cases she had helped them with. He also knew she would not have phoned him had she not been reasonably confident of what the outcome would be.

He quickly drove back to the courthouse and found Macha in his office. "We've got him," he said.

The time had finally come for the district attorney to do something he'd been waiting fifteen years to do. "Let's get to work on a search and arrest warrant," he responded.

The following day, Archer County D.A. Tim Cole and his chief investigator, Paul Smith, traveled to Wichita Falls and sat in Macha's office as he described the evidence that Little had assembled and the report they had received from Judy Floyd. By then she had finished the complete series of DNA tests and had matched the victims' samples to that on the discarded cup.

Smith, a veteran of almost two decades of law enforcement, was quick to praise Little's work. "This is great," he said, extending a hand to the younger investigator. "I guess it took a new set of eyes looking at what we had."

It was Cole who asked if any thought had been given to how to proceed with Wardrip's arrest. Macha turned to his investigator.

For the first time during the meeting, Little spoke. "He's got quite a support system down there in Olney," he said. "His wife, his parents, his boss, members of his church. From everything I've seen and heard, they're gonna rush to his defense the minute word gets out that he's in custody. And he'll take full advantage of that kind of backing. Down there. I don't think he's likely to do much talking. What I'd like to do is see if we can get him up here, then arrest him."

Already Little had begun to formulate a plan that he felt sure would lure the suspect to Wichita Falls.

CHAPTER FIFTEEN

On a sunny and crisp mid-February morning Faryion Wardrip woke early, opted against the delay of having breakfast, and was driving his wife's aging Honda northward on Highway 79. He made no effort to hide the enthusiasm he was feeling about the scheduled meeting with his parole officer. Normally reserved, his mood bordered on giddy as he talked almost nonstop during the drive. John Dillard had phoned to say he wanted to talk to him about the possibility of removing the ankle monitor. Finally. No promises, he'd said, but, hey, why else would he want him to come to his office so early on a Saturday morning? So confident was Wardrip that he would soon be free of the electronic monitor and the restrictions that went with it that he'd already confided to a few fellow workers at Olney Door & Screen that he and his wife would be leaving on a short vacation the following Monday.

Assured that he would not likely be long at Dillard's office, Glenda Wardrip had suggested that he drop her off at Wal-Mart so she might attend to some much-needed shopping. He could pick her up after his meeting, and they could have an early lunch before heading back to

Olney—finally free, she hoped, to move about where and when they wished.

Her husband's high spirits had quickly spilled over. Glenda, who hadn't seen him so happy in some time, felt good about what the day promised. And while she had been praying for good fortune since learning of Dillard's call, she could not escape a certain degree of worry over how Faryion might react to news that, for whatever reason, he would be required to continue wearing the monitor a bit longer. Her husband, she felt, had dealt with enough misfortune and bad news in his life. So, feeling a need to brace him for the possibility of such disappointment, she warned that it might not be such a good idea to get his hopes too high. "Let's just see what he has to say," she advised.

"It's going to happen," Faryion said, pounding his hand against the steering wheel for emphasis. "I just know it. Praise the Lord."

He was smiling as she waved back to him before entering Wal-Mart.

However, Faryion Wardrip's euphoria would vanish minutes after he entered Dillard's office.

During the drive to Wichita Falls, Wardrip had not noticed the car that had slowly pulled in behind him as he left the apartment and turned onto Olney's main street. Inside the car, which remained a safe distance behind him throughout the trip, was Texas Ranger Dick Johnson and investigator Paul Smith. In the unlikely event that Wardrip decided to go anywhere other than the office of his parole officer, they had orders to pull him over and detain him.

And even as they followed Wardrip, John Little and fellow investigator Danny Martinez had arrived at the Fre-Mar Valley office of John Dillard to give the parole officer and his supervisor, Lydia Ecks, a more detailed explanation of their reason for being there.

"We've got a search and arrest warrant," Little said after explaining the evidence they had collected connecting Wardrip to the two homicides. "Just introduce me to him and I'll take it from there." The nervous investigator made no mention of a concern he'd wrestled with through a sleepless night: What if Wardrip remembered him from the brief encounter in the Olney Door & Screen yard when he'd feigned need of a spit cup? What if he was sharp enough to pick up on the fact that something other than a discussion of removal of his ankle monitor was taking place and had the good sense to keep his mouth shut?

Thanks to the DNA matches, they had Wardrip on the Sims and Gibbs cases. Little was confident of that. But tying him to the murder of Ellen Blau depended on catching him off balance and getting him to talk before he had time to think his situation through.

The investigator's worries that he would be recognized had been unfounded. As Dillard pointed Wardrip to a chair across from his desk, Little made his entry from an adjoining room. "Faryion," the parole officer said, "this is John Little. He's an investigator with the D.A.'s office."

Wardrip, anxious to get on with the business he'd come for, quickly nodded and extended his hand. If any alarm bells were going off, he hid them expertly.

"I heard you were coming up today," Little said. "I've been down in Olney lately, working on a case."

Wardrip leaned forward in his chair. "A case in Olney?"

"Yeah, and since you live there and know people in town I was hoping you might be able to help me. Maybe you could come down to the office for a few minutes."

Wardrip flashed a questioning look in the direction of his parole officer and Ecks.

"They'll be here when you get back," Little assured. "My office is just right down the street."

Shrugging, Wardrip suggested that he follow Little. "I'll take my ol' car so I can come on back here when we're through, okay?" Then, before getting to his feet, he repeated, "A case down in Olney?"

Little nodded. "Yeah, an old one I got assigned to me."

On the third floor of the Wichita County courthouse, beyond a maze of hallways and small offices that house the operation of the district attorney's office, a lengthy corner room serves a multitude of purposes. It is part library, part interview room, and the location of occasional staff gatherings. Most important, it is where the office coffeepot is located.

Even before Little escorted Wardrip into the room, Barry Macha and Archer County D.A. Tim Cole had shut themselves into an adjacent office where a television monitor, connected to a ceiling camera aimed at the seat where Faryion Wardrip would sit, had been set up.

"Have a chair," Little said, motioning to the head of the long wooden table that filled the center of the narrow room. "There's another investigator who'll be joining us." As if playing to a cue, Paul Smith entered and introduced himself.

Little, careful not to appear too anxious, played down his enthusiasm for the case to which he'd been assigned. Insisting that it was little more than a formality, he read Wardrip his Miranda rights. "As I told you," he said, resting his elbows on the table, "it's a real old one. But in the course of my investigation your name came up."

"About what?"

"Ellen Blau. . . . A woman who was murdered here back in the mid-1980s."

Wardrip shook his head, his facial expression nonchalant. "I don't know her. Seems like I do remember reading something about her in the paper not too long ago, though. Some kind of a memorial or something. But I don't know her. Wasn't there a reward?"

The gamesmanship had begun, Little thought. He didn't respond to Wardrip's question, instead asking another of his own. "You know a woman named Janie Ball?" he asked. "Lived upstairs from you on Bell Street?"

"Nope. I don't know her."

Though he freely admitted he had at one time resided in the Bell Street apartment building Little mentioned, he insisted he had never met anyone else who lived there. He'd only stayed there briefly, with his former wife, but had left when they decided to separate.

"Look," Wardrip said, "you know that I've been in prison. You know what I did. I'm sorry about what happened to Tina Kimbrew. I never meant to do it. She was a nice girl, a friend of mine. I just went over there looking for some drugs and everything went crazy. It is a tragedy I'll never get over, a terrible accident. I'd never hurt anybody before that, not even my first wife. We never got along, but I never once hit her. Maybe I grabbed her a time or two, but I never once hit her."

Speaking rapidly, he began telling of his mediation meetings with Tina's parents. "It gave her family a chance to see that I wasn't the monster they'd thought I was," he said. He spoke of being a pioneer participant in the Victim Offender Mediation/Dialogue program. The network news show *20/20* had even contacted him about doing an interview. Death Row inmates had written him, applauding the courage it had taken for him to face the mother and father of his victim. Before leaving prison he'd even begun speaking to young offenders at several Scared Straight gatherings. The strength to do these things, to speak out and accept responsibility for his actions, he said, stemmed from the fact he was a born-again Christian.

"And since I've been out I've really tried to live my life the right way," he added.

Smith, who had been leaning against a wall, silently looking on while Little conducted the interview, stepped toward the table and placed a photograph in front of Wardrip. "You recognize her?"

"That's—" The next word froze in his throat. Wardrip stared at the picture of a smiling, alive Ellen Blau for several seconds but would not speak her name. For the first time since they'd entered the room, his composure seemed shaken.

Placing his forefinger on the picture, Smith leaned toward the seated Wardrip. "That's Ellen Blau," he said.

"I don't know her and I never had anything to do with what happened to her. I know in my heart I never met this person," Wardrip shot back. "I'm a man converted with God and to be converted with God is to be honest. I'm being as honest as I can about this."

"I'll tell you what," Little interrupted, demonstrating impatience for the first time. "Seems to me the quickest way to get this cleared up would be for you to give us a sample of your blood and let us take some fingerprints. Would you do that for us?"

Almost immediately the investigator recognized a change in Wardrip's body language. Even as the request was being made he leaned back in his chair, moving slightly away from the table as he began shaking his head. "No," he said, "I can't do that. I know how things like that can get all twisted up." All strength disappeared from his voice. "I couldn't agree to do that without talking to an attorney first."

In the adjacent room Barry Macha turned his attention

from the monitor, slumped in his chair, and looked over at fellow district attorney Cole. Both men shook their heads, resigned to the knowledge that connecting Faryion Wardrip to the death of Ellen Blau was going to be an all-but-impossible task. By invoking his right to an attorney, Wardrip had effectively brought the interview to a halt.

In the conference room, Wardrip straightened himself, glanced at a wall clock that indicated it was nearing 11 A.M. "Is that it?" he asked. "Am I free to go?"

For the moment he was back in control, his composure briefly reestablished.

"I'm afraid not," replied Little, struggling to mask the disappointment he was feeling over getting no information that would help connect his suspect to a third homicide. Standing, he said nothing for several seconds as he stared down at the man seated before him. Finally he spoke: "Faryion Edward Wardrip," he said, "I have a warrant for your arrest . . . for capital murder."

Wardrip's face went ashen. "Oh, my goodness," he whispered. "Oh, my . . ." He stood and placed both hands on the table.

"Mr. Wardrip," said Paul Smith, "I will ask you not to respond to what I'm about to say, since you've invoked your right to counsel. But for your information, this is not just about Ellen Blau but also the murders of Terry Sims and Toni Gibbs which occurred in 1984 and 1985."

Wardrip's response was barely audible. "But I didn't . . . Oh, my . . . Oh my . . ."

Wichita County Sheriff Tom Callahan entered the room to take custody of his newest prisoner and escort him downstairs to the booking desk.

"I dropped my wife off at Wal-Mart," Wardrip said as Callahan handcuffed him.

The bearish sheriff, who had attended several of

Wardrip's parole hearings in the company of Tina Kimbrew's father to protest of his early release, assured him that a deputy and a female investigator from the D.A.'s staff would get the car to her and notify her of what had transpired.

Wardrip nodded, then looked at the sheriff with a pleading expression. "Why now? I know somebody was tried for one of these murders a long time ago. Maybe fifteen years ago—"

"Son," the sheriff interrupted, "you've been warned and you've already said that you want an attorney, so you don't want to be telling me anything you don't want me to know. Understand?"

"Yeah, I know. But I ain't got nothing to hide." As he moved toward the door, the sheriff a step behind him, Wardrip was again shaking his head. "I know one thing, though," he said. "This is in for a big circus. I can see it right now. I can see it now because I'm not guilty of this. I didn't do this. This is crazy. And it's going to be a big circus."

Though he did not respond, Sheriff Callahan knew his prisoner, soon to be the most infamous man he'd ever taken into custody, was dead right.

"I guess I'm in for an uphill battle," Wardrip conceded, "but, you know, I've got a lot of people who are going to support me. My wife, my friends and family, my church."

John Little bit his lip to avoid voicing the question running through his mind: How long would that support last when they learned the truth? When the monstrous side of Faryion Wardrip was finally exposed?

Downstairs in the sheriff's office, Wardrip continued to plead his innocence. "Why?" he said. "Why after all these years? And capital murder? That's when you're charged with two felonies, right? Like murder and robbery. Or murder and kidnapping, or something like that." Looking first at the sheriff, then Little, his hands were shaking as he spoke.

Little made a mental note of the fact that as Wardrip listed the possible basis for a capital murder charge, he had been careful not to mention rape as a second offense.

"You know, I'm diabetic," he said to Little.

"You need something to eat?"

"That would help." Wardrip nodded. "Thanks."

Little left his paperwork and disappeared into the jail kitchen where the inmates' lunch of sandwiches and Kool-Aid was being prepared.

The prisoner steadfastly maintained his confused, resigned demeanor as he was transported to the hospital where samples of his blood and hair would be taken. It was not until Alicia Pruitt, a nurse trained in sexual assault investigation, entered a small examining room and asked him to stand that his attitude changed visibly.

With his hands cuffed behind his back, it fell to the nurse to unzip his trousers so that she might take a sample of his pubic hair. As she performed the intimate procedure, the look on Wardrip's face hardened into a spiteful glare. The piercing look in his eyes was not lost on the man who had arrested him.

Leaning against a nearby wall, hands buried in his pockets, Little said nothing, but thought: *You don't like it when a woman's in control, do you, Faryion?*

The "circus" Wardrip had predicted was soon to begin.

It was late afternoon before he was booked into jail. Grumbling reporters, not pleased that their weekend was being interrupted, gathered at the courthouse for a press conference that Macha had called to announce the arrest.

Soon television camera crews and print reporters were in a convoy, headed toward Olney in hopes of getting reaction to what had transpired. And, just as Wardrip had predicted, the sleepy little community immediately rushed to his defense.

Fellow members of the Hamilton Street Church of Christ insisted that the quiet, polite man who had been scheduled to teach a Sunday School class and then read scripture during communion the following morning could not possibly be guilty of the horrendous crimes he was being accused of committing. His employers assured visiting reporters that Wardrip was a man devoted to making something of his life with a good job, a new wife, and the admiration of the entire community. Stunned by the accusations relayed by reporters, Betty Duncan insisted that Wardrip had been an excellent employee during the year he'd worked for her and her husband at Olney Door & Screen. "I just can't believe this," she said. "We'll certainly back him all the way. For as long as I've known him he's done everything right. My husband and I were aware of his background, what happened to him before— he was upfront with us about all that—but we were willing to give him a chance. And I'm glad we did. It's worked out just fine. Since Faryion's worked for us he's been nothing but good, a fine person."

Bryce Wardrip angrily lashed out at the district attorney's office, insisting that the arrest was nothing more than a desperate attempt to clear some old cases, using his older brother's troubled past as a convenient tool to achieve some kind of convoluted closure to the cases. "There is no way," he told interviewers, "that my brother did this."

George Wardrip, weak from cancer treatments he'd been undergoing at the VA hospital in Wichita Falls, was home for a weekend stay when reporters found him. Not only was he certain that his son had not been involved in the deaths of the young women back in the 1980s, he said, but he was convinced that he had not been guilty of murdering Tina Kimbrew. Kimbrew's death, he was certain, was only the result of a tragic accident. Faryion had told him so.

"We didn't have the money to hire an attorney back then," the elder Wardrip said, "so my boy wound up taking that plea bargain. See, he didn't want to put us, the family, through a trial and all that kind of mess. He wasn't a murderer, but he did his time. And when he got out he started over to make something of himself.

"Now he's got a wonderful new wife. A good job. He goes to church and teaches Sunday school. My boy doesn't drink or smoke anymore and has been clean of drugs for at least twelve years. This just isn't right. He's a good . . ."

Wardrip's voice trailed off, the little energy he could muster gone. "I'm in the hospital five days a week," he finally added, "and I get to come home for the weekend . . . to this."

As George Wardrip stood on his front porch, responding to reporters' questions, John Little was finally driving home, speeding through the late-afternoon traffic in an effort to keep another commitment he'd made earlier in the day. He'd unsuccessfully tried to beg off attending the press conference called by Macha and had felt no small amount of discomfort when his boss had publicly singled out his efforts in the investigation.

He was relieved, upon arriving home, to find that his son Coleton's birthday party was still going on.

Downtown, long after the adrenaline rush had faded and the dark chill of night had settled in, a solitary figure remained on the third floor of the Wichita County courthouse. Alone in his cluttered office, Barry Macha, tie loosened, his jacket tossed onto a nearby couch, sat at his desk, dialing the final number from the list that lay in front of him. He was more tired than he could ever remember being.

One by one, he had been placing calls that he'd hoped against hope he would one day be able to make. Finally, after so many years of anger and disappointment, assurances he knew had routinely been judged as false, he was informing the families of the victims that the cases which had so haunted their lives had finally been solved. The man he was now absolutely certain had taken their loved ones from them was finally, after fourteen years, behind bars. There would be the formality of grand jury hearings, indictments and trials, likely to be a slow process that would add to the angst and frustration of those he was notifying, but at least he now had the answer to the question each had been asking so long. This time he would not have to make the same promise he'd been voicing over and over; would not have to try—one more time—to assure them that their daughters and sisters had not been forgotten.

At last, he had good news and had shared it with the family of Toni Gibbs, then Terry Sims.

It was nearing midnight in Connecticut when Murray Blau, the last name on Macha's list, answered his phone to hear the familiar voice. How often over the years had they spoken? How many times had the elder Blau traveled to Texas to sit in the very office from which the call was originating, hoping to learn that some step, however small, had been taken toward finding his child's killer? And how remarkable that out of the nightmare that had brought them together there had developed a strange bond, a genuine friendship. Murray Blau never forgot the birthday of Macha's daughter, always sending along some small gift. The families had been exchanging Christmas cards for years now.

"I know it has taken a long, long time, but I finally have some answers to your questions," the district attorney said. For several minutes he re-created the remarkable sequence of events that had led to suspicion and arrest of Faryion Wardrip. "For a time, he even lived in the same building Ellen did," he told the speechless father.

"Did she know him? Were they friends?"

"Not as far as we can tell," Macha replied.

While confident that Wardrip was responsible for the deaths of Sims, Gibbs, and Blau's daughter, Macha explained that in all likelihood it would be either the Sims or Gibbs murder for which he would stand trial.

"You'll do what you think is best," Blau said. "Just keep me posted, okay?"

"You can count on that."

"I know. And, Barry . . . thank you so very much." Murray Blau made no attempt to hide the fact that he was crying as he said good night.

For several minutes Macha sat at his desk, then he rose and walked to a nearby window. Staring out into the blackness of an empty parking lot, the city over which he had presided for a decade and a half silent and peaceful, he felt the sudden warmth of tears sliding down his own face.

A few miles away, John Little had helped his wife clean away the aftermath of their son's party, stopping regularly to answer congratulatory phone calls from those who had heard of the arrest on the evening news. His sister-in-law, who had been a friend of Toni Gibbs, was among the first to call. Then there had been one from an old high school classmate he'd not expected to hear from.

"John," the caller said, "this is Donnie Goodson." Little knew that the man once the prime suspect in the murder of Terry Sims was now married, had kids, and had moved out of Wichita Falls into the same Lakeside City community Little called home. "Look, I just wanted to call and say thank you. For fourteen years a lot of people have thought I was the guy who did this, you know. Thanks for proving they were wrong."

Little was at a loss for words. What Goodson had endured over the years was beyond his imagination. The suspicion he'd lived with had cost him a lifetime of friendships, including that of old classmates. Under different circumstances, the Goodsons and Littles might have enjoyed occasional backyard cookouts, their kids might have gotten to know each other, but the role of suspect and investigator had made all that impossible. Like so many others, Little thought, Donnie Goodson had also been horribly victimized by Faryion Wardrip.

Finally he spoke. "Donnie," he said, "I appreciate your calling."

Lisa Little looked across the kitchen as her husband hung up the phone, reading his face. "It's not your fault," she said.

Long after everyone had gone to bed, Little sat alone, his thoughts turned to the myriad things he would need to do the following day. It was almost midnight when he wearily made his way down the hallway to join his wife. It had been thirty-six hours since he'd slept. As he approached their bedroom he stopped and, for the first time all day, a broad smile crept across his face.

Attached to the door was a handmade poster fashioned by his daughter, Breann. In her best eight-year-old penmanship, it was addressed to "My Hero."

"Way to Go, Daddy," it read. "I Love You."

CHAPTER SIXTEEN

Those whose knowledge of the law is limited to what they learn from police dramas generally view the arrest of a suspect as the final event in a criminal investigation. In truth, it is only the beginning, a first step that sets off a flurry of paperwork and the careful addressing of judicial requirements, endless double-checking, dotting of i's and crossing of t's. In the frantic hours following the disappointing interview in the D.A.'s office and the taking of hair and blood samples at the hospital, Wardrip was taken before a magistrate for arraignment, Little's search warrant and affidavit were filed with the court, forensic evidence was prepared for delivery to laboratories in Dallas, and dozens of long-distance calls were placed in an attempt to begin gathering background information on the prisoner.

Meanwhile, a steady buzz whistled through the Wichita Falls legal community. The guessing game had begun. Who would be chosen to serve as counsel for the most notorious defendant in the city's modern history? Smart money was on the Public Defender's Office despite the promise of Wardrip's fellow church members to begin gathering donations for a defense fund.

And even before he knew who his legal adversary would be, Barry Macha had begun his preparation for trial, mentally cataloging the material he would present to a jury at some future date. Early Sunday he picked up Little for a drive to Olney, where he wanted to photograph and videotape the trash barrel from which his investigator had taken the discarded coffee cup, the single most important piece of evidence in the prosecution's possession. It alone served as the wellspring from which everything else the jury would ultimately hear would come. He wanted to be absolutely certain there was no way it might be ruled inadmissible. Macha planned a second-by-second re-creation of the manner in which the cup had found its way into an evidence bag and finally to Gene-Screen for testing. From Wardrip's telling Little to "help yourself" to the chain of custody thereafter, the district attorney wanted to be absolutely certain that no judge or defense attorney could find even the suggestion of a problem that might poison his legal findings.

The otherwise worthless paper cup and the DNA proof it had triggered would form the foundation of the state's case.

Even as they drove southward through the barren winter landscape, services at the Hamilton Street Church of Christ were already under way. Minister Scott Clark had wasted no time getting directly to the issue that occupied the thoughts of his congregation.

It really was not necessary for him to explain why Faryion Wardrip had not been on hand to teach his Sunday school class or read scriptures as the church bulletin promised. The news had spread quickly through the small community.

"We need to talk about this," Clark said from the pulpit.

"Each of you will have to make up his own mind, but I ask that you don't judge Faryion too harshly. Wait until you hear all the facts before you decide what you think. Remember what you know about this man. And let's show everyone how God's family can respond to a crisis like this.

"We're in the business of loving people. All we can offer as comfort is the love we have for Faryion Wardrip and his family."

From the congregation came a scattering of "amens" and prayer requests.

"Folks," the minister urged, "this is a wide-open opportunity to show everyone what we're made of."

With that a church member was called on to offer a prayer for Wardrip: "Father, we have watched him grow and we feel we know him and he loves you and he loves your son, Jesus," a man in one of the front rows said. "We know at times the problems we have seem overwhelming. This is one of those times, God . . ."

Later that evening, when several members of the church appeared on the ten o'clock news, promising support and voicing certainty that there was no way their friend could have been involved in the terrible crimes of which he was accused, Catie Reid lost her composure for the first time since learning of the arrest. Cursing, she stormed from the den and hurried into the kitchen to phone her sister.

Vickie Grimes had also been watching the news and was, if anything, more angry. How, she asked, would these people feel once they learned the nightmarish details of what their wonderful Sunday school teacher had done to their sister? "If I could take him out behind the courthouse and put a shotgun to the back of his head," she said, "I could pull the trigger. I really could. That's how much forgiveness I have in my heart right now."

. . . .

Early the following morning, as Little was preparing to leave for Dallas to deliver Wardrip's blood and hair samples and fingerprints, the receptionist buzzed his office. There was, she said, a man named Bryce Wardrip in the lobby.

Bracing himself for a confrontation, Little made the short walk to where Faryion's younger brother was seated and invited him into his office.

"I know you're busy, so I won't take but a minute," he said. "I just came to apologize. When I said the things I did—you know, about you guys just looking for somebody to clear your cases and all that—nobody had mentioned anything about what evidence you might have." Only after reading in the morning paper and learning that there was strong DNA evidence linking his brother to two of the victims had he begun to feel bad about his remarks.

Surprised by his visitor's attitude, Little remained noncommittal. "Mr. Wardrip," he said, "I appreciate your coming in, but if you're here to discuss the case, you should know that I'm not at liberty to talk about it."

"No, I understand. I just wanted to let you people know I'm sorry about the things I said."

With that the sad-faced young man rose to leave. He had taken only a couple of steps toward the door, when he turned back to the investigator, shaking his head. "He did it," he said, his voice little more than a resigned whisper. His brother had not told him as much, he quickly added. But he knew.

In time, others in the family would share his feelings.

Since she was approached by sheriff's deputies in the parking lot of Wal-Mart and told of the arrest Glenda Wardrip had not seen or spoken with her husband. In the days since traveling back to Olney alone, her life had been one of stunned confusion and paralyzing fear. Unable to sleep, she had spent much of her time praying for an end to her nightmare.

Finally, on Tuesday morning, she sat in the jail visitation room, looking through the Plexiglas that separated them into the tired eyes of her husband. She was immediately troubled by an emptiness she had never before seen and began to cry.

During the half hour they talked, her husband did not speak the words she'd prayed to hear. Absent was the indignation she'd expected. And while she had not been able to bring herself to ask directly if he was responsible for the horrible things he was being accused of, he had not once suggested his innocence.

It was shortly before 10 A.M., when jailers Edward Ayers and Paul Martinez escorted Wardrip from the visiting room back to his cell. The prisoner had said nothing until locked away, then, as the jailers began walking away, he called out. "Tell that D.A. guy, John, that I want to talk to him," he said.

"And you better tell him to hurry . . . before I change my mind."

Since the weekend, John Little had found it difficult to share in the excitement that had been vibrating through the D.A.'s office. That it didn't appear they would be able to tie Wardrip to the murder of Ellen Blau gnawed at him. Even when Barry Macha had urged him not to worry himself over it and instead focus on the fact two other murders had finally been solved, Little had been unable to dismiss the feeling that his job had not been completely done.

When the call came from the jail, however, his spirits lifted immediately. He contacted fellow investigator

Smith and urged him to meet him at the jail annex as quickly as possible. Then, hurrying down the hallway, he detoured by Macha's office. "I think we're going to get another shot at him," Little said.

The man escorted into the room looked nothing like the confident, self-assured person Little had first confronted at the parole office. Dressed in the standard-issue white jumpsuit with WICHITA COUNTY JAIL stenciled across the back, Wardrip's hair was uncombed, his shoulders slumped. Several seconds passed before he lifted his head and his eyes met those of the visitor he'd summoned.

"I had a talk with my wife this morning," he said, "and we agreed that I've got to get right with God."

"You tell her what you did, Faryion?" Little asked.

"Naw, I didn't tell her. I couldn't. But she knew." With that his voice broke and tears welled in his eyes. Taking a deep breath and folding his hands, he said, "I'm ready to talk about it."

With a tape recorder and video camera chronicling the conversation, Little carefully established that the prisoner had called for him, that he was waiving his right for an attorney to be present, and that he was fully aware of the rights that had been previously read to him during their Saturday conversation.

"You understand that you have the right to terminate this interview at any time," Little warned.

Wardrip nodded. "I do."

Little shifted in his chair, hoping the anxiety he was feeling was not evident to the man seated across from him. The questions, which he'd begun rehearsing back on those days he watched Wardrip through the window of the Olney Laundromat, ran through his mind like exploding firecrackers. Go slow, he told himself; don't rush it.

"Okay, Faryion, what I'd like to do is just go back to the beginning . . . in your own words . . . and start with the events surrounding December 21 of 1984. This would be in reference to the death of Terry Sims."

Wardrip's fists clenched, then opened. He looked toward the ceiling, then at Little. While specific dates escaped him, he recalled it as a time when he was heavily involved in drugs, a time when his life had become a dysfunctional nightmare. He and his first wife fought constantly. His only escape from the hate he felt for her was to leave the apartment and take long walks.

It had been, he said, while returning from hours of walking that he had seen Terry Sims at the front door of the house on Bell Street. He had seen several people that evening—total strangers—and had thought about lashing out at them but had managed to restrain his anger until he saw Sims on the porch of Leza Boone's house.

"She was at the door," he said. "I went up and forced my way in. I slung her all over the house in a violent rage. Stripped her down. Murdered her."

Little asked a quick series of questions that established that Wardrip had lived only a short distance from the scene of the crime at the time, then said, "Can you describe to me how you killed Terry Sims?"

"I think she was stabbed. It's hard to remember. She was stabbed. It was such a violent rage. I don't recall all the details, but I know I'm responsible for it."

Little stared silently at Wardrip for several seconds. *Nine stab wounds to the chest, slash wounds on the arms and hands, blood all over the house, and it's hard to remember?* The investigator pushed his thoughts aside and asked only about what happened immediately after the crime.

"I walked," Wardrip responded. "Just walked until I finally ended up back at the house. It seemed like hours. I remember that it was raining by the time I got home."

"Did you have sex with her?"

"No, I don't think I had sex. I'm almost sure, pretty sure, that I didn't have sex with her. I do remember stripping her down out of anger, but I don't recall having sex with her."

The investigator again quietly fought the urge to press the matter, to ask the questions that had haunted him since first reading the autopsy report on Terry Sims. *What about the sperm in the victim's vagina and anus and mouth, Faryion? What about your body fluid that was left on the bedsheet? If you're going to confess, why not just stop playing games and do it?*

"What did you do with the knife?"

"It could be laying anywhere. I'm surprised it wasn't there."

Little's questions came more rapidly. "You didn't have a knife with you?"

"I don't think I did. I can't remember if I had a knife or not."

"Ever carry a boot knife . . . own a black-handled hunting knife?"

Wardrip emphatically denied that he'd ever owned a knife. "I never was a hunter or nothing," he said.

"You've talked of all this rage that was building up," Little said. "What was causing it?"

Shaking his head, Wardrip answered, "Just all the things that go into life. I thought my family hated me. I hated them. My wife kept coming in and out of my life. She'd come to me when times were good and then when times were hard she'd leave. I just kept turning to drugs. I thought everybody was out to get me.

"The drugs made me paranoid. The way I grew up with drugs and drinking made me have these violent outbursts. I just kept drinking and doing drugs to cover it up, thinking it would go away. But it never did. I'd just reach a boiling point. Satan had a firm hold on me. Boy, he had a firm hold."

With that he pointed to an irony that wove through those tumultuous times. "The crazy thing," he said, "is that back when I would get so angry, so mad at my wife, I never done anything to her. Never hit her or nothing like that."

Little redirected the conversation to the night of Sims's murder. "Did you go into the bedroom with her?"

"Yeah, probably. I think we were in all different parts of the house."

"Did you tie her hands behind her back?"

"Yes."

"With what?"

"Rope. I believe it was a rope."

"Could it have been an electrical cord?"

"Could have been. I don't remember. But I do remember tying her hands behind her back."

"Do you remember where you left her? What room?"

Wardrip again shook his head. "Boy," he said, "I've blocked this out of my memory for so long. Maybe the bathroom, maybe the kitchen. I'm trying to picture it." Putting his hands to his face, he was silent for several seconds. "Maybe the bathroom," he repeated.

Inside the small room, the air was growing stale. Despite the fact the air-conditioning kept the temperature at a comfortable level, Little could see that Wardrip was perspiring. Concerned that at any minute his prisoner's faulty, selective memory might completely shut down, the investigator tried to move the conversation along as quickly as possible. If it was minute detail he wanted, that would have to wait for another time.

"Okay," he said, "let's move to a time approximately a month later—January 19, 1985," Little said. "Mr. Smith would like to ask you some questions about a case he's investigating."

Silent since Wardrip had entered the room, Paul Smith made no attempt at mock warmth. If John Little was understated and soft-spoken, the good cop in this three-man drama, Smith was the bull-charging, let's-cut-the-nonsense bad cop.

"We're referring to a nurse that worked at Wichita Falls General Hospital. Toni Jean Gibbs. Do you remember that?" Smith began.

"Yeah," Wardrip replied, nodding. "Again, I was out walking. Been walking all night and somehow wound up downtown. By the time I started home it was almost daylight. I was walking up by the hospital and Toni saw me and asked me if I wanted a ride. I told her yeah.

"When I got in the car I started seeing these images of anger and hatred and started in on her. I told her to just drive. I don't remember which direction we were going. As she was driving I grabbed her and started slinging her around. She swerved off the side of the road and stopped. I had her by her jacket and told her to turn down this little dirt road that went into a field. I was slinging her and screaming at her. Screaming as loud as I could. I finally told her to stop the car and when she did I took off her clothes and stabbed her."

"Was there some kind of structure out there in that field . . . ?"

Wardrip shrugged. "Maybe trees. That's the only thing I can think of."

"What did you do with her clothing?"

"I don't remember doing anything with her clothes. They should still be there."

"Do you remember the weather that day?"

"Cold, it was really cold."

"Do you recall if there was some kind of old bus or trolley car body out there? Anything like that?"

"No," Wardrip insisted. "I don't remember that. I just don't remember. When I went into those rages I just blacked out."

"Do you recall what you did with the knife?"

Again Wardrip's memory became selective. He was able to describe the white Camaro Toni Gibbs had been driving and what she was wearing, even the color of the jacket she'd worn, but he said he had absolutely no recollection of having a weapon with him or of what might have happened to it after he committed the crime. "Probably," he finally said, "it stayed right there."

He had, he said, begun removing her clothing while they were still in the car. "I think she got away from me," he told Smith. "She got out the door and started to run. I think that's how we got out in the field. I'm not sure, though."

Smith's impatience began to show. "Did you have sex with Toni Gibbs?"

"I don't really remember. I just remember screaming at her, screaming that I hated her. I don't remember if I had sex. I just remember screaming and screaming and screaming how much I hated her, how much I hated everybody."

"You said that you knew Toni and she asked if you wanted a ride," Smith said. "How did Toni know you?"

"From the hospital," Wardrip said. "I met her when I worked there. But she never had anything to do with me. I just knew her from there. It could have been anybody. She just happened to be in the wrong place at the wrong time. I never set my sights on anybody.

"I would just get mad and just get out and walk. I'd be in such a rage. I would just scream at the sky, scream at the trees, scream at God. Then, afterward, I would just lay down for a while and sleep. Then I'd see it on the news, realize that something bad must have happened, and I'd trick myself into believing it wasn't me.

"I'd hear all these things, like that she was shot. I knew that couldn't have been me because I never shot anybody. Didn't have a gun. Then I heard that she'd been abducted from her apartment and I knew that wasn't me because I'd never been way out there to her apartment. I just kept tricking myself into thinking it wasn't me."

Looking over at Little, he continued: "Same with Terry Sims. There were reports that she was some kind of karate person and it must have been a gang thing. All these kinds of reports kept coming in and convinced me more and more that it wasn't me. I just blocked it out of my mind and wouldn't think about it. Not for a long, long time."

That Wardrip had directed his remarks to Little was the cue to move the conversation to Ellen Blau. "I'd like to talk to you about another case I'm investigating," Little said. "About the disappearance and murder of Ellen Blau in September of 1985. Do you know anything about that?"

For several heartbeats time seemed to freeze before the investigator heard Wardrip's almost whispered reply:

"Yeah," he answered. "Same thing. I was out walking. Just walking."

"Where were you walking that night?"

"I was walking down the highway out by the air base. I was at a stoplight there by where the McDonald's is and she pulled up to it, then turned into this little store. I walked over to the side of the building where she parked and asked what she was doing. She told me she was looking for somebody. There wasn't nobody around so I just grabbed her and slung her up against the side of the car and pushed her in. I told her we were going to take a ride."

He described how he'd forced Blau to drive out to a road on the outskirts of town. "About a mile or so out on that road, I just started grabbing her and screaming at her, telling her that I hated her. We went on a little ways and turned onto a dirt road.

"I drug her out of the car, took her in a field, and stripped her clothes off. I don't believe I raped her. And I don't remember how she died. She probably broke her neck because I sure was slinging her. I was just so mad, so angry.

"It was weird. I was always so mad, but I never hit them; I just slung them, just grabbed them and slung them. But I never struck her. Never struck any of them."

"Did you try to have sex with her?"

Wardrip shook his head. "No, I was too mad."

It was, he insisted, never the victim he was seeing, but instead the face of his first wife. Each time it was his wife's face he looked into as he committed the crimes.

"Like with Tina Kimbrew. I remember I was screaming at her and had my arm across her throat. I was screaming bloody murder at her but it wasn't Tina's face. It was my wife's. I was just so consumed with hatred for her."

Attempting to contain his relief at hearing the confession he'd so badly wanted, Little pressed ahead. What, he asked, had Wardrip done after the murder?

"I started to walk down this dirt road and it was dark and I didn't really know which way to go. So I turned around and went back and got her car and drove it back into town. I just parked it where I knew where I was and started walking home."

"Had you ever seen Ellen Blau before that night?"

"No, no, I didn't know her. At least I didn't think I knew her," Wardrip said. It was, he went on to explain, a time during which he was doing a lot of drugs. "I was just going from drug dealer to drug dealer," he added.

Little leaned back in his chair and glanced over at Smith to see if he had additional questions. Smith wearily closed his eyes and shook his head.

"Faryion," Little said, "did you kill Ellen Blau?"

"Yeah. I don't remember how. I might have broke her neck when I was slinging her around. She wasn't heavy at all."

"Did you kill Toni Gibbs?"

"Yeah."

"Did you kill Terry Sims?"

"Yes."

And so, in less than an hour, Faryion Wardrip had resolved questions that had, for fourteen years, eaten away at the city of Wichita Falls like a cancer. The murderer who had struck fear into the hearts of so many young women so long ago had a face and a name. Finally it was over.

Or so Little and Smith thought as they made ready to return the prisoner to the custody of the jailer.

"My conscience tells me to keep going," Wardrip said. "There's one more."

And with that he began another horror story as the two investigators sat in stunned silence. "It ain't here," he said. "This one's in Fort Worth. I'd left Wichita Falls and gone there, hoping I could find a job. I was staying at this Travelodge that was full of people selling drugs. So I just stayed there, shooting drugs. One night I went to this bar. I had somebody's car but I can't remember whose. Anyway, there was this girl there and we got friendly and started dancing. She was coming on to me and after a while we decided to leave.

"We went out into the parking lot around back and I made my advance toward her. She said no and slapped my face. When she done that I just snapped. I slung her around and I killed her."

Quickly regaining his composure, Little responded. "How did you kill her?"

"I think I strangled her. I had her on the ground and I think I used my forearm. I put her body in the car and drove up the interstate and when I found a road to turn off on I just threw her out.

"I think her name was Debra Taylor."

For several minutes Little questioned Wardrip in an attempt to pinpoint the date of the Fort Worth homicide. Wardrip could remember only that after he murdered Ellen Blau he had hitchhiked to Fort Worth and while there committed the crime.

"I know it was after Ellen," Wardrip offered. "Ellen was the last one here in Wichita Falls until I killed Tina Kimbrew."

Smith and Little looked at each other, neither saying anything. Hoping to clear three homicides, they now had confessions to four.

"Will you be willing to cooperate with authorities in Fort Worth to help them with that case?" Little asked.

Wardrip shrugged, then nodded his head. "Yeah. It's all over with now. I've done what God said I should do. I've confessed to my sins."

"Were you promised anything in return for giving me this statement?" Investigator Little was cleaning up the loose ends of the interview.

"Eternal life with God is what I was promised," Wardrip answered. "I was promised that I won't burn in hell. What I've told you is the truth. It's all over. I give up. I can't go no more. You can kill me now, I don't care. I'm tired of living on this earth, tired of the pain and suffering that Satan brings to people." And then, for the first time during the interview, he broke down.

"Oh my God, what have I done?" He moaned. "I'm so sorry. My parents didn't deserve this. My wife doesn't deserve this. My kids don't deserve this. My brothers and sisters . . . God, they don't deserve this."

With that he began slowly rubbing his clenched fists against his temples. Tears welled in his eyes. "I'm so tired," he said, "and I've got such a terrible headache."

Genuine sympathy evaded the two men seated across from him. Too often and for too long, they had looked at the photographs of Faryion Wardrip's evil handiwork and read autopsy reports detailing the horrors his victims had been forced to endure.

Maybe God would forgive what he did. The grim-faced investigators, however, were concerned only with what a judge and jury might decide. And each had a similar thought as they stood to leave:

As Wardrip had spoken of those who didn't deserve to be involved in what he had done, he had failed to mention Terry Sims and the grief he had heaped upon her family, Toni Gibbs and her family, Ellen Blau and her family, Tina Kimbrew and her family, and now someone named Debra Taylor and her family. Five lives taken, five families shattered.

There was a dull monotone to John Little's voice as he spoke into the tape recorder a final time. "The date is still February 16, 1999," he said. "The time now is 11:18 A.M. That will conclude the interview."

Suddenly feeling drained of all energy, he slowly reached to the center of the table and pressed a finger against the OFF button.

It was midafternoon when Little and Smith returned to the jail and escorted a handcuffed Wardrip to their car. Their purpose: having him show them the routes he'd taken to the abduction sites and crime scenes from so long ago. Though street names and highway numbers escaped him, the prisoner found familiar landmarks that enabled him to re-create his movements of fourteen years earlier.

As they were headed back toward the jail, Wardrip leaned forward in the backseat and spoke to Little. "I'm just curious," he said. "How is it that you came up with me after all these years?"

The investigator explained how, while reading the case file on Ellen Blau's murder, he had happened on his name. "For a while she'd lived in the same apartment house you did," he said.

Wardrip slumped back into the seat. "I honestly don't remember that," he said. "I don't remember ever seeing her."

And then he had another question: "How long you been doing this?"

Little turned his head slightly toward the back of the car. "Working as an investigator? About nine years."

Wardrip nodded. "Well, you're obviously good at what you do," he said. "Keep it up."

CHAPTER SEVENTEEN

W ho was Debra Taylor?

From nowhere had come this fourth name—fifth if you counted Tina Kimbrew—to be added to Faryion Wardrip's dark legacy, giving rise to yet another question: Was it possible that there were even more victims whose murders had gone unsolved? Were there other families still not notified, crying out for justice years after suffering losses of their own? Or was it possible that by confessing to the Fort Worth murder, Wardrip had honestly kept his spiritual vow and finally wiped the slate clean?

Less than twenty-four hours after his confessions, Fort Worth Police Detectives Ray Sharpe, no longer working homicides and just a few months from retirement, and Diane Tefft were in Wichita Falls. Accompanied to the jail annex by Little and Smith, they questioned Wardrip and heard much the same recollection he'd given earlier.

"Did you have sex with her?" Sharpe asked.

Again Wardrip claimed a fuzzy memory. "I don't think so," he mumbled. "Probably not. See, the drugs I was using at the time made it hard to get an erection."

For years the murder of Taylor, a young mother of two, had been handed off from one investigator to another with no success. By the time the Fort Worth Police Department was notified of Wardrip's confession, it had become a cold, forgotten case, one of those mysteries not likely to ever be solved.

Even the details of the events leading up to the crime had begun to fade.

On March 24, 1985, a Sunday evening, Debra and her husband, Ken, had argued. Over the course of their five-year marriage, such events had become increasingly frequent. Always tight finances, two young girls to raise, too little time, too many responsibilities had pressured their fragile relationship.

Feeling the need to escape the claustrophobic confines of the house and her marriage, Debra waited until her husband and daughters—Tara, seven, and Jennifer, four—had gone to bed, then telephoned a cousin and suggested they meet at a neighborhood bar for a drink.

Her cousin had stayed only long enough for a quick beer before saying she had to return home. The twenty-six-year-old Debra, energized by the music that blared from the jukebox and the good-time laughter that ricocheted through the Peppermint Club, chose to stay a while longer. And then she had vanished.

On Monday, a distraught Ken Taylor spent most of the day telephoning friends and family, asking if they had seen his wife. Finally, early in the evening, he called the police and filed a missing persons report.

In the days to come, friends went door to door on Fort Worth's east side, showing a photograph of the missing woman, asking if anyone might have seen her. There was no way, everyone who knew her insisted, that Debra would just leave. She loved her children too much. And, despite their differences, she also loved her husband.

Detectives, following the time-honored rule of thumb

that suggests the spouse is generally the most likely suspect, quickly focused their investigation on Ken Taylor. If
there had been some manner of foul play, if the missing
woman was, as they had begun to fear, dead, odds were
good that he was responsible.

Though distraught and nervous, he readily agreed to
take a polygraph test. The results were judged inconclu-
sive. Medication he'd been taking to calm his nerves and
help him sleep had flawed the procedure. He took a second
exam, which indicated no deception. A third demonstrated
that he was being truthful when he answered questions
about his wife's whereabouts. Still, the detectives remained
convinced that he was more involved in the disappearance
than he was letting on. They appeared at his front door with
search warrant in hand and methodically went through the
house, never hinting to him what they might be looking for.
A weapon? His wife's body? Bloodstains?

The suspicion quietly spread. Once-friendly neighbors
began turning away when they saw him. His father-in-law
refused to return his phone calls. His young daughters began spending most of their time in the home of their
grandparents. Even when interviewing neighbors and
family members, the police made little effort to hide the
fact they believed Ken Taylor knew far more than he was
telling.

By week's end things got worse.

It was the following Friday morning when a worker at the
construction site of a new apartment complex being built
at the intersection of Loop 820 and Randol Mill Road
walked across a dirt road and into a clump of mesquite
trees to relieve himself. What he found made him sick to
his stomach. Lying beneath a small tree was the nude,
bloated body of a woman.

Detective Sharpe took the call about the discovery and drove immediately to the location to coordinate the crime scene.

In the week Debra Taylor had lain dead, decomposition of her body, particularly on her face and neck, where injuries had been inflicted, had been swiftly cruel. Identifying the body, Detective Sharpe knew, would be no easy task. In his years of investigating homicides, however, he had learned to trust his gut instincts. Even before the victim's blue denim overalls, underwear, and sandals were found in a neat pile, twenty-five yards away, he was certain that he knew who she was.

Despite the growing tension and fear that had haunted the family for days, they decided to go ahead with daughter Tara's eighth birthday party, which her mother had been planning before her disappearance. It was during the celebration, amid the carefree laughter and anticipation of cake and punch by the youthful party guests, that Ken Taylor received a call asking that he meet the police at the Tarrant County morgue.

Tara, moving away from her playmates to eavesdrop on the adults' whispered conversation, overheard words that would ring in her memory for the remainder of her life. Her mother, she learned, was dead. The party ended before gifts were opened or candles were ever blown out.

At the morgue, Taylor identified his wife by jewelry that was still on the body—two rings on her left hand, one her wedding ring, and a small necklace he had given her at Christmas.

Later, as he performed the autopsy, Tarrant County assistant medical examiner Dr. Mark Krouse made note of severe bruises and hemorrhaging to the victim's face and neck. The cause of death would be ruled manual strangulation. He estimated that it had taken only five to seven minutes for the young woman to die.

To make a more positive identification, the examiner compared dental records to the teeth of the victim. It was, without doubt, Debra Taylor.

In the months, then years, that followed, Ken Taylor lived his life under a cloud of suspicion. For weeks after his wife's funeral, he was aware of police following him everywhere he went. The bereavement of Debra's family slowly turned to frustration, then anger as the case remained unsolved. Taylor eventually lost track of the different detectives who visited him, asking the same tired questions he'd responded to over and over. He could convince no one that he had nothing to do with his wife's death.

Unknowingly, he had come to share kinship with Donnie Goodson and Danny Laughlin, waking day after day to the knowledge that he was the target of the most horrid of accusations.

When, finally, he received news that Faryion Wardrip had confessed to the murder of his wife, a shaken Taylor was unsure how to react. He had, over the years, managed to summon the strength to deal with his loss, even the suspicions that still lingered, and move forward with his life. His daughters were grown and happy. On some days so was he. The past had begun finally to fade.

And then, with one phone call from the Fort Worth PD, it was again March of 1985. The old agonies again gnawed at the pit of his stomach, the tears returned. Instead of an easing of the pain, the revelation signaled a reopening of old wounds. There would, he was told, be trials and, no doubt, a great deal of media attention in the days to come. He would be forced to live the nightmare all over.

This time, however, he wouldn't have to do so cast in the role of a killer.

In Wichita Falls, John Little's work days were consumed by the investigation. Tracing Wardrip's life from his youthful days in Illinois, Little put together a history far different from what had been suggested to the parents of Tina Kimbrew during their Victim Offender Mediation/ Dialogue prison meetings. Instead of the bright student Wardrip had claimed to be, Little gathered information on a poor-performing, eleventh-grade dropout. His brief service record included an unfavorable discharge after it had been discovered he was using drugs. There had been a string of minimum-wage jobs, a rocky marriage that ended in divorce in 1986, but nothing to suggest that before arriving in Texas he had left a string of unsolved homicides in his wake. All indications pointed to the fact that the killings had begun in 1985 and ended with his arrest for Tina Kimbrew's murder in 1986. Still, Little's phone rang constantly as law enforcement agencies throughout the Southwest phoned for information, wondering if Faryion Edward Wardrip might be the man who could solve some of their cold cases. In Fort Worth, homicide detectives reopened eight unsolved murders that occurred around the same time Debra Taylor had been abducted and killed.

Little routinely suggested that if fellow investigators had DNA evidence from their cases they should contact GeneScreen for a comparison. All the while, Wardrip insisted that he had confessed to all his misdeeds. Little, though still maintaining a healthy skepticism, was more convinced than his boss.

"What," Barry Macha suggested one late afternoon as they sat in his office, "if he's just throwing us a bone on the Taylor case? He knows we have him on the others.

What if he just added the Taylor confession to make us think he was coming clean on everything? And then some day, when they're about to stick the needle in his arm, he starts promising to clear more murders just to stay alive?"

It had, the district attorney knew, been done before. Ted Bundy, the charming and infamous Washington state law student who ultimately was tied to the murder of more than twenty women, came to mind. In the final weeks prior to his execution, Bundy had attempted to buy himself more time with the promise to give details of countless unsolved crimes.

Little shook his head. "I don't know," he said. "I'm not sure we'll ever know. But right now my feeling is this guy isn't really that smart. He's a manipulator, but he's no rocket scientist."

"I hope you're right," Macha replied.

By the end of March 1999, Faryion Wardrip had been indicted for murder in three Texas counties: Wichita County, for the murders of Terry Sims and Ellen Blau; Archer County, for Toni Gibbs; and Tarrant County, for Debra Taylor. And while district attorneys in each jurisdiction spoke of their eagerness to prosecute Wardrip, it was agreed that the first trial would take place in Wichita County.

Appointed to represent Wardrip was public defender John Curry, a respected young attorney who had been defending indigents since 1992. In the course of his career he had served as counsel for a dozen clients charged with capital murder, but few had ever gone to trial. Curry had a reputation for sizing up the evidence, weighing the defendant's chances, and, when the facts merited it, negotiating the best deal he could.

This case, he knew, would be different. There would be no plea bargains for Faryion Wardrip. The public outcry for justice had grown in volume since the arrest and confessions. Once burned by allowing Wardrip to plead to Kimbrew's murder in exchange for a thirty-five-year sentence, there was no possibility that any talk of another such arrangement would merit even the slightest consideration by the prosecutors. This, Curry knew, was the type of case on which district attorneys forged their legacies. This was a case that was absolutely going to trial.

Thus Curry set about to position himself as best he could. In a series of pretrial hearings, most of the motions that he offered fell on deaf ears. Though he attempted to have his client's statement in which he admitted to the crimes suppressed, it was ruled that it was voluntarily given and thus would be a part of the prosecution's case. Forensic evidence collected also was ruled admissible.

Curry filed a motion requesting that presiding judge Robert Brotherton be disqualified, pointing to the facts that while still in private practice, Brotherton had represented Wardrip's wife, Johnna, in her 1986 divorce proceedings, had been the attorney of record for Donnie Goodson when he was considered a suspect in the murder of Terry Sims, and had been appointed to represent Danny Laughlin in the event he was ever retried for the murder of Toni Gibbs.

Retired Wichita County district judge R. Temple Driver heard the public defender's arguments and routinely denied the motion to disqualify Brotherton.

On the morning of the hearing, the local paper had published a brief item about John Little being honored as Wichita Falls' Law Enforcement Officer of the Year by the Optimist Club. As the investigator was leaving the courtroom, he heard Wardrip call his name and turned back to the defense table where he was still seated.

"Congratulations on your award," Wardrip said. There was not the slightest hint of sarcasm in his voice.

Nonplussed, the speechless Little simply turned and walked away.

It was not until later that evening at home, as he recounted to his wife what Wardrip said, that a response had finally come to mind. "If I'd been a little quicker on my feet," he told Lisa, "I'd have told him I couldn't have done it without him."

Public defender Curry's only victory came when he asked that the trial be moved from Wichita Falls to a jurisdiction where the overwhelming media attention given the case had not already poisoned the jury pool.

Wardrip's fate, it was decreed, would be decided by a jury of his peers who resided 150 miles to the east in Denton County.

CHAPTER EIGHTEEN

When historians reflect on the decade of the 1990s, one of the most troubling issues they must face will be the headline-grabbing litany of violence that all too regularly visited the most unlikely places. Misguided outcasts sprayed lethal gunfire into schools in tiny Pearl, Mississippi; quiet, upscale Littleton, Colorado; and rural West Paducah, Kentucky. The same inexplicable horror found its way into a Jewish children's day care center in Los Angeles and business offices in Atlanta.

Then, on a hymn-filled Wednesday evening, Wedgwood Baptist Church on the southern edge of Fort Worth felt the terror.

In mid-September, as preparations for the Wardrip trial moved into high gear, a forty-seven-year-old man named Larry Gene Ashbrook became the nation's latest time bomb. Armed with two handguns, ten clips of ammunition, and a homemade pipe bomb, he suddenly appeared at a youth rally, screaming obscenities and spraying gunfire. Before ending his bloody rampage by putting a pistol to his head and taking his own life, seven people, total strangers to the insane gunman, had been killed.

Just hours before the senseless massacre, Ashbrook's final fury had begun in the privacy of his modest home, where he bashed holes in the walls with a shovel and crowbar, poured concrete into the toilets and motor oil onto the shower heads. He destroyed family photographs and ripped the family Bible apart, page by page. In the front yard, he poisoned fruit trees.

He became the nation's newest poster boy for madness.

In the wake of the tragedy at the church, Fort Worth police quickly pieced together a profile: Like Wardrip, Ashbrook had been discharged from the service in 1983, after it was discovered he was smoking marijuana; then he had drifted in and out of a succession of menial, low-paying jobs. Since the previous July he had been living alone following the death of his eighty-five-year-old father. Strange and solitary, the neighbors called him "Weird Larry."

They could have added "paranoid" to the list. In a series of rambling letters and phone calls to a reporter for *FW Weekly*, an alternative newspaper, Ashbrook had ranted about how local law enforcement officials had targeted him as a serial killer. There were murders on the Texas Christian University campus that he was being "blamed for." He insisted he had been the prime suspect in a series of mid-1980s abduction–sex murders for which a man named Ricky Lee Green was ultimately arrested and convicted. Then he told reporter P. A. Humphrey that for years "they" had been after him for the murders committed by the recently arrested Faryion Wardrip.

Though Humphrey had little knowledge of the cases to which her strange caller referred, nor could she find any evidence that any law enforcement agency had been keeping watch on Ashbrook, she was amazed at the lurid details he provided of the homicides committed by Green and Wardrip. Ashbrook knew dates and places where bodies had been found. He knew the names and ages of each victim and background on their killers. He had saved every newspaper article published on the murders. Clearly, the crimes and the men who committed them fascinated Ashbrook.

In the sick world of deviant crime, Wardrip had apparently found at least one admirer.

Relatives of his victims, however, viewed him much differently. For them, the upcoming trial had become a driving force in their daily lives, something on one hand dreaded, on another eagerly anticipated. Husbands of Catie Reid and Vickie Grimes, while making every effort to comprehend the effect the loss of a sister-in-law neither ever knew had on their spouses, could not understand why they felt it necessary to attend the proceedings in Denton, putting themselves through the ordeal it was certain to be. "It's not something I'm doing for myself," Catie tried to explain. "It's something I have to do for Terry."

Sister Vickie felt the same way.

Marsha Bridgens's friends, upon learning of her plans to attend the trial of the man accused of killing her daughter, began collecting funds for her lodging and meals. In San Diego, DeeDee Bridgens shared her anxieties with members of the Homicide Support Project group she continued to attend regularly and was urged to travel back to Texas in hopes she might find long-searched-for peace.

And while Wardrip would be on trial only for the death of Terry Sims, District Attorney Macha made it clear his intent was to seek justice for all of the victims. Thus the courtroom was certain to be filled with families of the other young women who had been killed. Elaine Kimbrew Thornhill and ex-husband Robert, once so deceived by Wardrip, had talked often of what their responsibility should be as their daughter's murderer came to trial. Their place, they agreed, was alongside the families of the other victims. Ken Taylor, still shaken by news that his wife's killer had finally been arrested, would accompany his now-grown daughters to Denton. Jeff Gibbs, brother of Toni, made plans to be there. In San Antonio, Janie Ball, aware that the parents of Ellen Blau were in poor health and unable to travel, promised to attend the trial and call with daily reports.

Though each would arrive with private motivations—hope for pain's end, a chance finally to express pent-up anger, a last gesture of the love felt for lost sisters and daughters and friends—a similar unspoken truth rang through their planning: Even among strangers, drawn together by the nightmarish sequence of events they'd lived through for so long, there was certain to be some measure of strength in numbers.

A last way station before travelers along Interstate 35 reach the Oklahoma border, the city of Denton sits invitingly on the rural blackland prairie of northern Texas. Named for a pioneer Protestant minister, it is an architectural montage of old and new, populated by third- and fourth-generation wheat and cotton farmers who stubbornly maintain small farms on the outskirts of town while bright, energetic college students annually enroll at either North Texas State University or Texas Women's University, expanding the population to just over 70,000.

Crop-raising and higher education aside, there is no better trace of the city's history than its judicial system. In the mid-1800s, long before Denton County could even claim a courthouse, trials were held beneath a billowing elm tree, jury deliberations conducted in a nearby thicket. In time there would be a log courthouse, then, as progress continued its march, a two-story building. Popular legend has it that members of the notorious Sam Bass gang were responsible for its burning to the ground on a night in 1875.

From its ashes, the first brick building in Denton was constructed, only to be repeatedly struck by hail and lightning during a savage spring storm twenty years after its completion. It would be a grand jury that unanimously voted that the structural damage caused by the elements had rendered the building unsafe. Thus yet another court-house was erected, this time on the town square, and it served the county's judicial needs for a century, until progress called out one more time.

The courthouse where Faryion Wardrip's fate would be decided had not even existed when the crimes of which he was accused had been committed. In 1986 the site of today's modern Denton County Courthouse was nothing but an open field on the eastern edge of town. The irony of change and the march of time was not lost on prosecutor Barry Macha on his first visit to the new build-ing as he stood near the entranceway reading a cast-iron plaque that noted it had been opened for business only on May 5, 1998.

The repetitious voir dire process by which the jury pool was finally whittled down to the eight women and four men who would hear the case consumed the entire month of October. Finally, on an overcast Monday in the first week of November, a trial many had thought would never occur got under way with an announcement that sent re-porters running into the hallway to alert editors back home.

Before the jury was seated, Defense Attorney John Curry rose to address the judge, stating that despite his advice not to do so, his client wished to enter a plea of guilty. There had, Curry acknowledged, been no plea bargain arrangement, no life-saving deal offered by prosecutor Macha and his assistants.

Judge Brotherton questioned Wardrip to make certain that the defendant understood that a guilty plea in a capital murder case did not prohibit the state from putting on its case, nor was it an automatic escape from the death penalty in the event the jury, after listening to the evidence, determined that it was warranted.

Wearing a white shirt and tie, Wardrip adjusted his glasses and nodded. "I'm fully aware of my rights," he said to the judge, "and my decision is made."

A few feet away, seated between her daughter Catie and Elaine Kimbrew Thornhill, Marsha Bridgens glared at the defendant as the jurors made their way into the courtroom, silently praying that he would turn in her direction and see the hatred she felt for him.

After Macha read the indictment, the judge acknowledged Wardrip. "Sir," he said, "do you wish to make a statement?"

Wardrip faced the jury and rapidly uttered the words none of them had expected to hear. "I plead guilty," he said.

And so, in a matter of minutes that early morning, the course of the trial changed dramatically. Much of the time-consuming testimony Macha had so carefully planned was no longer necessary. What most had anticipated would take as much as six weeks had now been reduced to an abbreviated matter of days.

The trial of Faryion Wardrip would go directly to the punishment stage. The prosecution's sole purpose became an exercise in convincing the jury that the defendant deserved to die for his crimes.

Traditionally, the presentation of a capital murder case is a methodical, almost surgically planned practice, a volley of point-counterpoint during which the prosecutor and defense attorney carefully connect dots of evidence designed to prove guilt or innocence to the jury. A far cry from the high drama of television and movie depictions, it can be bone-achingly tedious, filled with a dry drone of testimony that moves toward a critical point at a speed that can best be described as leisurely.

Such would not be the case in Denton. With the matter of the defendant's guilt legally established even before the jurors were seated, Barry Macha's task became greatly simplified. His sole agenda was to prove to those sitting in judgment that Faryion Wardrip would pose a continuing threat to society for the remainder of his life and therefore should be put to death.

The D.A. attacked his goal with a rapid-fire vengeance that at times seemed to suck the very air from the courtroom. First, he would graphically detail for the jury the terrifying death of Terry Sims. Then, without allowing time for those sitting in the jury box to catch their breath, he would remind them of the other heinous crimes that had been committed.

It would, as he had promised, be a proceeding that demanded justice for all of Wardrip's victims.

Quickly time spun back fourteen years as a parade of witnesses took the stand. Leza Boone, her soft voice filled with reluctance to revisit a scene that she admitted continued to haunt her, told of that December morning when she returned to her Bell Street house and encountered the scene of horror that Wardrip had left behind. She turned her eyes away as the prosecutor introduced evidence that validated her testimony—diagrams and photographs that told of the death struggle that had occurred. There was a close-up picture of Terry's glasses lying on the living room carpet. Overturned furniture. Her purse and wallet shown lying open on the bedroom water bed, then the victim's crumpled work smock, underwear, and pink tennis shoes. Wadded tissues scattered about. A bottle of Windex, a scrub brush, and a towel used in a futile attempt to clean away the nightmare. The electrical cord that had been used to strangle the life from a terrified victim.

Each mood-setting picture led to another more graphic, as if the crime scene photographer was methodically telling a story which he dreaded. Several jurors grimaced as a photograph of the bloodstained bathtub was exhibited. Then the blood on the bathroom wall. So much blood, so much violence.

Boone, pale and shaken, was crying as she stepped from the witness stand.

It was left to Joe Shepard, who had moved to nearby Seymour to become police chief after a seventeen-year-career with the Wichita Falls Police Department, to provide the more graphic details. Reflecting back to that holiday season morning when he was called to the crime scene, he told of finding Terry Sims's body, nude, covered in blood, her hands tied behind her back with a piece of yellow extension cord. As a photograph of the body was shown, Catie Reid reached out for her mother's hand as both bowed their heads and focused their attention on the floor in front of them.

It would get no easier. As the courtroom lights were dimmed, Marsha Bridgens placed her palms against her eyes in anticipation of the playing of a police video John Little had warned her about earlier in the morning. While the still photos, standard evidence in such trials for decades, had been dramatic and disturbing, they paled in comparison to the sweeping images of the moving pictures that led viewers through each room, ending with an almost surreal walk down the hallway and into the bathroom where Terry's body lay.

In the gallery, Elaine Kimbrew Thornhill gently placed an arm around Sims's mother, who rose and walked hurriedly from the darkened courtroom. At the defense table, Wardrip, hands folded in front of him, fixed a stare at the wall and slowly chewed his gum.

At the conclusion of both Boone's and Shepard's testimony, Defense Attorney Curry had no questions for the witnesses. The jurors, he hoped, could not read his thoughts: The video of the Terry Sims crime scene was the most savage thing he had seen in his twelve-year career as a public defender.

Before the noon break, forensic pathologist Dr. Allan Stilwell detailed the autopsy he had performed so many years earlier, methodically explaining the dozen stab wounds, the blows to the face, and the cuts on the victim's fingers and thumbs. "At some point," he explained, "the victim apparently grabbed the blade of the knife in an effort to defend herself."

When the defensive wounds occurred, he somberly told the jury, Terry Sims had, in all likelihood, known she was going to die.

For some time after Dr. Stilwell was excused, Macha sat in silent review of the testimony given. Had the quick and graphic parade of evidence he'd put on made the case? Was there anything overlooked that might eliminate any question in the minds of the jurors? Finally looking up toward the judge, he recalled Leza Boone.

"Leza," he asked, "did you or Terry know Faryion Wardrip?"

She shook her head. "No."

"At any time had either of you ever allowed him into your house?"

"No."

And how, the prosecutor finally asked, had the death of her friend affected her?

As if searching for the right words, Boone did not immediately respond. Then, as tears began to stream down her cheeks, she said, "It changed my life. To this day I won't go into a house alone." Her voice grew faint, old grief rekindled by her ordeal. "I still miss Terry," she said. "I miss her every day."

"No further questions," Macha said.

After almost a decade and a half of waiting, he had presented the evidence of Terry Sims's death in less than three hours, leaving the jury stunned and without appetite as it paraded from the courtroom.

The intensity that the prosecutor was so purposefully driving did not lessen during the afternoon session. Having established the facts of the Sims murder, his plan now was to show the jury the pattern of angry, brutal crimes Wardrip had committed during his mid-1980s rampage.

Toni Gibbs's older brother, Jeff, took the stand, his eyes warily searching the surroundings. Responding to Macha's questions, he remembered his sister when she was still alive, then described that day when he had been notified that she was missing, of the agonizing three weeks of fruitless search and dwindling hope that preceded the mid-February day her body was found. While attempting to express the agony he and his family had endured during the time Toni was missing, he broke into heaving sobs. "It was," he finally managed, "a horrific nightmare."

Bill Gerth, the Texas Ranger who had been summoned to the Archer County field where the body was found, recounted the crime scene investigation. Constantly shifting his weight in the witness chair, he spoke with a dispassion fashioned over his thirty years in law enforcement. He spoke of the event as if it had happened only days earlier, providing exacting detail gleaned from the reports he'd written long ago. From the crispness of the day to the fact a section of the barbed wire fence surrounding the pasture was down, Gerth took the jury through another nightmare. He described the landscape and the abandoned trolley, and told of the discarded woman's clothing found beneath its decaying floor.

And then, as a second crime scene video began to play, he switched to the role of narrator. "Inside the trolley car there was a lot of debris," he said as the camera panned the interior. "There were blood splatters at the entrance . . . We could see the nurse's uniform . . . It was obvious there had been a lot of violence. . . ."

Only the Ranger's steady baritone voice broke the palpable silence that had fallen over the shadowy courtroom. As the camera focused on Gibbs's nude body, its frail arms frozen in a gesture of surrender, Gerth's voice lowered, his descriptions becoming more halting. He described the visible wounds to her chest, the evidence of frostbite to the feet and hands, the small gold chain that remained around her neck, then paused briefly before continuing. "Part of one of her arms and her calf," he said, "had been eaten away by animals."

Again Marsha Bridgens had avoided viewing the video. This time, however, she remained in her front-row seat, glaring across the room at Wardrip, praying that for even a fleeting moment he would look in her direction and know the unparalleled hatred she was feeling for him.

By the time Dr. Fossum had returned to the stand and completed his testimony about his autopsy of Toni Gibbs, those who had come to observe were physically and emotionally drained. Robert Kimbrew and his ex-wife walked toward the double doors leading out into the hallway as if weights had been attached to their legs. Marsha Bridgens remained in her seat until long after Wardrip had been escorted out a side door, back to his holding cell. Some gathered in small groups to share whispered evaluations of the opening day.

Jeff Gibbs, jaw set, his head down, said nothing, hurrying toward the exit as if only a deep gulp of fresh air would save him from the suffocating surroundings.

Long after the courtroom had cleared, John Curry remained seated at the defense table, occasionally whispering to assistant Dorie Glickman, a young woman working her first high-profile trial. Already showing signs of weariness, her boss slowly shook his head. How could someone he had found to be mild-mannered and reasonably intelligent, someone whom he believed had made a serious effort to redirect his life toward a spiritual path, do something so vulgar, so evil? Even though he knew the details of the crimes Wardrip had committed, Curry had come to have feelings for him. There was a part of the public defender that felt genuinely sorry for his client.

But Curry forced himself to also keep in mind the irreparable suffering Wardrip had caused those who had come in hopes of seeing justice finally done.

Before returning to his hotel, he stopped by the jail where Wardrip was being held, seeking out a deputy who would be working the evening shift to ask a favor. "My guy had a pretty tough day," he said. "Would you get him a milkshake tonight?"

One of the things he'd learned about his client in recent weeks was that he had a passion for chocolate milkshakes.

The jailer smiled and nodded. "I'll see what I can do," he said.

Rather than make a daily drive from Wichita Falls to Denton, Catie Reid had made plans to stay at the home of her remarried grandmother during the course of the trial. Marna Todisco had briefly considered attending the trial herself but in the end decided it was not something she could deal with. Catie had promised to be her eyes and ears, returning daily with details of what transpired in the courtroom.

It was late afternoon by the time she got on the road to Bridgeport to begin her solitary commute. Throughout the trying day, she had managed to maintain a stoic manner, feeling a responsibility to give whatever strength she could to her emotionally fragile mother. Now, though, alone on the highway and reflecting on things she had heard and seen, she allowed the pain to escape and the tears to flow. She gripped the steering wheel so tightly that she felt a pinching sensation, which drew her attention to the small silver ring on her right hand. It had been Terry's. After it was returned to her grandmother by the authorities, it had become hers. Yet for reasons she couldn't explain, she had never been comfortable wearing it, instead putting it and the memories it evoked away into her jewelry box.

But as the date for the trial had neared, she had sought it out, polished away years of tarnish, and placed it on her finger. Terry, she found herself thinking as she drove, would be pleased to know that she had worn it into the courtroom.

That evening she sat in the den with her grandmother, watching as the evening television news recapped the first day of testimony. During the report, one of the crime scene photographs that had been introduced into evidence briefly appeared on the screen. The two women looked on in silent horror at the picture of Terry, dead, blood-soaked, and so robbed of dignity. Marna quickly pointed the remote and turned the screen to black. For several minutes neither woman said anything.

Finally Catie leaned across the couch to plant a kiss on her grandmother's cheek. "I'm going to bed," she whispered.

"Let me fix you something to eat first."

"I'm not hungry."

It was only after her granddaughter had disappeared into an upstairs bedroom that Marna rose and tearfully walked toward the bathroom. Closing the door behind her, she knelt in front of the commode and began to vomit.

Alone, waiting for the dizziness to pass, she wondered how Catie could get through the trial. How any of them could.

CHAPTER NINETEEN

A chilling morning wind, a reminder that winter had not yet forgotten north Texas, drove those who generally stood outside the courthouse, smoking a last cigarette before beginning the work day, into the warmth of the building's spacious lobby. Long before Judge Brotherton would call the second day of testimony to order, the victims' family members had gathered outside the doors of the 367th District Court, exchanging quick smiles and greetings. Drawn together by their common purpose, they were fast becoming comfortable in each other's presence.

Already inside, having spoken to no one upon her arrival, was Wardrip's wife. Sitting stiffly in the front row directly behind the defense table, she focused on the side entry to the courtroom, the door through which her husband would eventually appear. When he did so, carrying a Bible, he looked her way, brightened, and mouthed the words "Good morning." He then handed a small envelope to Dana Rice, the defense team investigator. Rice silently passed the note along to Glenda Wardrip.

The case had been a particularly difficult one for the young investigator from the moment it was assigned to her. For the first time in her career, she found herself working on behalf of someone accused of murdering someone she knew.

She had been a senior at Vernon High School when Tina was a freshman. And while they were never close friends, small-town life had naturally dictated their being in each other's company a good deal. And, too, their parents had been acquainted for years. A parole officer for four years before joining the Public Defender's Office, Rice had not spoken with Tina since their school days until seeing her one evening while visiting the Sheraton Hotel lounge. They had spent the evening revisiting old times, laughing about the time Dana and other senior girls had put Kimbrew and some of her classmates through a freshman initiation ritual that required them to ride around the local Sonic Drive-In on tricycles. And of the time Tina's mother, working at the Vernon bank, had helped Rice with a loan. They had promised to stay in touch.

And then, just two days later, Rice heard the news that Tina Kimbrew had been found dead in her apartment.

After placing her briefcase on the defense table, Rice walked over to where Tina's mother was seated. "Do you remember me?" she whispered.

Elaine, aware that the young woman speaking to her was part of the defense team, looked surprised for a moment, then began to smile. "Oh, my goodness," she said. "You're Dana . . ."

The investigator reached for Elaine's hand. "I just want you to know," she said, "how sorry I am about what happened to Tina."

Keeping with the pace he had set the previous day, Macha called forensic experts to detail autopsy findings, then Ken Taylor walked to the witness stand, his slow movements a contrast to the speed with which the trial was proceeding. As if shouldering the weight of the nightmare he had lived since his wife's body had been found, he slumped into the chair and was still staring at Wardrip when the district attorney began his questioning.

As he had done more times than he cared to remember, Taylor recounted the night Debra had left their Routh Street house and the agonizing days of searching and wondering that followed. In a measured, halting voice he described the trip to the morgue to identify his wife's body and how, in the days that followed, it had become clear to him that he was being viewed as a suspect.

"And how did others respond to you in the days after Debra's murder?" Macha asked.

"Her family," Taylor acknowledged, "her father in particular, blamed me and went so far as to threaten me. It was a long time before we could even talk to each other. It was a nightmare from day one."

Macha stopped short of asking Taylor about a search warrant brought to his front door soon after his wife's body was found, forcing him to remove his clothing so the police could search his body for scratches and bruises that might prove that he had been engaged in a death struggle with the victim. Nor did he ask Taylor about the endless series of polygraph tests that followed.

The D.A. had made his point. Just a few feet away, Taylor's daughters, both now grown, were crying.

Artfully, the district attorney had begun painting a broader picture of Wardrip's crimes, demonstrating the emotional destruction that had spread in the wake of the murders he'd committed. There were, he was determined to prove, far more victims, more lives damaged, than any juror might have imagined.

Janie Ball had traveled from San Antonio to tell of the close kinship she had developed with Ellen Blau, of the fact she had even named her daughter, now thirteen years

old, Ellen. With obvious pain in her voice she spoke of
those days living in the apartment house on Bell Street
and of the strange neighbor whom she had met on occasion but had gone out of her way to avoid. Turning to look
at Wardrip, she recalled advising Ellen to ignore the man
living in Apartment A if she ever encountered him in the
yard or hallway.

Then, nervously, Shelley Kelley told of growing up
with Tina Kimbrew and of the day she and her grandmother had walked in on the horror in her cousin's apartment. "That," she told the jury, "was the worst day of my
life . . . and it hasn't gotten any better."

The emotional barrage aimed at the jury continued as
Wichita Falls police officer Steve Pruitt took the stand to
describe the scene he had encountered after being summoned to Kimbrew's apartment and then of the surpris-
ing call from Galveston police, who said they had a man
in custody who had confessed to the murder. Then Dr.
Mary Gilliland returned to detail the autopsy she had performed on the young victim's body.

By day's end, the spot occupied by Wardrip's wife was
vacant. During a conversation the previous evening her
husband had urged her not to return and subject herself to
the torture of the testimony she was certain to hear.
"You're still my husband," she had argued. "I'm trying to
show my support."

She had managed to do so only through the first half
of the second day's testimony. There were tears in her
eyes as she sought out Dana Rice to tell her she was leaving. "I just can't hear about any more murders," she told
the investigator.

During the afternoon, Wardrip turned to steal a glance
at those in the gallery and was surprised to see that his
brother Bryce and the parents of his first wife were
there—seated directly behind the families of the women

he was on trial for murdering. His own parents, he'd been told, were en route to Florida to attend a wedding.

Except for a handful of reporters, the benches on the defense side of the courtroom were empty.

For the first two days, John Little's primary responsibility had been to escort witnesses in and out of the courtroom and see that Macha's presentation stayed on schedule. Now, on the third day, he had separated himself from the crowd waiting for the proceedings to get under way, pacing the hallway, occasionally tugging at a tie, which clearly felt uncomfortable to him. Though he'd done it dozens of times in recent years, testifying in court never failed to set his nerves to grinding.

Robert Kimbrew, who, in recent months, had developed a friendship with the investigator that went beyond their common interest in the case, saw Little as he was stepping off the escalator and walked toward him. "Ever think the day would come when you would regret giving up bricklaying?" Kimbrew chided.

Little smiled and rolled his eyes.

On the stand he displayed no sign of nervousness as he methodically recounted Macha's assigning him to the case and detailed how he had come to focus on Wardrip as the prime suspect. In the jury box there was the first hint of bemusement as the investigator described setting up his survellience outpost in the Laundromat across the highway from Wardrip's workplace and finally securing the all-important coffee cup by suggesting that he was in dire need of a "spit cup."

Before he was dismissed, he detailed Wardrip's arrest.

"Subject to recall, your honor," the prosecutor said. The knockout blow he planned for Little to deliver would have to wait until forensic experts linked the defendant to the crimes.

The jury's obvious interest in the events that had led to Wardrip's arrest was quickly replaced by twelve tired faces as GeneScreen lab supervisor Judy Floyd, her voice pleasant, told of her firm's DNA findings. For all its importance, it was not the kind of testimony that evoked the response Macha had hoped for. Even when Floyd explained that the frequency in which the sperm DNA found in Terry Sims might appear was "one in three-point-twenty-three quadrillion—which is equal to the earth's population multiplied by 500 million," not a single eyebrow raised.

"Faryion Wardrip," Floyd said, "is the only person who could have left that sperm." Yet even as she spoke she knew full well that she was not providing testimony that would sway the jury. Its mind had been made up for it when the defendant pled guilty, its feelings about the defendant solidly formed as they had viewed the crime scene videos and photographs.

Still, the D.A., determined to make his case airtight, added one more forensic fact to the stockpile of evidence. Latent print examiner Glenn Unash of the Texas Department of Safety slowly described the fourteen points of comparison he had discovered, matching Wardrip's left middle finger to the bloody print discovered on Sims's tennis shoe.

Then, as Little returned to the stand, the jury shifted in its seats, again alert and eager to hear more of what the investigator had to say. He would not disappoint.

Describing the events leading up to Wardrip's decision to confess to the murders, Little immediately recaptured the jury's attention. It was, however, not until Macha handed his witness the eighteen-page transcript of the statement given by Wardrip following his arrest that the jurors collectively leaned forward in their seats.

The prosecutor had, after considerable debate, decided

against playing the audiotape and video of Wardrip's confession. The off-and-on static and echo-chamber quality,
he felt, might serve as an unnecessary distraction. Defense attorney Curry viewed the decision quite differently. He was convinced that Macha did not want those
sitting in judgment to see his client in tears or be allowed
to view the pained expression on his face as he spoke. The
district attorney, he believed, didn't wish the jurors to
hear even the slightest hint of remorse in the voice of the
man for whom he was seeking the death penalty.

What would occur, then, would be something akin to a
dramatic reading, with Macha asking the questions posed
by John Little and Paul Smith while his investigator read
Wardrip's responses.

Carefully and without lending emotion, Little spoke the
words that reconstructed the horrors that had resulted from
the defendant's self-described fits of rage. First, he read
Wardrip's admission of the murder of Terry Sims— *". . . I
think we were in all parts of the house . . . I tied her hands
behind her back . . ."* —and Toni Gibbs— *"I think she got
away from me and started running. That's how we got into
the field . . . I remember screaming that I hated . . ."*
—then Ellen Blau— *"I was so angry . . . She was just in
the wrong place at the wrong time . . . I just started grabbing her and shaking her . . ."* —and finally Debra Taylor—
". . . I found the first road I could and just dumped her . . ."

Aside from the sound of someone softly crying, the
moments between Macha's questions and Little's responses passed in still silence. A female juror briefly
glanced in Wardrip's direction, her hand clasped over her
mouth as if to hide the revulsion that had swept over her.

The exchange ended with Little reading Wardrip's
thoughts about the spiritual awakening he'd experienced in
the years since the murders. *"All the guilt, all the shame is
gone,"* Little read. *". . . I was promised I won't burn in hell."*

At the defense table, Wardrip buried his face in his hands and sobbed.

As Little stepped from the witness stand, there was no visible evidence inside the courtroom to indicate the slightest belief that the promise might one day be kept.

After showing a video that reconstructed the routes Wardrip had taken during his self-described angry walks, his abductions, and, finally, the visits to sites where bodies of his victims were ultimately found, the prosecution rested.

For defense attorney John Curry, the case had been one littered with roadblocks from the moment he'd taken it. His efforts months earlier to work out some kind of plea bargain arrangement with the district attorney had, as he'd expected, fallen on deaf ears. Even before jury selection was under way, Wardrip had regularly argued to take the stand, not so much to tell his side of the gruesome story but to offer a public apology to the families of his victims. And finally, there had been the open court plea of guilty as the trial got under way. Curry had little to work with.

He called Wardrip's employer, Fred Duncan, who described the defendant as "pleasant" and a good worker, one he'd ultimately promoted to the responsible position of purchasing agent at his Olney Door & Screen. Then came parole officer John Dillard, who testified that Wardrip had been one of the best clients in his program. "He was required to come to my office for visits seven times a month and never failed to show," Dillard said. "I made a number of unscheduled visits to his workplace and home and always found him where he was supposed to be. He participated in alcohol and drug abuse programs as well as anger management classes.

"Mr. Wardrip complied with all the rules."

As the parole officer stepped down, and all eyes in the courtroom shifted to the defense table, the question on everyone's mind was obvious. Would Wardrip speak in his own behalf?

The answer came quickly. "Your honor," Curry said, "the defense rests."

The prosecution had one more emotional volley to level at the jury. Allowed to introduce rebuttal testimony in response to the defense's abbreviated case, Macha called Tina Kimbrew's parents and Terry Sims's sister Catie to the stand.

For several seconds after he was seated, Robert Kimbrew glared at Wardrip before explaining to the jury how he had done everything in his power to keep the man who murdered his daughter from being paroled. And he spoke of the 1996 mediation meeting with the defendant. "He looked me in the eye and swore to me that he'd never hurt anybody other than Tina," the angry father said. "He assured me that he knew right from wrong and that he was deeply sorry for what he'd done."

"And how did it make you feel to find out it was all a total lie?" Macha asked.

"It made me feel terrible."

His ex-wife followed him to the stand, telling the jury of that morning she lay in the hospital, wondering why her daughter had not visited as promised. She, too, spoke of endless letters and petitions and phone calls made in an effort to keep Wardrip in prison. And, finally, of her own mediation meeting with him.

Wardrip's head was down, avoiding eye contact with the witness, as she recalled the daylong talk they'd had. "He painted such a good picture," she said. "Yes, he did."

Then came Terry Sims's sister Catherine, her shining blond hair pulled into a ponytail, to tell of a time when she was younger and of the caring older sister she'd once had. She remembered Terry taking her to movies, to ride go-karts, and to the State Fair of Texas. There were, she said, even times when she had been allowed to accompany her sister and a boyfriend on their dates. When she had broken a kneecap while playing softball, it had been Terry who had taken her to the hospital.

Since asked to testify, the young woman on the stand had searched for the right anecdote to demonstrate the kind and caring person her sister had been. Slowly, as tears began sliding down her cheeks, she told of a time when she had decided to try out for the junior high tennis team. "That first day," she remembered, "I was the only one out there with a wooden racquet. It embarrassed me to the point where I'd made up my mind to just forget it, to quit. The next morning, as I was getting ready to leave for school, there was a new aluminum racquet sitting by the front door. Terry had gone out the night before and bought it for me."

Lifting her head and making no attempt to wipe away her tears, she looked across the room at the solemn faces in the jury box. "That," she said, "was the kind of person my sister was."

Finally, all that remained was closing arguments.

For Barry Macha, all reference to time had vanished in the preceding days. That his case had been presented in less than a week seemed impossible. The night before, as he and his associates hosted a dinner at a local steakhouse for the families of the victims, someone had suggested that he looked tired. His reply was that he felt as if he'd been trying this case forever.

He was relieved that he'd outlined his argument to the jury well ahead of time, as was his practice, rather than facing a long night of preparation. He had, he admitted, no more midnight oil to burn.

Still, the following morning he seemed crisp and energized as he left his chair and moved to a position in front of the jury box and immediately began discussing the special issues that were to be considered. With Wardrip's guilt established, the prosecutor's sole purpose was to convince the twelve people he was facing that the defendant deserved to die for his crimes.

"There is no question that he deliberately caused the death of Terry Sims," the D.A. said, "and there is no better evidence that he is a continuing threat to society than the fact he committed four other murders after killing Sims. Clearly, this is a situation that calls for the death sentence. You've heard no evidence that would warrant a life sentence."

With a large montage of victims' photographs resting on a nearby easel, Macha reviewed the evidence that had been presented. Then, turning to the pictures, he fell silent for several seconds, as if admiring the beauty and life they once represented. "This," he said as he returned his focus to the jury, "is about a lot more than Terry Sims. Five young girls, beautiful people, were killed in a seventeen-month period."

Before yielding the floor to the defense, Macha pointed out that other suspects—victims in their own right—had been cleared thanks to the advances in DNA testing. Donnie Ray Goodson committed no crime. Danny Laughlin had murdered no one.

Turning to look at Wardrip, the prosecutor reminded the jury of the day John Little had secured the coffee cup from a trash barrel at Olney Door & Screen. "That cup," he said, "would forever change the complexion of this case."

Then he reminded jurors of the horrifying confession they had heard the previous day. "Ladies and gentlemen, that's the brief overview of this case."

Then came John Curry's final chance to save his client's life.

"For me personally," the public defender began, "this week has been one of unbelievable agony and heartbreak. It has been hard not to have an emotional reaction to the things I've seen and heard. What my client has done is so horrendous . . ." With that he paused and breathed deeply. "But I would hope that you will not simply act on the anger you are feeling."

Yes, he pointed out, Wardrip had initially lied to John Little. But, after speaking with his wife, he had confessed to four murders. "He said, 'I know I'm responsible,' " Curry pointed out. "Does that mean he was a changed man? I'm not going to argue that. More likely, it says that he was resigned to his fate."

That fate, the attorney suggested, should be to spend the remainder of his life behind bars.

"In eleven years in prison, he was involved in only one argument with a fellow inmate, one assault resulting from a disagreement over what TV show to watch. There is, I believe, evidence that in a prison setting Faryion Wardrip would not pose any threat to society."

With that he yielded the floor back to the prosecutor.

Moving the photographs of the five victims closer to the jury box, Macha slowly pointed to each of the smiling faces. "At one time," he began, "they were living, breathing human beings with their futures ahead of them." Then, pointing in Wardrip's direction, he said, "He took their lives . . . and their dignity.

"My greatest concern in recent days has been that I wouldn't be able to convey the true horror of these crimes." Pointing to Terry Sims's photograph, he asked,

"How did things get from this to lying on a bathroom floor, hands tied behind the back and the taste of semen in her mouth? You have to imagine what was said, the absolute horror that Terry was forced to experience.

"He forced himself on her, knocked her glasses off, hit her in the face. And then produced a knife, a knife he had taken with him to the crime scene and later took away with him.

"If Terry were here today, what would she say? 'I tried to defend myself. I even grabbed the knife.' She was screaming and fighting for her life. But he takes her into the bedroom, ties her hands behind her back. He puts his penis in her mouth, then her vagina. Then he takes her into the bathroom . . ."

Among the new faces in the courtroom, Terry Sims's aunt, DeeDee Peters, who had arrived from San Diego the previous evening, wrapped her arms across her chest in an attempt to ward off the sudden chill that had invaded her body.

Macha then pointed to the picture of Toni Gibbs. "Three weeks later," he continued, "a nurse is driving home. Toni had some level of comfort with Faryion Wardrip since he'd worked at the hospital at one time. She offered him a ride. The last ride of her life. A ride from hell."

For several silent seconds, the D.A. let his fingers trace the photographs of each of the victims. "It has been over five thousand days since these people died," he said. "During that time, innocent people have been held up to great scrutiny. One was even tried. Ken Taylor was accused of murdering his own wife.

"All of this," he reminded, "was about power and control, dominating women and making them do what he wanted.

"And who convicted this man? These girls did; their

discarded bodies did. They're telling you what happened to them . . . and I hope you're listening. Just remember, please, that at one time they were somebody's little girl, being bounced on a knee, dearly loved."

Turning toward the gallery, Macha looked at Robert Kimbrew. "Two years ago—to this very day—Faryion Wardrip sat across from Robert and told him, 'I never hurt anyone other than your Tina.'

"This defendant is not the only person in this court-room who has rights that should be protected. These young girls had rights, too. This is not something I say very often, but this man deserves to die for what he did."

And with that he turned to the photographs one last time. "I ask that you remember that the last thing these girls ever saw was the menacing face of Faryion Edward Wardrip."

Down the hall, away from the soft whispers of a mingling crowd that seemed unable to decide what it should do to pass the wait, Barry Macha sat alone, elbows resting on his knees, staring at an unopened soft drink he had placed on the floor near him. Either because it was sensed that he was seeking a moment of well-deserved privacy or sim-ply because he wanted escape from the quiet praises for his closing argument and speculations about how long the jury might take to make its decision, the tired-looking district attorney had distanced himself from all that sur-rounded him. His jacket unbuttoned, tie now loose at the collar, he brought to mind the figure of a battle-wearied athlete, the last drop of energy spent in pursuit of victory.

Around him ironies abounded. The unspeakable crimes that he'd so meticulously re-created for the jury had, quite literally, been with him throughout his entire career as the Wichita County district attorney. Fourteen years had passed and now, finally, he, like those waiting nearby, was nearing an end to the tragic saga.

Yet, regardless of the jury's answers to the all-important questions posed it, he had to wonder if it would ever really be over.

At the opposite end of the tiled hallway, Robert Kimbrew stood, hands buried in his jacket pockets, looking out the second-floor window into the busy parking lot below. People were hurrying toward their cars, some off to a quick lunch, others away from whatever legal matters had brought them there in the first place. His eyes bore the same sadness he'd brought to Denton just a week earlier, but now there was a new strength, a new confidence in his voice. Taking the stand, speaking out about his dead little girl while only a few feet from the man who had committed the crime, had not been easy. But it had helped in a way he'd not anticipated.

"I look at all those people down there," he said, "and wonder who they are, what their lives are like. Do they have kids? Are they happy? What kinds of problems do they have to deal with when they get out of bed every day? Over the years I've found myself wondering a lot about things like that.

"But today's different. Standing here in this God-forsaken place which I hope never to see again in my life, I find myself thinking something else."

A friend standing at his shoulder finally spoke. "What's that?"

"For the first time in fourteen years," Kimbrew said, "I feel like I just might get my life back." And with that he nodded agreement to his own self-assessment and again fell silent, looking out into the clear blue Texas day.

CHAPTER TWENTY

Defense attorney John Curry had also sought a quiet place in which to do his waiting. Seated in an out-of-the-way corner in the first-floor lobby, away from those gathered in hopes that his client would soon receive the ultimate penalty for his crimes, he had long ago resigned himself to the role of the enemy in such settings.

He was, then, surprised when Elaine Thornhill approached him after closing arguments and shook his hand. "I know," she said, "that this must have been so very difficult for you. I just wanted you to know that I respect the job you've done." And moments later, as he had entered the elevator with Ellen Blau's friend Janie Ball, she had smiled at him.

"I must tell you," Curry told the young woman, "that your testimony had a strong effect on me. You did an excellent job."

Ball thanked him and then said, "You did a good job, as well."

Though it was not said, she, like Tina Kimbrew's mother, was acknowledging the fact that at no point during the trial had he exercised the time-honored defense strategy of attacking the reputations of the victims, attempting in a perverse way to suggest their actions might somehow have provoked Wardrip's attacks.

When the deliberations stretched past the lunch hour, Curry allowed himself the first glimmer of optimism he'd felt since the trial began. If the jury was taking this long to reach its decision, he told himself, it was viewing its responsibility seriously, not quickly voting on raw emotion as he'd feared it might.

Unknown to him at the time, the first vote on the question of whether Wardrip would remain a threat to society—one that demanded a unanimous decision if the death penalty was to ultimately result—had received "no" votes from two women jurors. Since going behind closed doors at shortly after 9:00 A.M. there had been tears and several angry exchanges. Those stunned at the suggestion there was even the most remote reason for discussion quickly grew impatient with those who had cast the negative votes. Did the word "society" include the world behind bars? one female juror wanted to know. "Just look at the evidence," a male accountant had responded. "I don't think there is anything to question here." Still, a note went out to the judge for a more specific definition.

Finally, with tempers flaring, the foreman suggested a lunch break might be in order. By the time they returned from a nearby Luby's Cafeteria, the number of holdouts had dwindled to one.

Then, at 2:30, Assistant D.A. Jerry Taylor hurried down the hall to pass along the words Macha had wanted to hear. "The jury's reached a verdict," he said. The prosecutor raised a clenched fist into the air and reached for his jacket.

Wardrip's pretrial guilty plea had made the first of the three questions the jury was required to answer moot. Still, as a matter of formality, Judge Brotherton was required to ask if the jurors had unanimously agreed that "the defendant had acted deliberately in causing the death" of Terry Sims.

"Yes," the foreman replied.

"And on the second question: Do you believe beyond a reasonable doubt that the person you have just convicted of capital murder represents a continuing threat to society?"

"Yes, your honor."

"And, finally: Do you believe there are any mitigating factors which would warrant the individual spend his life in prison, rather than be put to death?"

"No, your honor."

Wardrip stared ahead, showing no sign of emotion, as the judge thanked the jury members for their service and dismissed them. Even as he spoke, Macha was on his feet, moving to a position at the entrance to the jury box. Standing there, he shook the hand of each departing juror.

Beyond the railing, family members were sharing embraces, wiping away tears, and exhibiting smiles they had not worn in days. Lisa Little had driven from Wichita Falls to hear the verdict and stood near the back of the courtroom, patiently waiting for others to offer their congratulations to her husband before she approached and gave him a kiss. "I'm so proud of you," she whispered.

As Wardrip was being escorted from the courtroom, Janie Ball borrowed Little's cell phone and dialed the number of the Blau home in Connecticut.

All that remained was for the judge to issue the formal sentencing.

There was one more extraordinary occurrence to be played out in this trial, which from its first day had featured the unusual and unexpected—from Wardrip's open-court guilty plea to the judge's allowing witnesses access to the proceedings even before they were called to the stand. As court reconvened, the heads of those already seated turned collectively to the doorway and saw the jury members enter and take their place in the gallery. Minutes earlier in chambers, the judge had heard the request brought him by the foreman. "Your honor," the man said, "we would like to be able to show our support of the families."

Judge Brotherton, hearing such a request for the first time since he'd been elected to the bench, suggested that by their verdict they had already done so. "But," he added, "I see no reason for you not to be in the courtroom."

And so, suddenly returned to the role of private citizens, they listened as the judge sentenced Faryion Wardrip to die by lethal injection. And they allowed themselves to shed tears as Vickie Grimes, Terry Sims's sister, nervously read the victim's impact statement .she had prepared the previous evening.

"For almost fifteen years I have thought of what I would say to the person who killed my sister," she read. "I know now that he is a sick person who not only killed Terry but also took the lives of Toni Gibbs, Ellen Blau, Debra Taylor, and Tina Kimbrew.

"I remember the day my papa came to my house and told me Terry had been murdered and took me to my grandmother's house where Terry lived. That was one of the hardest days of my life.

"He not only killed my sister but also my great-grandmother because every day of her life after Terry died in December of 1987, she said that your great-grandchildren should not die before you do."

Only then did she pause and turn to look in Wardrip's direction. "I don't see how you could live with yourself. But, then, I don't understand how anyone can take another persons life."

Grimes's voice gained strength as she continued. "Even though my children were born after Terry's death, they know just how great a person she was and how much she meant to our family. I'm sure the families of Toni, Ellen, Debra, and Tina feel the same as I do.

"I have one last thing to say to you and that is I will be there the day they put you to death. I only wish you would have to suffer the way they did."

Her rising anger evident, she no longer referred to her written notes. "I will," she spat, "always remember you as a coward."

She was not the only family member whose emotional temperature was rising. As deputies led the convicted murderer from the courtroom, he turned in the direction of his victims' family members and blurted the words, "I'm sorry."

Before he could be hurried through the door leading to the holding cell, Robert Kimbrew angrily shot back: "You certainly are."

Returning to his hotel room, John Curry sat alone, the shades drawn, exhaustion sweeping over him. The boxing of the disheveled stacks of papers and law books, file folders, and legal pads that had been part of his preparation would have to wait. Clothing bagged and ready to be taken to the dry cleaners could be tended to another day. Though eager to put the trial behind him and return to the comforts of his Wichita Falls home, the public defender was not able to summon the energy for the drive. Tomorrow would be soon enough.

After a while he reached into his jacket pocket for a small piece of paper that Glenda Wardrip had given him on that day she'd said she could no longer bear to remain in the courtroom. Written on it was a phone number with an Oklahoma area code. Curry realized that his job was still not completed.

Dialing the number, he waited with eyes closed as he

listened to the rings, and finally heard the voice of Wardrip's wife on an answering machine: "Please leave a message."

The attorney briefly felt the urge to hang up, to try the number again later when he could speak to Glenda in person. But then he thought, no, it is time for it to be over.

"Glenda," he said. "This is John Curry. Faryion was given the death sentence this afternoon. . . . If you would like to talk, please feel free to call me."

He never heard from her again.

Even with the Denton conviction and death sentence, it was not over.

On December 5 Faryion Wardrip had been bench warranted from prison and found himself back in familiar country. In the Archer County courthouse, just a thirty-minute drive from Olney, he stood before a judge and pled guilty to the murder of Toni Gibbs. In a prearranged agreement reached with the district attorney, Wardrip received a life sentence and waived his right to appeal.

Sitting at the prosecution table with the Archer County D.A. was Barry Macha. The whole thing took no more than fifteen minutes, and the early-morning courtroom was virtually vacant. Of those who had regularly been in attendance in Denton, only Gibbs's brother Jeff, having driven over from Iowa Park, was on hand, seated alone in the rear of the courtroom.

Then, three days after Christmas, in an all-but-deserted Tarrant County courthouse in Fort Worth, Wardrip, dressed in a green jail-issued jumpsuit, with his hair closely cropped, pled guilty to the murder of Debra Taylor. Again he received a life sentence. For some time after the brief formality presided over by a prosecutor from the local D.A.'s office, Barry Macha sat in the hallway with Debra Taylor's daughter, Tara. Her father, she explained, had been having a difficult time dealing with the renewed memories of her mother's death and had decided against attending.

Referring to the brief victim's impact statement she had just given, she said she had not made up her mind to do so until arriving at the courthouse. "I didn't know if I wanted to do it or not," she said, "but now I'm glad that I did. I've waited a long time."

Tearfully, she had reminded Wardrip that it had been during her eighth birthday party that she had learned that her mother was dead. "I'm glad I got a chance to let him know that," she said.

Macha hugged her as she began to cry. "I'm glad you did, too," he said.

As they made their way out of the courthouse into the lingering holiday season chill, the district attorney waved good-bye to the young woman, then turned his attention to assistant prosecutor Rick Mahler. "One more to go," he said.

Two days later Wardrip was walking the familiar hall that led to a side entrance to the Thirtieth District Court in the Wichita County courthouse. A woman television reporter nervously pointed a microphone in his direction and asked if he had anything to say. Never looking in her direction, Wardrip said, "I live with remorse every day. I'm so sorry." With that he was led inside the courtroom.

This time Janie Ball, having made her first trip back to Wichita Falls since shortly after Ellen Blau's death, sat in the front row. Beside her were Catie Reid and Marsha Bridgens. The previous day, in the company of John Little, Ball had visited the site where her friend's body had been discovered and left flowers.

Lips pursed, her hands twisting a knotted handkerchief, she listened as the man who had introduced the long-lasting nightmare into her life pled guilty and was again sentenced to life in prison.

Even in the unlikely event that Wardrip's death penalty should be overturned, Macha had explained to her, the three life sentences he had received—"stacked" so that time for each must be served consecutively—ensured that he would be in prison for a minimum of sixty years before he would be eligible for parole. One way or another, Wardrip would spend whatever remained of his life behind bars.

Later, as he sat among the clutter of his spacious office, Barry Macha leaned back in his chair and pondered the framed photographs of Wardrip's victims that hung on a nearby wall. Just one day remained in 1999.

"It's hard to believe," he mused, "that when this year began we still didn't know who killed Terry Sims or Toni Gibbs or Ellen Blau. We'd never even heard of Debra Taylor. Yet within a year's time we've gone from an arrest to four convictions."

He breathed an audible sigh and allowed a faint smile to emerge. "It's amazing," he said. "Absolutely amazing."

One morning, as Little sat at his desk, attempting to redirect his attention to other cases he'd set aside, Catie Reid arrived at his office, bringing with her a fitting token of her family's appreciation. On an ordinary red brick, a reminder of another time in his life, were inscribed the words "Our Hero, John Little."

POSTSCRIPT

As I wrote this book, attempting to maintain focus on the mountain of misery created by one misguided and darkly evil person, I could not help but occasionally reflect on the sad and puzzling manner in which Faryion Wardrip had lived his life and the seemingly random manner in which he selected his victims. As I pondered the growing list of questions for which there were no satisfactory answers, I was reminded of a magical and provoking novel read many years ago. In *The Hobbit*, a character named Bilbo Baggins discusses the complexities and dangers of the life roads available to us all: One can leave his house, thinking he'll only stroll down the front walk. But not so. At the end of the walk is the street, and there one can turn left or right and continue the journey. Then, at some point, there is yet another street, another choice. And then another. The journey expands to avenues, freeways, then highways leading out into the whole wide world. The journey becomes endless, lasting a lifetime.

During his travels, Faryion Wardrip had taken every wrong turn possible. And, even as this is written, he continues to do so.

Whatever sympathy he might have generated with his willingness to plead guilty to his crimes quickly fell away once he took up residence on Texas's Death Row. In the immediate aftermath of his convictions, he had insisted that he had found a new inner peace and was ready to meet his maker. "I've told God to take me, that I'm ready to go home," he said. He spoke again of the overwhelming regret he felt for his victims and their still-grieving families and of the apology he had so badly wanted to make from the witness stand in Denton before his attorney had persuaded him to remain silent.

Beyond the state-ordered appeal process that automatically accompanies any death sentence, he insisted that he planned no legal fight to avoid his fate. The blame for his wrongdoings, he added, extended no further than his own wasted life.

Soon, however, he fell back to his old manipulative and dishonest ways. From prison he talked of how a troubled childhood, filled with poverty, abuse, and an ongoing battle with attention deficit disorder, had set the stage for an adult life of drug and alcohol addiction and violent rages.

He again pled that he had grown up on the "wrong side of the tracks," that the rich kids had constantly picked on him, criticizing his hand-me-down clothes and the cramped two-bedroom house the Wardrip family called home.

When such claims appeared in the Wichita Falls paper, Bryce Wardrip reacted with outrage of his own. There had, he insisted, been no abuse and no financial hard times back in Marion, Indiana. Had his brother forgotten the bicycles and minibikes bought for them, the family trips, the love and generosity of their parents? Their home, Bryce pointed out, was two stories, not two bedrooms. Their parents had provided a comfortable living.

He had no recollection of his older brother being picked on or shunned. Quite the contrary. He remembered Faryion being popular with his peers, praised for the talent he displayed in art classes.

Didn't Faryion remember his father helping him purchase his first car, a new Firebird, then taking up the payments when his son fell behind? To say their dad was an alcoholic was blatantly false.

His brother, he said, is a killer, a con man, and a liar.

It was Faryion's horrendous misdeeds, Bryce is convinced, that caused his parents to age prematurely. "He has literally sucked the life from them," he says. "And despite it all, he still wants everyone to feel sorry for him."

Bryce had long since quit accepting Faryion's collect calls from prison, tossed letters and Christmas cards into the trash, unread, and refused to travel to prison for visits, when he learned of the latest of his brother's self-absorbed decisions.

In 2001, on the December anniversary of Terry Sims's murder, Faryion Wardrip filed papers seeking a federal appeal to his death sentence. He now wishes to pursue every appellate avenue available to him. The man once eager to look into the eyes of a forgiving God today wants only to be assigned a new attorney whom he hopes can derail his scheduled trip to the death chamber.

While such changes of heart are not unusual, the origin of the outcry that followed was. It wasn't the families of the victims who collectively spoke out against the decision that was announced just days before Christmas. Rather, it was again Bryce Wardrip.

"He's hurt people enough," the younger brother said. "He needs to let it go and quit wasting the taxpayers' money. This case is closed. He's guilty, he admitted it, and he was tried and convicted. Take him down to Huntsville, put a needle in his arm, and execute him."

In all likelihood, that's where the twisting road Faryion Wardrip has traveled will eventually lead.

ACKNOWLEDGMENTS

In the summer of 1982, police in Waco, Texas, discovered the bodies of three teenagers on the shores of a nearby lake, victims of brutal murders that immediately became a local sensation. The crime and the remarkable investigation that followed evolved into the first true crime book of my career. *Careless Whispers* told of a bizarre and twisted murder-for-hire-gone-wrong plot that claimed the lives of a young man named Kenneth Franks and friends Jill Montgomery and Raylene Rice.

In the years following its publication, I received interesting and welcomed responses from numerous strangers. None, however, compared to the long-distance call that came one evening from Wichita Falls. The voice on the other end of the line belonged to Catherine (Catie) Reid.

"My sister," she said, "was a close friend of Raylene Rice." She described how the girls had met while both briefly lived in Dallas, of their attending rock concerts in the Cotton Bowl together, and driving around in Raylene's Ford Pinto, the same car that was ultimately found at the Waco crime scene.

Her sister's name, Catie said, was Terry Sims. And she, too, had been among the victims of a deranged killer years earlier. Perhaps, she suggested, I would find the case interesting.

Which, in capsule form, is how I came to write the book now in your hands. And why a great deal of gratitude is owed a loving sister who wished to have the lives—and deaths—of Terry Sims, Toni Gibbs, Ellen Blau, Tina Kimbrew, and Debra Taylor remembered.

Over the years, as I've ventured into the dark corners of society to chronicle crimes both senseless and savage, there has always been one remarkable constant: As I've come to know family and friends of those whose lives were prematurely ended, I've encountered amazing strengths and willpower, a collective goodness and resolve that has helped to lend an uplifting tone to my efforts. I told Catie Reid during one of our many conversations during my research on this project that if I'd had a daughter, I wished she would have been like her. For her summons to Wichita Falls, I will be forever grateful.

She, however, is not the only one due a sincere nod of gratitude. Those who welcomed me into their homes, shared recollections, and offered trusting insights are numerous. If their names are not mentioned here, it is only because they requested anonymity. To them my thanks is as genuine as it is to:

Vickie Grimes and her husband, Scott; DeeDee Peters; Marna Todisco; Marsha Bridgens; Leza Boone; Janie Ball; Robert and Rae Kimbrew; Elaine and Larry Thornhill; Shelley Kelley; Ken Taylor; Jeff Gibbs; Tarra Shirley; Lisa Little; Wilma Hooker; and Bryce Wardrip.

Judith Floyd patiently explained the mysteries of DNA testing while Raven Kazen and David Doerfler of the Texas Department of Criminal Justice's Victim Services Division provided valuable recounting of the relationship between Faryion Wardrip and the parents of Tina Kimbrew. Roy Hazelwood of The Academy Group became a friend while sharing the personality profile of the killer Wichita Falls authorities so long searched for. And attorney Roger Williams was generous with his time, pulling out old files and reliving the trial of Danny Laughlin.

In the Wichita County Public Defender's Office, John Curry, Dorie Glickman, and Dana Rice were equally hospitable and helpful, as was Leslie Ryan-Hash, as professional a court reporter as one will ever come across.

Without investigator John Little and District Attorney Barry Macha, the cases would not likely have ever been solved. Nor would this book have been a possibility. For their willingness to welcome in a stranger with a notepad, I'll be forever grateful.

Carroll Wilson, editor of the Wichita Falls *Times Record*, and his talented staff kindly offered a starting place for my research. Over the years a small army of reporters were assigned to write about the case and each provided valuable insight. My sincere thanks to Matt Curry, Monica Wolfson, Steve Clements, Lee Anderson, Patricia Poist, Armando Villafranca, Rodney Rather, Kristen Dietz, John Hamilton, Michelle Locke, Graham Underwood, Joe Cutbirth, Lee Williams, Tom Chaney, Katti Gray, Gail Fields, Brett Jones, Jim Mannion, Troy Bryant, Joe Lackey, and Karen Ball.

Thanks also to Stephen Michaud for sharing.

The encouragement, counsel, and patience of executive editor Charles Spicer, and his assistants, Anderson Bailey and Joe Cleemann, at St. Martin's was, as always, a big help. And to literary agent Janet Wilkens Manus, I'm constantly indebted for expertly pointing the way. You'll notice that several of the photographs included were taken by Pat Stowers, my wife and my beacon. I thank her here as I should every day. To the other photojournalists and family members who offered pictures, I appreciate their making the book better.

At times, you have read some detailed scenes and dialogue that there was no way I could have seen or heard firsthand. Know that they are fashioned from the recollections of those who were there at the time. In addition to the numerous interviews conducted and visits to courtrooms in Denton, Wichita Falls, Archer City, and Fort Worth, I also reviewed numerous legal documents relative to the cases and their prosecutions. Too, some names have been changed. It was all part of a sincere attempt to provide as honest a retelling as possible.

JEROME
313
461-8809